Unlimited Realities

ALSO BY ELIZABETH JOYCE

Books

Psychic Attack, Are You A Victim?
Ascension—Accessing The Fifth Dimension
Ascension—Accessing The Fifth Dimension Workbook
Opening To Your Intuition and Psychic Sensitivity
Developing Your Sixth Sense
BOOK ONE
BOOK TWO and
BOOK THREE
Seeding and Nurturing the Garden of Your Soul
The New Spiritual Chakras
And How to Work With Them

CD Programs
Spiritual Healing and Meditation
Healing Depression the Natural Way
The Chakras and Your Body
Opening The Spiritual Chakras
Inserting the Divine Seals
Distant Healing with the Divine Seals

All of the above items are available from
Amazon.com, Ingram, Book Stores, and
Visions of Reality
PO Box 277
Chalfont, PA 18914
WEBSITE: www.new-visions.com

Unlimited Realities

BORN WITH THE GIFT OF SIGHT
AND NATURAL HEALING

A Memoir

Elizabeth Joyce

Unlimited Realities
Born with the gift of sight
and natural healing
A Memoir
By Elizabeth Joyce

ISBN-13: 9780997208306
ISBN-10: 0997208309

Copyright
July 7, 2017
Cover Artist: Jim Warren
Cover Art Copyright by Jim Warren.
www.jimwarren.com/site/
All Bible quotes are from the
King James version (KJV)
Publishing, Editing, and Page Layout by
Visions of Reality
PO Box 277
Chalfont, PA 18914
WEBSITE: www.new-visions.com
215-996-0646

Printed in the United States of America

Dedication

Kathleen Hemphill Dalrymple

and in memory of
Ella Russell Hemphill,

Caroline Henning DiVone and Nilas Henning

and
Linda Banks

To another, the word of prophecy...To another,
the ability to distinguish between Spirits....

—1 Cor. 12:8-12:10

They will place their hands on sick
people, and they will get well.

—Mark 16:18

And She hath put a new song in my
mouth, singing praises to God.

Amma has never asked anyone to change their
religion. Only to go deeper into their values or
faith, and live by those essential principles.

—From Amritanandamayi

Stay true to yourself even when the circumstances
may seem to be against you!

In the silence, once I hear, see, or feel the
answer, I must follow through.

If one Soul is harmed, injured, or removed, then the tapestry
of the Universe becomes disturbed and incomplete.

Happiness, balance, success, and inner peace come from
applying your metaphysical principles to your everyday events.

—Elizabeth Joyce

Table of Contents

Acknowledgements

WHAT I HAVE DISCOVERED OVER the past thirty years while sitting at the feet of the Divine Mother, Amritanayanda Maye, is that thoughts, devotion, and experience transcend dogma and tradition. She has given to me a new understanding of the importance of decision, which brings us the evolution of human consciousness, our inner connections, and the unlimited opportunities that are with us every moment. She is a shining example of what selfless service is, and her charities embrace the world.

Thank you Kathy Hemphill, Batbara Meirose Cole, Brenda Hayes, William Vitalis, Richard Shulman, Marc Tremblay, Elizabeth Hepburn, Gordon Clark, Judith Sudha Greentree, Adrian Gilbert, Ann Walker, Donald L. Swaim, Kathy Sasso, Betty Jane and Ed Heemskirk, John F. McHugh, George, Carol, and Alison Reich, and all of you who have stood by my side in loving friendship, for your unwavering support.

Thank you Linda Banks and Barbara Cronie for your precise editing, and Nora McDevitt for your editing contribution, Mary Carol Sullivan for your graphics, and Jim Warren for your spectacular cover art.

I give special thanks to my film Executive Producer and advisor, Harvey Rochman, along with the skillful and supportive suggestions over the years from Joe Franklin, Prof. Hans Holzer, Dick Clark, Bobby Darin, Paul Anka, Connie Francis, Dick Summer, Shirley MacLaine, Ed Asner, David Gere, and Ben Bryant.

Thank you to every teacher I have met, listened to, meditated with, and grown from your message.

Thank you, thank you, thank you Grammie Hemphill.

Foreword

ELIZABETH JOYCE HAD DEDICATED HER life to helping others, inspiring them to realize their inner growth and begin their transformational process. She is truly a gifted teacher of spirituality, especially for beginners. As producer *of the Joe Franklin late night talk show,* I met Elizabeth through Joe's friend, Prof. Hans Holzer. He recommended her to be a guest on the show. Dr. Holzer was following her predictions and keeping a record of her accuracy. He reflected that in two books he published.

Now, I don't necessarily believe in psychics because so many have been frauds, but Elizabeth Joyce is different. Not only did she appear on *the Joe Franklin show,* but she became our "in-house psychic." Her life is truly unique and bears witnessing. She has a true gift for awakening others to the magnitude of their own gifts, held within the depth of their heart.

I am also a retired police officer and Elizabeth has advised me more than once in solving a mystery. The insight and clues she offered helped us apprehend and convict criminals. Three come to mind, the president of Exxon murder in 1992, the first twin tower bomb in 1993, and a murder case here on Long Island in 1999.

I have known Elizabeth for more than three decades, and still call on her for help and guidance. This book, *Unlimited Realities,* is her life story, and brings us many of her true life experiences. Her life has been very diversified, as she is a lady of many interests, music being one of them. As an *American Bandstand* regular from 1957-1960, Elizabeth met many stars before they got there, and also knew her music history. Joe would have me walk with Elizabeth down memory lane on his Saturday night show on WOR-radio.

Her teachers, who I respect, have undoubtedly helped her build a strong foundation and basis for her ongoing work. What I like about

Elizabeth is that she never wants to stop learning. All in all, this amazing book offers a beautiful template of how to live a richly rewarding spiritual life.

Richie Ornstein
Executive Producer
The Joe Franklin Show
Freeport, LI, New York
February 1, 2017

Preface

I FIRST HEARD ABOUT ELIZABETH Joyce when I picked-up her fascinating book *The New Spiritual Chakras and How to Work with Them*. As someone who has been on a healing path, I found her step-by-step process on how to access the spiritual chakras to raise one's consciousness and embrace the new energies empowering and timely. Her energy intrigued me and I knew I had learn from this beautiful soul.

Her earlier book, *Ascension: Assessing the Fifth Dimension* takes us further. In it, she reminds us that all is in divine and perfect order in the Ascension process. We have chosen to be born into our current lives to help move mankind forward.

Elizabeth is a spiritual pioneer in transformative energy from which others can draw strength, wisdom and understanding. Her stimulating writings and teachings have resurrected many souls and inspired people globally to embrace their highest spiritual potential and surpass their limiting beliefs. Her life mission is to help people connect with their multidimensional natures and walk in Divine Love. She is offering a new teaching concept and webinar series designed to help people manage the fifth dimensional energy field titled: *Embracing Spiritual Frontiers—Ascension Clearing.*

As described in her lectures, the vibrations are changing as we shift into the fifth dimension, a time she calls Ascension, where we connect to our Divine Higher Self. It's a new awareness or "wake-up" call inviting us to be transformed by embracing our unity and connection to the higher frequencies. This is being called "Unified Physics." This new vision for ourselves and the planet draws us to integration, collaboration, love, and oneness.

Elizabeth tells us that the powerful fifth dimensional energies that are pouring into the Earth's energy system are causing floods, earthquakes and plate shifts as the planet balances the higher frequencies. The chaos (destruction before reconstructions) is driving radical changes within our social, political, economic, and religious systems.

As we experience these new energies, old myths about reality are being shattered. Collectively, we will begin to co-create a multidimensional world where spirituality and science come together. Ultimately, it is a realization that at the deepest level we are One.

Her latest book *Unlimited Realities* is an honest memoir that will inspire and empower all of us on the spiritual journey. It is beautifully written, full of grace, humor, wisdom and above all love. It makes us think about who we truly are: perfect, whole and complete beings of Light having an earth experience. It reminds me of the exhortation of a Maori Tohuna, *"You are miracles in expression—now get on with your energies!"*

In her heartfelt life story she shares with us how Spirit works miracles in our lives, guiding and loving us and leading us to the answers within. I was deeply moved and inspired by her message. Despite however we were raised by our parents, we can heal our own stories and awaken to our true essence, which is love. I resonate with her profound message: that by embracing our Spiritual Light Body we can rise to the challenges of our present world and walk in the footsteps of the Divine. It is a message of hope and healing that is needed now as we move into the higher energies of this new millennium.

I am confident that this book will bring hope, comfort and inspiration for those seeking spiritual guidance and understanding. I encourage you to read *Unlimited Realities* like I did, with your higher self and an open heart. Allow yourself to be guided to find your truth in her words.

Elizabeth is a Woman of Light who shines it's rays in many ways in our World, and we are blessed to have her among us. I have enjoyed being in her Light!

Robert R. Maldonado, PhD.
Author, The Calling of the Heart:
A Journey in Self-Healing, and,
The Children of Atlantis:
Keepers of the Crystal Skull
www.authorrobertmaldonado.com

Introduction

CHILDREN NEED TO HEAR OFTEN from their parents that they are loved, no matter what! As babies, they need to be held, nurtured, and reassured. They need bonding with their mother, love during the preschool years, structure, order, and regularity. They need to know that when they mess up, when they make a mistake, when they try and fail miserably, they are no less deeply loved and cherished by their parents. This bonding and nurturing was not available to me during my childhood or adolescent years

I am the second born of the second set of identical twins. My mother endured an uncomfortable pregnancy as well as suffering during a thirty-two hour delivery. In the 1940's all that was available for anesthesia was ether. My twin and I could not come home from the hospital with Mother, because we only weighed three pounds each and were kept in an incubator for the next six weeks.

Mother suffered from ether pneumonia after her delivery, and it was impossible for the "little twins" to receive the proper care, so we were boarded at Hackensack Hospital for six months. Finally, in the fall, Mother's sister, Claramay, came from New Hampshire to Ridgewood, New Jersey, with her two daughters, to care for us. We were brought home, but our Mother could not physically hold us until our first birthday.

Children long for inner certainty, and hunger to know that nothing, absolutely nothing, can make their parents stop loving them. In our house, dishonesty, secrecy, disobedience, and wrongdoing were the norm. There was little sharing or joy, and obedience was enforced through corporal punishment and fear. On the heels of misbehavior came excuses and blame. Money, recognition, and fame were the life goals. There were prizes to reach for, and it didn't matter what you did to get there or who you hurt in the process.

Because of this breakdown in our family structure, we learned how to manipulate others, not to believe in them, and to take rather than give. We learned competition and control, pushing others back to gain the lead, *and were unaware of our underlying sense of disconnection to each other or to Spirit.* At the core, we were troubled, fearful, anxious kids, unsure of what caused our apprehension.

When unknowing is consistent, then lack of clarity eats at us and becomes a continuous source of self-doubt and self-recrimination. Since all of us are biologically programmed to survive, we naturally seek to reconcile the incongruity between ourselves and our home environment in order to provide a state of security, where we can feel safe and comfortable. Early on, I learned that if I was sick, I got attention and was rather safe.

The one thing my twin and I had going for us was our unceasing energy and our active minds. We were hyperactive and more than likely had a short attention span, coming from hyperglycemia and too much sugar. Our bodies did not reflect this however, as we were both tall *string beans* until our thirties.

As we grew, my twin became more and more difficult to be around. She lived to satisfy her own desires and her heart grew hard. She developed a heart that feared scarcity, a belief that there isn't enough to go around, and so she must grab what she can. Such a heart inevitably suffers decay, pain, and death. The reasons were many, but the fact was real. Every time I was with her, trouble brewed.

When I was eight, I became ill with a touch of TB. We lived in Ridgewood, New Jersey, but Mother had grown up in Warner, New

Hampshire, where her mother and family still lived. I was shipped up to grandma's to live for a year, which was the beginning of "saving my Soul" as well as my life.

During that precious time I learned so much. Grammie taught me *integrity of the heart.* There in the Mink Hills of New Hampshire, I received my first nurturing. I felt the touch of God's love, the glory of the animals, nature, clean air and water, honesty, integrity, and most of all, self-responsibility.

I came to see that the mark of true wisdom is twofold: First, it encompasses every aspect of our being, body, mind, and spirit. It touches our personal lives as well as our relationships with family, community, and the world. At the same time, this new lifestyle was so simple, with no need to run, hide, or fear. I was able to *feel inwardly* and thought, "Yes, I knew that!" or "Of course, this is natural." There was a sense of *reawakening to an understanding* that Grammie believed was inherited through her Penobscot Indian heritage, and her mother's ancestor generations. When we are open and touched on this deeper level, truth is instantly translated from a thought into active, workable solutions to our upsets and problems.

Such were the lessons of truth that flowed from Grandmother's shaman wisdom, ceaselessly. Not as platitudes, but as practical expressions of the supreme wisdom that brings success, health, enduring happiness, and love of the Divine into all circumstances of life. She filled my mind with a *universal harmony* and taught me that I could meet any challenge to my wellbeing. Her motto was, just listen. Get quiet, open your heart and your ears, and listen. *"The heart has its reasons which Reason knows nothing of."*

Never in my wildest dreams could I have imagined exactly what Grammie was preparing me for. Transformation, improvement of my family history, how to conquer any struggle between a variety of forces, as well as to locate my past-life talents and put them to use in this lifetime. To teach others how to enhance the understanding of who we are and release all that has constrained us in the past, to walking in Divine Love.

As our world civilization moves forward, the need for a means of achieving physical, mental, and spiritual harmony and balance is emerging as an absolute necessity. Today, those concepts and methods taught over the centuries are being adopted by scientists, religious leaders, and experts in the physical and mental health fields bringing Light and vital insight to help guide everyone with the current ongoing and vital challenges facing us humans.

In *Unlimited Realities* you will learn how to:

Find wisdom and strength in making your life decisions.
The antidote for stress, worry, and fear.
Transform your failures into successes
Develop inner security in an insecure world
Perfect and refine your human relationships
The power of setting conditions, affirmations, and prayer
Developing your personal relationship with the Divine using:
The Law of Surrender
The Law of Trust
The Law of Grace

As we move through the teens of this new millennium, and our *Spiritual Light Body* is ignited with new higher dimensional energy, we are ready to embrace the challenges and changes of this marvelous time and walk in the footsteps of the Divine, as an inherent *rite of passage*. It's time to embrace our connection to everything within this Universe, which is so willing to bring to us universal harmony and our own, personal *Unlimited Realities*.

—Elizabeth Joyce
July 25, 2016

CHAPTER 1

Grammie Hemphill

Come sit by the windowsill girls,
Listen to the raindrops as they touch the sill.
What message are they whispering to you?
Listen-can you hear their song?

WHEN I WAS EIGHT YEARS old, I suffered from a slight case of tuberculosis. "We caught it early, thank goodness," the doctor told my parents. "Betty Ann won't even have to go to the hospital. She should be just fine if she takes her medicine like a good girl and gets plenty of rest."

Luckily for me, my mother didn't agree with the doctor. "I don't care what he says," she announced after we got home. "The air is terrible in this part of New Jersey. Bergen County is practically on top of those oil refineries in Newark, and those refineries are polluting the air night and day. The atmosphere is stagnant here. If Betty Ann stays, she's only going to get worse. And then, well, I hate to think about what might happen. I know in the marrow of my bones that Betty Ann has got to get away. I want to take her to New Hampshire to stay with my mother for a while. The air up there is pure and good for the soul." Mother was born and brought up in Warner, New Hampshire, where the air was crisp and clear.

I expected my father to yell at her the way he usually did and tell her she didn't know what she was talking about, but, surprisingly, this time he agreed with her.

So off I went to Grammie Hemphill's house in the middle of the cool and sweet-smelling Mink Hills at the foot of Mt. Kearsarge. Looking back on it now, I'm certain that the year I spent with her saved my life. My injured lungs got a rest from the benzene and carbon monoxide that poisoned the air in New Jersey, and my heart got a rest from the anger and discord that poisoned the atmosphere in my parents' house. There weren't any screams and crashes at Grammie's. No shouting, fighting, or stomping up the stairs. Nobody snatched or pushed. Nobody, child or adult, punched anybody or pushed anybody down. Nobody had to hide in the corner and cry.

Grammie's house seemed very close to the outdoors. Sunshine could easily enter the house built by my Grandfather. The profound country darkness was there too, with its complex choruses of night birds, frogs and insects. When it rained on the tin roof of the garage, it sounded like cymbals and drums playing to God's rhythm. There seemed to be time enough for everything there. There was plenty of room for peace, for quietness. There was plenty of room for me.

Each night Grandmother Hemphill read me a story from the *Old Mother West Wind* books by Thornton W. Burgess. I devoured every one of the stories and begged her to read them to me over and over again. I fell in love with Grandfather Frog and the Merry Little Breezes. I would pretend to be a fairy flying along with the Merry Little Breezes, so I, too, could sit on a lily pad and listen to Grandfather Frog's stories.

Grandmother Hemphill was short, a bare five feet two inches with piercing blue eyes, but she was a woman with profound common sense. Born in Maine, her mother Jenny Patch was part Penobscot, a section of the Algonquin Tribe. Grammie was a true shaman, although I had never heard of that word at the time.

Every morning at ten o'clock Grammie would have me sit in the living room, and look out the window, while she went outside and sat in the middle of the front yard. She would sit cross-legged on the ground in front of the porch where I could see her. She always took dried corn, birdseed, peanuts, and other little bits of food. She lay some of the goodies on the ground near her, and others she would hold out on the palms of her hands. She sat very still and patiently. She was a small, sturdy woman with beautiful, capable hands. Because her mother had been part American Indian, her face had something of the Indian peace and calmness about it. After a while, as she told me later, she would begin to do what she called "breathing with the wind." She would take deep, slow breaths, becoming one with the atmosphere around her, making her as connected to the natural world as the rose bush or the white daisies in the garden.

Suddenly a black raven would land on her shoulder, staying long enough to gobble up the corn kernel that was placed there for the magnificent bird. A little chipmunk we fondly named Chippy would crawl towards Grammie's open hand, ever so slowly, then pounce and grab the peanut waiting for him and scuttle away. Other small creatures would come too: robins, cardinals, sparrows, mourning doves, the little yellow finches called Ohio canaries, squirrels, sometimes even wild rabbits.

My Grandmother taught me patience. I was not allowed to bang on the window, laugh, or make any kind of sound at all until all the creatures had eaten and gone away. "We don't want to scare them, because if they're frightened, they might not return."

I could barely contain myself the first time I saw her feed the animals like this, and I jumped up and down for pure joy when she came back into the house. "How do you do that, Grammie?" I stammered through my excitement. "I want to do that too! Please, please teach me."

"Of course I will," she said. "I'll tell you all about that and much more, too. I'm glad you're going to be with me for a whole year because I want to have the time to teach you many things of the Earth.

"You know, Betty Ann, that I love you and all your sisters. Nancy, Claramay, Pricilla, they're all extremely dear to me. But you are very different from the rest of your family. You were born with a special gift. Not everyone has such a gift. It was given to you by the Lord, and you must learn to work with it and treasure it. This gift is as special as a good singing voice or the natural ability to play the piano."

"I don't feel like I have a special gift," I said. "I just feel like there's something funny about me. I try to tell the truth, but people keep saying that I tell lies all the time. They say I get carried away by my imagination. I can't always tell when something really happens or when it only happens in my mind. It seems like I always say the wrong thing. Sometimes I wonder if I'm crazy."

Grammie gathered me into her arms. "Don't worry, little one," she said. "Trust me, you have a great gift, even though it doesn't look so wonderful to you right now. We have the entire year ahead of us, and if we put our heads together, I know we can make some sense out of everything."

A bit shy, I asked, "What is my special gift?

"You have several but the important one is the *Gift of Knowledge*," she answered. "You'll understand better as the year unfolds," Grammie answered softly. "First of all you have come up here to rest and get well."

I always felt such a great love around my Grandmother. She gave the greatest hugs! It seemed as if, when she enveloped me in her arms, I could escape off the planet safe within her protectiveness.

Whenever I was feeling weak and tired and it became hard for me to breathe, my grandmother got the special sit-upon she had woven for me out of straw and told me to go out across the brook to a certain big pine tree on the hill. She explained that the tree could help me get strong again.

"Sit down by the roots of the tree and lean back against it," she instructed. Soon you will feel strength coming into you from the tree. Wrap yourself within that energy. Pretend you are becoming the tree. Imagine yourself melting into it. After a while, when you begin to feel stronger, come on back. And don't worry; I'll watch you from the back porch window while I do the washing and ironing.

I was amazed to find that it always worked. I would sit against the tree with my back against the trunk, and I would pretend to be a branch of the tree or a bird in flight. I would daydream about nature and the little animals. I pretended that the tree could breathe and talk to me. That pine tree told me some amazing things! After about an hour, feeling stronger and breathing more easily, I would reluctantly get up and walk back across the little brook to the house. During those times under the pine tree I was filled with a particular kind of delight.

I felt as if the tree were a cushion, a back rest, soft and enveloping like a great big pillow.

A verse I remember singing a Hymn in Sunday School has something of that same feeling:

> *This is my Father's world*
> *And to my list'ning ears*
> *All nature sings*
> *And round me rings*
> *The music of the spheres.*

I did *Time Out* before it became the fad of nowadays. In the early fifties, it seemed that most parents routinely yelled at or spanked their children when they misbehaved. I certainly got plenty of spankings, slaps and smacks at home. Grammie, however, had her own way of correcting children. "What good is disciplining a child, or giving her some kind of restriction, such as *time out,* unless she can understand why?" Grammie said.

When I did something to upset my grandmother, she would put her hands on her hips, while tapping her right foot. Then she would hand me my sit-upon and instruct me firmly to go out to my pine tree. "Don't come back in this house until you can tell me what you did to get me so angry," Grammie would say." "You must strive to understand your mistakes and learn by them. If you can explain to me what the upset is all about, in your own words, I will know that you learned something about yourself. After all, what good is punishment or spankings unless a child can see the error of her ways? Now go!" Grammie would stand over me with her finger pointing out the back porch toward the tree. She did point her finger a lot when she explained things, but she never pointed it directly at me.

How my heart would break when Grammie was upset with me. I loved her so much. Off I would go and sit and sit, replaying the actions in my mind until I could begin to figure things out. When I would return to Grammie, I felt tears of sorrow and regret but also a great relief. Vowing I would never make that mistake again, I would put my sit-upon away and try to reassure myself that everything was back in order again. Grammie listened patiently as I explained to her my folly. If at times I didn't completely understand what I had done wrong, she would guide me and show me through examples until I understood the mistake. She never scolded me if I couldn't explain clearly, but guided me to think some more. She always had a chore for me to do when I returned from the pine tree, like sweeping the porch or putting the lunch dishes away. Then she would smile, thank me for helping her, and all my sorrows would magically disappear.

I had to go to the pine tree every time I was naughty, even in the rain, just as long as it wasn't too cold and there wasn't any lightning. "A soft, summer rain never hurt anyone," Grammie would explain. "The birds and little creatures love a summer rain. God sends many messages with the rain, as he does with all natural life."

Even now, after all these years, I smile as I step outside to feel the raindrops against my face in a soft, summer rain. I can often feel my grandmother's presence then. It brings me sweet peace.

"I had a dream last night," Grammie said one morning. "I was told in my dream that I should explain to you how God and His angels write down everything we do."

"But how can they do that?" I asked. "On a pad? With so many people on Earth, how do they keep it all straight?"

Softly she responded, "They put a mark on your Soul. An indent. When you die, you go over it all. You see your lies and deceits, as well as all those people or animals you have ever hurt or cheated. Then it is decided where your Soul will rest, in Heaven or Hell. When you come back again, you must correct all the mistakes. You have a chance in a new life to make up for your past-life errors. Don't think you get away with anything, Betty Ann. Not with God watching! Every lie, no matter how small, gets recorded. There is a payback, a karma that each Soul collects as they walk through a lifetime. If we all understood this here on Earth, life would be very different. Perhaps we could all live in peace."

Smiling, she looked deeply into my eyes. "Little Betty Ann, the girl who almost didn't make it. Such tiny little things you and Priscilla were when you were born, like twin baby robins. Priscilla looked as if she was about to fade away back to Heaven, and you looked even weaker than that. It's a wonder you ever survived your nine months in your mother's womb.

You have quite a challenge as you grow up. You have been given a mission and you must fulfill it. You are very different from your sisters. You and your twin are opposites. Almost exact opposites, except you both have so much energy! But it's character that counts. You must eventually break away from your family roots and continue on alone, teaching God's work."

Continuing, Grammie explained, "You are shrouded by God and protected by His angels. One day you will teach others about the work of nature and the work of God. You will guide and help many people. You will write and communicate with thousands of people through your books.

"I know too that you will travel great distances in your search for truth. You will go to Egypt. You have a discovery to make there at the Sphinx. Your heart has a strong connection both to Mother Mary and the Goddess Isis.

"You will see the beginning of what are called the Last Days, and your children will live through the latter part of that time. This is your destiny."

I knew what Grammie said was important, but I wasn't sure I was especially happy about it all. Writing books and flying around the world to see Egypt and the Sphinx sounded good, but who was this goddess I was connected to? The words "Last Days" gave me the shivers. I remembered hearing something about the Last Days in church, and I remembered being terrified.

"I can see you've had enough of the future for one morning," Grammie said, smiling while taking my chin in her hand. "It's time to fix lunch now. Do you want to ask your cousin Kathy to come over today and eat with us?"

Jumping up and down while clapping my hands, happy to forget about adulthood and the wrath of God, and even more happy to think about playing with Kathy, I exclaimed, "Yes! I love her so much and we have such fun together."

"I know," Grammie responded. "It's a shame my son's daughter isn't your twin. She might as well be, as close as you two are. Run over and get her now while I fix the sandwiches."

Kathy and her brother Chuck lived around the corner on Kearsarge Street, the road that went to the top of that mountain. Their father, Uncle Charlie, was Grammie's fourth child and my mother's younger brother. My cousin Chuck was fifteen that year, and he was full of mischief. One afternoon we suddenly heard Chuck screaming out on the front porch, accompanied by the voice of an older man shouting out things along the order of "I hope this will be a lesson to you, young man," and, "It's lucky nobody got hurt."

Grammie hurried to open the door, and there was Dick Cogswell, the town postmaster, holding Chuck by the ear. Mr. Cogswell had caught Chuck and some of his friends by the railroad tracks which were across Main Street and down the hill. The boys had picked all the crab apples off a neighbor's tree and were lining them up along the tops of the tracks to watch the freight trains roll over the fruit and squash it. As soon as one train passed, they lined up more crab apples for the next exciting show. By the time the postmaster caught the boys, the tracks were awash in juice and pulp.

"These boys are trouble, Ella," Mr. Cogswell said. "Always stealing apples and putting them in front of trains. One of the engine men might slip on all that slime and hurt himself. Cleaning up the mess is very time consuming. You've got to try and stop Chuck from doing this."

Looking Chuck straight in the eye, Grammie said, "Go outside over to the field across the road, young man, and cut a switch of goldenrod. Right now!"

Chuck cowered, but he took his pocketknife and walked over to the field. "Make sure it's a long and supple one," Grammie called. She always used goldenrod for a switch because it would sting but not cause any real damage.

Kathy and I watched from the back porch. "He's going to get his," Kathy whispered, giggling.

When Chuck came back, Grammie told him to take all of the leaves and flowers off the switch. Then she turned him over her knee and switched him on his rear several times. "You know what you've done wrong," she said angrily. "You not only stole, but you wasted good food and put other people's lives in danger. I cannot allow you to do that. I'm going to tell your father to give you more chores to keep you out of trouble." Chuck was trying not to sob.

"I know you weren't alone in this foolishness," Grammie went on. "One of the most important things you can learn is that we are judged by the company we keep. Not only that, we become like the company we keep. If you travel with the riff raff of life, you will become the riff raff. As you grow up and become a man, your character must grow along with you. As the saying goes, *one bad apple spoils the bunch!* I don't want to see that happen to you, Chuck. You are basically a good boy. You need to tell those other boys that you can no longer be friends with them because of the pranks they play. That doesn't mean you should dislike them or want to hurt them. No! It simply means that you are recognizing your own weakness and prefer not to be near any negative influences. If one of your friends picked up a cigarette and told you to try it, I suppose you would, or perhaps light a match on dry leaves. You need to be with boys who share your God-given talents. Learn to play baseball or practice throwing basketball: Good healthy competition never hurt anyone and develops character.

Grammie always made us be responsible for our actions. Although she did not like giving spankings and usually used other means of discipline when someone put another's life in danger from misbehavior, a spanking seemed to be most appropriate. Grammie taught us there is a consequence for all behavior, and sometimes it was most unpleasant.

"Have you young girls finished your lunch?" Grammie called out to us. "Come and have some gingersnaps and milk. After that it will be naptime."

Oh, but those cookies were delicious! No one could make homemade gingersnaps or chocolate chip cookies like my grandmother. And her fresh biscuits in the morning! Yum

I can sometimes remember the smells of her kitchen, even now. Her gingersnaps actually snapped! Eagerly we ran from the back porch to the kitchen table to enjoy our snack. A nap was worth this anytime.

Some afternoons Grammie would work on the spinning wheel on the back porch as Kathy and I watched. It was almost like magic the way Grammie could keep the wheel going with a regular tap-tapping of her foot on the wooden pedal and, at the same time, change the cloud of wool into yarn as it passed through her fingers. The spinning wheel made a whispery, clickety sound as she spoke.

"This wool comes from our sheep family," Grammie explained to us. "It has to be made into yarn so we can knit it into clothing and blankets. Many people don't think about how a sheep gives its coat for our benefit and how we give that sheep food and a safe place to live. We and our animal kingdom depend on each other, and we both benefit each other. Our connection to the natural world is a wonderful thing, but most people don't feel a part of it at all. There is little connection to it down in New Jersey where you and your sisters live, Betty Ann. People there have little concern for animals, trees, and the rest of nature. Many people lack respect or understanding about why the animals, birds, insects, plants and water were put on this planet.

"When you learn the mysteries of the natural world, you will learn about universality and balance. Knowing about the natural laws can open your eyes to compassion and sharing. You begin to see beyond yourself and into the needs and wants of others. Every animal, every insect, every flower has a purpose, as does every human being. Each one brings a gift to planet Earth. It is very important to understand this lesson.

"Harmony and balance are the keys to a successful life. You must never hate or want to hurt someone back. God takes care of karma, or getting even, not us humans."

In the late afternoon after our nap, while Grammie was preparing the vegetables for supper, Kathy and I began to play the game of *Sorry*. This is a board game where you draw a card and move spaces within the squares and try to go around the board and back Home. Each card tells you how to move and how many spaces. When you pick the *Sorry* card, you get to remove someone's piece from the board. The first one to get all their pieces back to Home wins. Each group of pieces (or men as they were called) have a different color, so you can recognize them easily. I loved winning! I loved it so much that sometimes I didn't mind moving my man ahead a few extra spaces when no one was looking. Sometimes I would try to move more than the space allowed and I hated it when my opponent got the *Sorry* card because, even with three or four players, I was sure mine would be the one picked to be taken off the board.

Suddenly Kathy drew the *Sorry* card, which meant she could take one of my men from the board and I began to cry. She already had two of her men Home and I wasn't half way around the board with mine. I knew she would probably win. Of course, Grammie heard me!

"Betty Ann," she called, "come in this kitchen right now!"

"Uh oh," I thought, frustrated with the game and with getting caught. What were you and Kathy doing?" Grammie asked.

"Playing *Sorry*," I responded.

"And who wins most of the time?" Grammie continued.

"I do," I answered.

"Now, your young cousin has spent all day with you. You girls have had a lot of fun playing and learning how to make yarn. I thought you would have learned another great lesson, the lesson of sharing and honesty in your actions." I felt as if my grandmother was looking deep into my Soul!

"There is a law of balance and equality working within this Universe and this law sees to it that you win as many games as you lose in life," Grammie explained sternly. "For each win there must be loss. For every happiness, a sadness, and for every positive move forward, a negative challenge. That is the law of polarity. You cannot have one without the other for that would be like having moonlight without the sunshine. You'll win the next game, and Kathy another one after that. Trust the universe and know that everything happens as it should. Play the best you can, have fun and let your mind relax. Don't concentrate on winning, but rather concentrate on sharing and having fun with your cousin. When you cheat, you cannot share! You will throw off the law of balance within your own life, and this is what brings in disease, upsets and unhappiness.

"Now girls, put the *Sorry* game away and set the table for dinner. There will be six of us tonight. Chuck, Uncle Charlie and Aunt Alice are joining us for supper."

After I apologized to Kathy for my anger, we set the table together. How I enjoyed my cousin during that year. We were inseparable. We still are very close.

Bedtime was always special at Grammie's house. I got my hair brushed, my face washed or was given a bath in the great tin tub in the kitchen, and was read my bedtime story. Order and regularity. Order and regularity. Every morning I made the bed, brushed my teeth and put my dirty clothes in the hamper. This is what Grammie taught. Put things back, be organized, don't overdo or over indulge and remember that children thrive on monotony.

Every night Grammie would come upstairs to my room to put me to bed. This was the only time I ever saw her ascend the stairs. My room had cream-colored wallpaper with tiny pink roses, and on the dresser was a pitcher and basin with big pink roses. The room was large and airy, with two windows that looked out onto a garage roof where I could watch squirrels playing. It was beautifully clean and neat, mostly because Grammie insisted that I make my bed before I could have any breakfast and that I hang up or put away all my clothes right away. Since, in the manner of most old houses, there was only one bathroom and that was downstairs, my bedroom also had a chamber pot that I was expected to use at night and empty promptly in the morning. Of course I hated this unpleasant procedure, but Grammie insisted it was my responsibility, and I had to do it.

My room had a big, old-fashioned brass double bed, and at times the mattress springs would squeak, especially if I jumped on the bed or sat down hard. I would lie on it, my arms and legs flung out wide, enjoying the open space of it and the clean smell of the sheets.

At bedtime I would pick a story from the Thornton W. Burgess *Old Mother West Wind* books, or Grammie would tell me a story of when she was a little girl and of her fraternal twin brother Edgar, Other times she would describe to me what was coming in the future of the world. She was training me and helping me to understand what my life would be like as I grew into adulthood.

Sometimes, after Grammie had read me my story, we would talk about the thing she called my special gift. The circle of the lamplight would shine around both of us: me, warm under the covers with my pillows propping up my back, and Grammie, sitting on the side of the bed.

"You know, Betty Ann," Grammie said, "this particular gift you carry within you is from God. *The Gift of Knowledge* is not just your imagination. You really do see things that other people can't. You know some things before they happen. I think you sometimes can tell what people are going to say before they say it, can't you?" With a big sigh, I nodded my head yes.

"From the day you were born I have believed that you were specially chosen. You were born with a veil over your face. Did you know that? It isn't like the kind of veil you see on hats, of course. It's tissue from the sac you grew inside of before your birth. This doesn't happen very often, and when it does, most people believe the baby will have the *Gift of*

Knowledge, just like you have. Even though Priscilla is your identical twin sister, she was not born with a veil, and she doesn't have the Gift. That's a mystery in itself.

"We have had several other seers in the family. My mother's sister, your great-aunt Lois, always knew when babies in the neighborhood would be born, and when anyone was about to die. In those days people didn't understand about second sight, and everyone was afraid of her and called her Mad Lois. Her family even locked her in the attic. There was another child, my niece, who was born blind, yet she knew the name of whoever was coming up the front steps. She could even tell people what colors they were wearing."

"What does having this *Gift of Knowledge* mean?" I asked again, remembering that I had asked her about it several times before during that year. "What do I do with it? It doesn't feel like a gift. I get so confused about it."

"You'll know when the time comes," Grammie assured me. "Our Lord has something special in mind for you, sweet girl. These things cannot be rushed. You will just have to wait and see what life brings to you." Then she held me close, and I felt safe. I knew the outside world could never hurt me here. Oh, Grammie, how many, many times since then have I wanted to have just one more of those wonderful hugs.

As it drew closer for me to return to New Jersey, Grammie stepped up the lessons. One evening she decided to tell me a story about the future. As she looked at me with my head on my pillow, she spoke with almost a different voice. "You are special child," she said with a tear in her eye. "You have quite a life ahead of you. Your life is about spiritual development.

As you grow up you will have many teachers and may want to even pull away from the teachings of the Lord. You must never allow anyone to let you do this. Hang on to these moments as you grow and try to remember always what I am saying to you tonight. I may never get another chance to guide you and help you as you begin to develop your special gifts.

"Betty Ann, you will be and have been a great teacher. You are a guide for the Lord. You have been given two of the seven gifts that He promised would be left here on earth after His departure. *The Gift of Knowledge* and the *Gift of Healing.* You are blessed and protected by the angels, always. You will spend much of your life doing and teaching God's work. You will meet, after the age of forty-five, a great being. It is a woman who will represent to you Mother Mary. She will be an Avatar and will be a great influence on you. Because you have chosen to work with her in your later years, you will be able to write books, teach groups and bring many tortured souls to Her feet, as well as the feet of God." I had a funny look on my face, not really being able to comprehend what Grammie was saying to me. I was squirming under the covers because a strange energy was coming up my spine and I was uncomfortable with that feeling.

"Your life is a great light and I am so pleased you are my Granddaughter, Grammie said with tears in her eyes. "I only hope you have listened well this year and will remember the lessons when the time comes. Put all this out of your mind for now and enjoy your life. It will all come back to you when the time is right. You will be tested, Betty Ann, and you will have to prove over and over again that you choose to be used as an instrument for God. You will not have an easy time of it, I'm afraid. But I know with these early teachings that you will do just fine. Remember that I love you and God loves you, and you will blossom.

"Now let me hear you say your prayers," Grammie said, hugging me again. "When you say prayers you connect with our Lord. Every prayer is heard, no matter how small and every prayer is answered. You may not understand how the prayer is answered because we don't always get what we want in life, but God gives us just what we need daily, for our Souls to grow strong. Connecting with God every day helps us to stay on the path to Him. When we wander off that path, we get mixed up, confused, things don't go our way and we become sick. This is the law of the Universe. You are here to get well, Betty Ann, and you are doing just fine. Remember your prayers when you go home and you will stay well."

After my prayers Grammie reached up to turn the light out and tucked me into bed. "Good night dear one," she whispered, kissing me lightly on the forehead. "See you in the morning. I'll make oatmeal with maple syrup and fresh biscuits. Maybe little Kathy can come over for breakfast." Smiling with delight, I turned over and fell into a peaceful sleep.

In late August mother came up to take me back to New Jersey to begin school. "Cilla dear," Grammie said to her daughter, "your last born child is very special. I am glad you named her Elizabeth because it is a regal name. I want to tell you something, which is not for her sisters to hear. Betty Ann is psychic. She sees pictures and has thoughts in her mind about people and future events. She hears messages from the angels. Betty Ann is a special child of God and is here to fulfill something grand. She does not lie. She really does not exaggerate, for it is quite difficult for a small child to understand the gift she is carrying. Be gentle with her and try to understand her. Try to support her and encourage her to use this gift. She has a good heart and would never hurt a fly deliberately. Listen to what she tries to tell you and see beyond it. She needs your love and understanding very much, as well as your protection at times against her sisters."

Mother smiled back, not sure of what she was hearing. "I'll try Mumma," she responded, "but she has to behave herself. I don't want her to feel self-important."

"Cilla, your daughter is shy," Grammie explained gently, "and sometimes lacks strength and self-esteem. Betty Ann is compared to her twin too much. Allow the girls to become their individual selves. It is extra hard for them because they have their older twin sisters as a pattern, and still have to compete with each other as well. These two girls are not a bit alike. Their lives will take different paths. While Nancy and Claramay are close and even have developed their own language, these two younger twins are separate, but look exactly alike! To remember this will be difficult for you, Cilla. Call me if you need me to remind you. What a cross she will have to bear." Mother nodded and promised Grammie she would try to remember that.

As we were packing the car for the long drive back to New Jersey, I had a deep ache inside. I did not want to go back and leave the protection of my Grandmother. I was looking forward to going home to see my friends, but not necessarily my sisters, who constantly teased me unmercifully.

Before Mother could start the engine, I dashed back into the red house with the white shutters that held so much love for me and walked through it for the last time. As I climbed the stairs to say goodbye to my room, I stopped short. Frozen in place, I looked up at the familiar picture hanging at the top of the stairs. It was titled *Rock of Ages*, but in my mind I had silently renamed it *Oh My Darling*. I loved that picture, and it was the first thing I would look for when we visited Grammie each summer. This time a cold chill ran up and down my spine when I saw the haunting print of a woman with long blonde hair. Clinging to a cross, she was kneeling on a rock in the middle of the ocean as waves lapped up around her. At that moment, I knew somehow that picture represented my life to come.

CHAPTER 2

The Early Years

I REMEMBER A CERTAIN KIND of Easter ornament popular when I was a little girl. It was a hollow egg, three to five inches long, made of hard, white sugar and trimmed with pastel frosting ribbons and flowers. There was a little round window at one end, and when you put your eye up to it, you could see a tiny, magic world inside -- all blue skies, green grass and blossoms. There were figures too, sometimes baby rabbits, chickens, or happy children

On the surface my family was like one of those eggs, all sweet and pretty and perfect: beautiful house in a genteel suburb of New York City; handsome corporate executive father; lovely Christian mother, and four attractive, talented daughters; two sets of identical twins. But a closer look through the window of our particular sugar egg told a different story. There wasn't any blue-skied paradise, that's for sure. Instead, there was a stormy, distorted landscape. Among the little figures under the gray sky, there were a cold, tyrannical father; frightened, submissive mother; and abused, resentful children. Love was there too, but all twisted up and hidden within the general chaos. This was my family. This was my life.

My parents were about as well matched as a ballet slipper and an army boot. Mother persistently proclaimed her born-again, fundamentalist Christianity and her purity. As a good 1950's Christian wife, she believed she should be submissive to her husband in all things, except when it came to alcohol. Dad accepted the role of emperor as his natural right and ruled with a microscopically critical eye and a cast-iron hand. If my mother put the wrong dessert on the table, or if she wanted to spend money on a pair of shoelaces he didn't think we needed, everybody heard about it, and in stereo sound.

Every Sunday we all went to church. My father always looked handsome in his beautifully cut suit and tie. Mother, my sisters, and I wore the full mid-twentieth century churchgoing regalia: hats, gloves, linen handkerchiefs, best dresses, best coats and best shoes. I'm almost sure my father thought that going up the steps before church and coming down the steps after church were the most important parts of the service. Mother, on the other hand, took the portion in between very seriously and very literally. She believed in a real Heaven and a real Hell, and she knew who in our family was going to which place.

Our church friends would have been astonished to see what happened the other six days of the week, days when my father went storming through the house. When he yanked open kitchen cabinets and searched bathroom shelves, then bounded down the stairs to the basement where he made bumping and scraping noises, he would yell something like, "Cilla, where did you put it? You don't have any business touching anything of mine. Tell me where it is, or I swear I'll make you sorry you were ever born."

Mother would respond, "I poured it all down the sink last night, every single drop. You've got to stop that drinking or you're going straight to Hell, and there won't be anything you can do about it. And the card playing has got to stop too. You're hanging around with the lowest possible element. If you were to die now, you would stand condemned before the Lord."

Then my father would turn up the volume, "I can't do it, Cilla. I'm one of the top bridge players in America. I write the bridge column for the *New York Times*. I'm not shooting seven-come-eleven in some back-room crap game. Teaching bridge helps pay our bills!"

"Cards are nothing but flattened-out dice," my mother would start sobbing. "The soldiers threw dice at the foot of the cross while Christ was dying. Is that what you want to do? Laugh in the face of our suffering Lord?"

One morning I went into my parents' room and found my mother sitting up in her bed. Her eyes were red, and I thought she might have a cold because she was blowing her nose into a handkerchief. My father's bed was empty.

Mercurial is the word that I think of when I picture my father, not only because of his volatile temper and changeable moods, but also because he was like quicksilver to live with: all shiny and attractive on the outside, but dangerous to be in close contact with for any length of time.

I remember seeing my father at a family party where he pulled his suit jacket over the top of his head like a crazy scarf and told jokes. Everyone was laughing except my mother, who sat rigidly erect with a stiff smile on her face, her lips drawn in thin line that always showed me she was angry.

Dad hated to see weakness in any of us. Once, when I was sick in bed with one of my many bouts with the flu, my father came into the room and looked at me with lightning in his eyes. "What, again?" he said to my mother. "This is unbelievable."

"The doctor says Betty Ann is anemic, and that's why she gets sick so often," my mother explained.

"That's ridiculous," my father said. "Priscilla is her identical twin and she's not anemic, so there's no reason why Betty Ann should be. Stop hiding under the covers, Betty Ann, and get up and get moving. You know you're not sick, so stop pretending. Nobody likes a liar."

Later that same year, my older sisters got the mumps. Nancy had them on the left side of her face, Claramay had them on the right. Then I got them on both sides. Priscilla didn't get them at all. I wasn't surprised – a double load of mumps fit in perfectly with the rest of my life.

It wasn't unusual for me to have various bruises here and there from where my father hit me. Once I had a bruise on my forehead from his belt buckle and tried to cover up the discoloration by combing my hair this way and that, but nothing worked. I was ashamed. Less shameful were the marks I got elsewhere because they were in places no one could see. I usually had at least one bruise somewhere or other, except in the summertime when I went to New Hampshire to stay with my grand-mother, where I was safe.

Wendy stopped suddenly, her blond curls still bouncing. Her eyes and mouth turned into perfect circles as she stared at me. "She's dead," I told her, as we skipped home from school one spring afternoon. "Mrs. Vail died last night," I said, a bit proud that I knew something Wendy didn't, even though she was a really big girl. She was the advanced age of fourteen, three years older than I.

"Mrs. Vail's body wasn't working right any more. She was so old that it was worn out. In the middle of the night her lungs just stopped and never started again. She's still in her bed right now. Her hair is in braids. She looks like she could sit up and have my mom bring her a cup of tea, like she always does, but she really can't because her soul went out of her body. She's really in Heaven." For a moment I could see Mrs. Vail again -- a still, gray figure lying on the bed in the shadowy room on the third floor of my house. The window was open a little, and the curtains were blowing softly outward.

I remembered the slow, painful "thump, thump" I used to hear as the old woman climbed the three flights of stairs to her apartment. Then more and more, it had been my mother and other ladies from church who went up and down the steps. Finally it was only my mother and the ladies. The women, in their pastel flowered dresses, carried laundry baskets and food and sometimes flowers. They had to help the old woman wash her-self and get dressed and undressed. It seemed strange that a grownup would need help with those things. The ladies spoke to Mrs. Vail in loud, cheerful voices, but when she was out of earshot they talked quietly and called her "poor thing." Now the ladies wouldn't be coming any more.

"I'm afraid of getting old, Wendy," I said. "I'm afraid of what will happen to me."

Wendy put her arm around my shoulders. "Want to come over and play awhile?" she said. "We could play Monopoly or Chinese checkers, or we could work a puzzle. I've got a pretty one with three cats in a basket."

"No, I have to get home," I said. "I wish I didn't. Priscilla and I have a piano lesson, and I hate piano lessons. I always get into trouble, and the teacher yells and gets so mad."

"Well, maybe we can play another time," Wendy said, "And I just bet your piano lesson won't be so bad today."

Wendy turned out to be right. The piano lesson really wasn't so bad. It was, in fact, completely horrible.

"Let's start out with your four-hands-on-the-piano piece," the teacher said. Miss Hudgens was the organist in our church, The Ridgewood Methodist Church, where my parents were active members. She had taught piano to my older sisters, Nancy and Claramay. They were accomplished pianists. We were expected to achieve the same musical excellence and have the same talents.

Priscilla smiled at me as we sat down next to each other on the piano bench. I played three notes, and then my sister leaned over toward me and pinched me on the arm as hard as she could.

"Yowp!" I yelled and hopped off the end of the bench.

"Really, Betty Ann," the teacher said, "you aren't going to start that again today, are you?" She refused to listen to any explanation. "Sit right back down again, young lady, and start over."

I began again, and quickly Priscilla jabbed my elbow very deftly so Miss Hudgens couldn't see. A jangle of wrong notes came from the piano. "Really, Betty Ann, have you been practicing at all?" the teacher said. I slid over on the bench as far as I could without falling off and tried the piece again. This time my sister kicked me in the ankle. I tried not to make any noise, but I reflexively threw my hands up and lost my place in the music.

"Here it cuh-ums," my sister said to me under her breath. The teacher took me by the shoulders, turned me around on the bench, and began a long and loud scolding. Words and phrases like "never seen anything like it," "outrageous," "disrespectful," "you should be ashamed," "sick and tired," "appalling," "cheeky," "your parents will hear about this," whizzed around the room like hornets. I wanted to quietly melt away and sink into the well-vacuumed carpet.

Priscilla, her hands folded in her lap and the smile still on her lips, seemed to be listening to an angel chorus. Of course, the words weren't directed at her. But even if they had been, I believed she would have looked the same. She shrugged her shoulders at things like authority figures and yelling and piano teachers. "They're nothing but a bunch of rotten prunes," she would say. "They don't mean a thing to me."

I had almost completely recovered from the music lesson by dinnertime. The piano teacher had stomped out of the house and down the porch steps, and she wasn't going to come again for ages and ages -- a whole week, in fact. My parents were both smiling, the kitchen was cheerful with light and with pleasant talk, and the taste of my mother's lamb stew was fast healing my injured feelings. My sister was making faces at me, of course, and opening her mouth to show what she was chewing, but I didn't mind. I bugged out my eyes, gave her my best Howdy Doody smile, and went right on eating. The troubles and trials of the day were over at last.

Then the telephone rang. My mother answered it. "Well, hello, Mrs. Quad. How nice to hear from you. Hmmm, I don't quite understand what you mean. What sort of arrangements are you talking about? What you're telling me is extremely strange. I can assure you that Mrs. Vail is just fine, or at least as well as can be expected for a woman her age and in her condition. Why, I had a nice little talk with her only an hour or two ago. You say one of the twins told your Wendy? Oh, yes, I have a good idea which one it was. We've had trouble like this with her before. No, I really must disagree. I don't think this is just a childish prank. A lie is a lie, Mrs. Quad, and with my daughter, lying is becoming a serious fault. Thank you so much for calling. I'll see that everything is set straight."

Mother came back to the table, but she didn't sit down. "That, as you probably heard, was Wendy's mother," she said, looking straight at me. "She just informed me, Betty Ann, that on the way home from school today you told Wendy some outrageous story about how our tenant Mrs. Vail died last night. Wendy's mother called to find out what the funeral arrangements were. You can imagine how I felt having to tell her that Mrs. Vail is upstairs on the third floor and just fine. She certainly did not die last night! I am ashamed that you told a lie. And such a wicked lie about that poor old woman.

"Betty Ann, I'm absolutely at my wit's end!" Mother stated angrily. "Don't you know the difference between the truth and a lie? A big girl like you?"

"But mother, she is dead!" I said, my eyes wild with fear.

"I won't hear it, Betty Ann; I just won't hear it. You have shamed yourself, and you have shamed your family too. There isn't any possible excuse."

"But I really did see..." I stammered.

I felt a hand clamp painfully onto my shoulder. "Your mother told you no excuses," my father said. His face had turned a dangerous red. "I'm going to march you right up to your room, Miss, and we're going to have a few words about this story you concocted."

We flew upstairs, his grip getting tighter and tighter as we went. I don't remember exactly what happened next, but his "few words" made the scolding from the piano teacher and my mother seem like sweet, gentle praise. It was like being with the lion that I saw in a Tarzan television show. Tarzan thought the lion was his friend, but all of a sudden it jumped up, snarling and showing its huge teeth, and then it started roaring so loudly that its mouth seemed bigger than its head. I was spanked so hard with his belt that my bottom was sore for days afterwards. I couldn't sit down without feeling searing pain.

After my father left, I crawled into my bed and curled up in a ball under the covers. I still had all my clothes on, even my shoes. I didn't notice. I cried until the sheets near my head were soaked and sticky with mucus and tears. "I want to die," I whispered, and I meant it.

My mind was tied up in misery-tangles. I knew that Mrs. Vail had died last night-- she really had! I saw the *misty thing* leave her body, and I knew it was her soul. I saw it for sure. But then she really didn't die. Mother talked to her today. So I'm a liar. But I thought it was true. How do other people tell the difference between what's real and what's not real? Everyone can do it but me. A liar is a terrible thing to be. If you are a liar but don't know you're a liar, does that make you even worse than a person who tells lies on purpose? They all were so angry and yelled so much. I must be a really horrible person. But I'm not trying to be a horrible person. I just said what I really saw. But I broke a Ten Commandment. I'm so scared. Is there really a God? How will I ever learn what things I should say and what things I shouldn't say? It's like I'm always falling into a hole that everybody else knows is there but me. Can't God send one of his angels down to save me or guide me in some way? My heart was breaking.

Suddenly on the ceiling I saw a shining light, comforting and vibrating towards my direction. When I closed my eyes, it became brighter. Then I had the sensation of being held in a woman's arms. She had blonde hair and was dressed in brilliant blue. A halo of rainbow of light surrounded her. Somewhere far away I heard soft music playing. She rocked me back and forth, back and forth, and I finally drifted off to sleep to her lullaby.

Two days later, my mother told me that Mrs. Vail had died in her sleep the night before. Mother seemed very sad. She remembered Grammie's words from two years before, "Your daughter will be tested, and she will have to prove over and over again that she chooses to be used as an instrument for God. She will not have an easy time of it, Cilla, and some of her experiences can be very misunderstood."

"Betty Ann, dear," she said, looking intently at my face, "I may have judged you a bit too quickly the other day." She reached her arms out to me and held me close, while she stroked my hair. She tearfully said, "I'm sorry your Father punished you so harshly."

Then she held me back and looked intently into my eyes. Sighing deeply she said, "Betty Ann you almost died at birth. You were only three pounds and had to spend over six weeks in an incubator. You have always been physically weak, just a wisp of a girl, but I envy your mind. Where, little one, do your thoughts take you?"

I asked her what she meant, but she just said that we would have to talk about it sometime soon.

When I was nine or ten, my Aunt Claramay took me aside and told me about the first year of my life. I don't remember my mother ever talking to me about that time, except to say that Priscilla and I were born six weeks early, and that Priscilla was twenty minutes older than I was. "When I first saw you, you were as light as two feathers lying side by side, not a drop of fat on either one of you," Aunt Claramay said. "Your little arms and legs were like baby chicken bones. You weighed three pounds apiece, and you looked like you could fit into the palm of my hand. Identical in just about every way, except that you were born with a veil over your face, and Priscilla was not."

"A veil?" I asked, picturing myself as a baby with a miniature white tulle headdress.

"Not the kind a bride has," said my aunt, smiling. "Being born with a veil means that your face is covered by a thin tissue, kind of like a very delicate piece of skin. The doctor had to take it off right away, so you could breathe. Grammie Hemphill was born with one; so were a few of your other ancestors. Old people say that when you are born with a veil, it means that you have second sight, that you can see and hear things other people can't. The nurses had to put you and Priscilla in an incubator to keep you warm and safe because your bodies weren't big enough to work on their own. You were connected to all kinds of tubes to help you breathe and get food. We didn't know whether either of you would live or die. It looked like a puff of wind could carry you away from us to Heaven. But you both held onto life.

"Your mother was very sick too. She was dreadfully weak, and she came down with pneumonia. Priscilla began to grow and thrive right away, but you were so little and helpless for such a long time. I had to come down from New Hampshire and stay at your house for a year to take care of you. The very first time your poor mother held you was on your first birthday."

This revelation was powerful and helped me throughout my life. I began to understand the feelings of separation, loneliness, and why I could never feel that I "fit in."

In the early 1980's, under the guidance of Dr Frank Alper, founder of the Arizona Metaphysical Society, I undertook what is called a present life regression. I was put into a hypnotic state, where I was able to send my consciousness backward in time until I was back in my mother's womb. I found myself huddled over to one side, facing my twin, our knees touching. My hands were raised, trying to cover my face, while my twin went at me with her arms and legs. "Please, please don't hurt me," I was soundlessly crying out. "I don't want to be born if this is what life is going to be like."

A friend of mine who has a fine, intuitive sensitivity, has a theory that twins who face each other in the womb tend to act aggressively toward each other after they are born. Twins who are prenatally positioned spoon-style, or back-to-back, or crossed like an "X" are usually much kinder to each other in later life. It makes all the sense in the world to me.

My older twin sisters, Claramay and Nancy, were as close to each other as my twin and I were far apart. They had the amazing ability to have fun and laugh together without any punching or yelling. When family storms hit, my older sisters would go up to their room and quietly ride them out, supporting and protecting each other. I wished I could be triplets with them. I remember often seeing them playing the piano and singing in the living room while my parents looked on and smiled. Claramay and Nancy took lessons from Miss Hudgens, the same piano teacher Priscilla and I did, but they were excellent students. One of them never poked the other as they sat side by side on the piano bench, and there weren't any wrong notes when they played, even though their music books were ever so much harder than ours

My older sisters were so close and they had their own language that no else knew how to speak. "Boddit tog lala," Nancy would say. "Lama boo," Claramay would answer, and they would both giggle. My older sisters lay across each other in the womb, and their hearts beat in exact time to one another. Mother didn't know there were two babies until almost delivery time.

Whoever thinks identical twins have identical personalities doesn't know my sister Priscilla and me. When we were young, she had glowing good health; I was scrawny and weak. She pushed; I got pushed. She smacked; I got smacked. She was daring; I was cautious. She didn't believe anything anyone said; I believed everything everyone said. She was all frills and lace and full skirts; jeans and a shirt were my favorite clothes. I didn't have many friends at all until I was a senior in high school. My twin, on the other hand, always seemed to have lots of people around her. In high school she hung out with the wild kids, the greasers from Paramus, kids my father classified as a form of life just a little above pond algae. "Tell Mom I went uptown," Priscilla would instruct as she jumped into a black 1955 T-Bird convertible. Off she would go with her Paramus buddies. She would be laughing, her dark hair and her pink rayon neckerchief flying. She never thought of the interrogation I would have to face at home.

When my twin and I were small, my mother used to bathe us together. Sometimes when Mother left the bathroom for a little while, Priscilla would push my head under the water and hold it there. I struggled, but she was the stronger one, so I usually couldn't get my head up. Often I was sure I would drown and knew she wanted me to. Finally she would let go just before mother returned. Then Priscilla, with that familiar lying mask coming across her face, would say, "Betty Ann splashed water all over the floor. I told her not to, but she did it anyway."

Sometimes Priscilla got me to play Indians with her, and the game usually ended up with her tying me to a tree. She liked to tie the ropes as tight as she could and haul me up along the tree trunk so that my feet couldn't touch the ground. Then she would leave me there and go off and forget about me. Usually I managed to escape, but sometimes I couldn't. Once I was trussed up so long that I must have come close to passing out, because when my mother drove up the driveway and saw me, I didn't recognize who she was.

I learned to give Priscilla anything she wanted, because if I put up any opposition, she would hit or scratch or bite. If I tried to retaliate, she would tell my parents that I started the whole thing. If she wanted one of my toys, I usually just laid it down on the floor and walked away. "Betty Ann," my mother told me years later, "if you had the money for everything you have given away, you would be a millionaire

I don't know exactly why God saw fit to make us twin sisters. I don't believe Priscilla is any more pleased about the arrangement than I am. I do know that God always has His reasons. I think we needed to work out some things between us in this lifetime, things that we didn't complete in a previous life on Earth. At that time I didn't know that we chose each other, and designed the opposition for our soul growth before we incarnated as identical twins. If I had, I would never have believed it.

My psychic sensitivities made my life more complicated. I had trouble sorting out my prophetic dreams and visions from the plain, everyday things that everybody sees all the time. I often heard what people were going to say before they actually said it. The words they were planning to say just inserted themselves into my mind. It all seemed perfectly normal to me. I assumed it happened to everyone. I couldn't understand why people would get so upset when they were talking to me. My father might want to ask me where the newspaper was, for example, so he would start to say, "Betty Ann, where's...."

Before he could finish the sentence, I'd say, "It's on the table by the front door."

Then he'd say, "You don't even know what it is I want."

"Yes, I do. You just asked me where the newspaper was.

"I didn't have a chance to ask you anything. You very rudely interrupted me, and rudeness is something I will not tolerate in this house."

"Then how did I know you wanted the newspaper?"

"I don't want to hear any more of your sassy mouth, Miss. Go up to your room and don't come down until I tell you to."

As a child, I had an unusual ability with words that I've completely lost as an adult. Until I was about twelve, I could sometimes understand people who spoke foreign languages, and I could speak those languages back to them. I was about seven when Mr. Taylor, a friend of my father's, came to visit us at Christmas. He brought my twin and me each a music box from Switzerland, where he had been living for some time. I was delighted with the lovely little thing -- round and shiny green, with a clear glass top so you could see the tiny machine going around and around inside as it played.

"*Danke viemals,*" I said to Mr. Taylor. "*Dieses ist sehr schon, und ich liebe es. Das war sehr nettt von Ihnen.*"

"She talks just like a little Swiss girl," Mr. Taylor said. "I didn't know she could speak German, Walter."

"I didn't either," said my father. "This is the first I've heard of it." He turned to me. "Betty Ann," he said, "what did you say to Mr. Taylor?"

"How did you know those German words?" Father asked.

"I don't know. They just came out of my mouth." I began to worry that I had done something wrong. There was an uncomfortable silence. "I just knew, that's all," I finally said.

Once a missionary to the Philippines visited our church, and, without thinking, I spoke to him in Tagalog about some native embroidery he had brought along. The missionary's eyes got big, and he didn't seem to be able to talk for a minute. "Oh, boy," I said to myself. "I've done something wrong again." I still wonder how he fit my little performance into his theology. I hope he didn't think I was possessed.

School in Ridgewood, New Jersey, was rough on my twin and me. World War II had ended a few years before, and the McCarthy Era was in full swing. Our last name happened to be "Reich." Gossip had it that because of our last name our family had somehow been connected with Nazi Germany. After all, wasn't Hitler's regime called the Third Reich? What more proof could anyone want? Some of our classmates' parents called us "those German brats," and they weren't at all upset when their children taunted us and beat us up

In ninth grade, our music teacher Mr. Phillips decided to put on a production of Victor Herbert's operetta, *The Fortuneteller.* Just about everyone in school knew that he had Priscilla and me in mind for the leads since the story was about two girls trading places, much like Mark Twain's *The Prince and the Pauper.* My sister's voice was beautiful -- strong and clear, and she had excellent stage presence. I wasn't too bad either.

A group of parents got together and waged a telephone campaign to keep us from getting the leading roles. They informed the principal that if 'The German Twins" (That was us, even though we were born in Hackensack, New Jersey) were chosen as the leads, they (the parents) would keep their children out of the show. The principal gave in to their demands, and Mr. Phillips was forced to give the parts to other girls. My sister was named understudy to the lead gypsy, and I was in the chorus.

Camilla, who got the leading role of Musette in the operetta, came down with strep throat just before the evening of the show. Numerous parents telephoned the school and threatened that their children wouldn't show up if Priscilla went on instead. Mr. Phillips was forced to put the show off for two weeks until Camilla was well again. When *The Fortuneteller* finally was performed, Camilla put in a strictly pedestrian performance. Priscilla, who only had a few solo lines, sang them so strongly and beautifully that she stood out from everyone else in the cast.

A few parents who were new to the school district and not in on the phone campaign came up to Mr. Phillips after the show and asked him why the lead hadn't been given to Priscilla. The music teacher had to give them some kind of phony story. Many years later, as he was dying of cancer, I went to visit Mr. Phillips. It was then that he told me about the phone campaign and everything else. He had tears in his eyes, and I could see that he was in great pain. The ninth grade operetta was an annual event throughout Mr. Phillips' reign as music teacher. We had anticipated starring in it ever since the older twins had leads in *The*

Ruddigore, five years before. I told him not to worry about it any more. "Our family has always realized it wasn't your fault," I said. "I know you had faith in Priscilla and me and that you wanted us to succeed." We held hands tightly for the remainder of the visit. Thanking him, I kissed him on the forehead and left.

When Nancy and Claramay were sixteen, they were picked to be one of sixteen sets of twins nationwide to be in advertisements for Toni Home Permanents on the exciting and new entertainment medium of television. In the commercials, the camera would come in for a close-up on my sisters' beautiful faces and hair while the announcer intoned, "Which twin has the Toni, and which twin has the expensive salon permanent?" My sisters would turn their heads this way and that, smiling prettily. Then the announcer would say, "Only her hairdresser knows for sure," and the twins would smile some more. It was practically as good as being royalty. Everyone in the United States knew about the Toni Twins, except maybe cloistered monks and prisoners in solitary confinement.

One week Nancy and Claramay were to do a live commercial on comedian Ed Wynn's Show in New York City. Our whole family went along. The studio was vibrating with excitement, people rushing this way and that and all kinds of bright lights and TV cameras.

While my parents went to see Nancy and Claramay rehearse, comedienne Beatrice Lillie, Ed's guest that evening, offered to watch us in her dressing room for an hour or two.

I marveled at her makeup mirror, with its surrounding halo of lights, and the enticing clutter of little different-colored pots of makeup, the round boxes of powders, the creams and brushes set out on the table. Sitting in front of it all was Miss Lillie, looking as exotic as everything else, with her peacock blue kimono dressing gown and her peacock blue eyelids.

Now my Deahs," she said, patting her knees, "why don't you just hop up heah, and I'll sing you something amusing." Then, with Priscilla on one knee and me on the other, she began to sing.

Three little maids from school are we,
Filled to the brim with girlish glee. ...
Everything is a source of fun,
Nobody is safe for we care none!
Life is a joke that's just begun!
Three little maids from school.
(W. S. Gilbert, The Mikado)

If only I could stay right here forever, I thought, I would be happy every minute of my life. I instantly began to dream of being a singer or a dancer on the New York stage.

When we got home, I begged my parents to let me take tap dancing lessons. Since I had failed at both piano and violin, my mother told me that there was no money for more lessons. I decided to practice dancing on my own. My parents weren't interested in watching my endless performances, nor were my sisters

Sadie was interested, though. Sadie McNeil, our housekeeper was short, black, and she liked to laugh. Sadie came up from Paterson, New Jersey, every Tuesday and Friday, so every Tuesday and Friday I knew I had an audience. I would rush home from school and in through the back door, straight to Sadie's territory, the blessed laundry room. Mother would be out and about somewhere, but Sadie was always right there waiting for me. I'd hop onto her lap and tell her all about my day, and then she'd tell me about her day. She made such a fuss over me. She listened to everything I had to say and respected my opinions and ideas. She even believed me when I told her about the way I knew what people were going to say before they said it, how I saw things that other people couldn't see, and how I dreamed about things that came true later

After our talk, it was Showtime. I'd jump off Sadie's lap and run to put on one of my many homemade costumes. A favorite ensemble was a Kleenex carnation or two pinned in my hair and an old lace curtain thrown around my shoulders. Then I'd leap back into the laundry room.

"Look at this, Sadie," I'd say. "I can do ballet. See, I can almost get up on my tiptoes. This is a ballet about a caterpillar who turns into a

34

butterfly." Then I'd flap my curtain-covered arms and hop back and forth in front of Sadie while she was ironing my father's white shirts or my sisters' ruffled Sunday dresses. As the steam rose from the iron, a good smell would come from the hot, clean fabric.

"Betty Ann, you're gonna knock my curls right down to Paterson." Sadie would laugh. "It's the best caterpillar ballet I ever saw, and that's the truth.

"Now wait a minute, don't go away," I'd say. "I'll change costumes and then you can see me do my tap dancing." Then I'd rush off and get changed for the next part of the performance. Sadie watched all the dancing I wanted to show her, which was a considerable amount. She was just as willing to hear my songs. I specialized in show tunes and anything else I could think of. Some times I read Sadie my poems and stories. One story, I remember, was about Tramp, a dog who died in an ice skating pond while trying to rescue a little boy. All my fiction featured a person in dire straits, needing to be saved, much like the girl in the *Oh My Darling* picture at Grammie's house.

"You're going to make a fine mother someday." Picking up the iron, Sadie began to press one of my favorite dresses. "Your children will love all your stories and songs."

Dancing on my toes, I began twirling around like a ballerina. "I want to live on a huge farm in New Hampshire, near Grammie. I want ducks, chickens, dogs, cats and twelve children. Oh yes, and lots of horses to ride."

Sadie laughed and laughed. "My curls just got knocked down to Paterson again. Your man better be awful rich to give you all that."

"No, "I explained. "We'll live off the land and grow our own food. Grammie says that if people don't stop their foolish ways, there'll be lots of pollution around here when I grow up, and we'll have to live in the country if we want to survive."

"Lord have mercy. What serious things go on in that little head of yours, Honey?"

Sadie's niece Hazel was tall, very dark, and stunningly beautiful. I looked forward to the times she would come to pick Sadie up from work.

Sometimes, especially when my mother wasn't home, she would stay a little while.

Hazel had long, elegant, scarlet fingernails. When she taught me how to take care of my own nails, she opened a little window into the world of glamour and grown-up ladies for me, and I couldn't wait for the time when I would be old enough to have nails as long and red as hers. She was kind and soft-spoken to me, but she had a sly smile that told me she knew a lot about the world. Sadie's niece, I somehow realized, didn't lead the same kind of life as quiet, God-fearing Sadie.

Hazel taught me an interesting game with numbers. We would play it while Sadie was out of earshot. Hazel would tell me to think of a series of numbers, usually three in a row. Then she would try to guess what they were. Most of the time she didn't get them right, so I would finally have to tell her what they were. Then Hazel would smile and tell me that they might come in. I didn't know exactly what "come in" meant, but if it made her happy, then it made me happy too.

Once Hazel brought me a list of horses' names in the newspaper and asked me which ones could run the fastest. I was studying this fascinating piece of literature when Sadie came into the room, and the fireworks began.

"Now don't you be betting no horses from what little Betty Ann says," Sadie yelled. I had never heard Sadie raise her voice before. "This is a good Christian house, and Mr. Reich would be furious if he ever found out."

"But she's usually right, Sadie," Hazel's eyes, with their long, curly lashes opened wide. "I made over five hundred dollars on the numbers because of her. She's a little witch."

"Don't you ever call my little Betty Ann a witch. Not this child. She has a true gift from God and don't you ever misuse it. I didn't have no idea why you were paying so much attention to her. Never thought you had any patience with children. Serves me right. I shouldda known you had a motive. Well, this is the last time I ever ask you to pick me up from work. I'll take the bus home from now on."

I was eleven and had no idea what was happening. I didn't want Hazel and Sadie to argue, and I didn't want Hazel to leave. "Please don't yell, Hazel," I said. "Buttermilk and Joe's Angel are going to win."

Sadie was pointing angrily toward the door, but before she left, Hazel turned and gave me a hug and kiss goodbye. "I'll let you know what happens, Baby," she said, tears welling up in her beautiful eyes. The next week Sadie told me that Hazel and her boyfriend had played the horses, and they had won over a thousand dollars.

About a month later I asked Sadie how Hazel was doing. "I just had a picture of her coming into my head. She has a tummy ache today. She's worrying about something."

"Yes, "Sadie nodded. "She was kinda under the weather this morning."

"There's another thing too," I said. "You're going to be a great-aunt soon, Sadie. Hazel is getting a baby girl to live with her."

"Oh, my," Sadie said. "I've been afraid of that. Her no-good boyfriend will most likely take off." Sadie paused a moment and stared down at her hands. "Betty Ann, how do you come to know all these things you do?"

Shyly, I began swaying back and forth and pulling my hair. "I don't do anything special. Sometimes pictures just come in front of my eyes, like a TV show. Other times I can't see things but I can hear them. Lots of times people don't believe me."

"Betty Ann," Sadie said, "I know you're telling the truth. I can tell it bothers you sometimes, all those things you see that nobody else does. But you know, you can just leave it all in God's hands and let him carry your burdens. He'll help you if you just ask."

I stopped my nervous swaying and crawled into her lap. I stayed there a long time.

CHAPTER 3

American Bandstand

"PLEASE, PLEASE, YOU JUST GOTTA let us do it," Priscilla and I begged our parents with the fervor of a pair of starving vacuum cleaner salesmen. "Please take us down to Philadelphia so we can dance on *American Bandstand*. Everyone in the world wants to be on."

It's all we'll ever ask you for, ever, ever again," I said. "Nancy and Claramay did TV commercials, so it's only fair for us to be on television too. We're fifteen, and that's just the right age."

My father looked skeptical. "What exactly is this *American Bandstand* thing?"

"Omigosh, Dad, I can't believe you don't know," Priscilla said, her fists pumping the air like mad pistons. "Everyone in the world watches it. They have performers come on and sing all the new music, and they have high school kids like us dance all the new dances."

"And it won't cost you anything at all," I cut in. "They let you dance for free. You'll get to see us on TV, and we'll make you proud, and we'll get to see famous singers, and it'll be great experience in case we become professional dancers." Our parents weren't sure at first, but finally they gave in. Maybe the fact that my twin and I were agreeing about something threw them off balance.

The four of us drove to Philadelphia the very next week. My father blew up when we got to the WFIL-TV studios on Market Street and saw at least two hundred teenagers lined up outside the front doors. "This really takes the cake," Dad roared. "A hundred and five-mile drive down the Jersey Turnpike in heavy traffic, just so you kids can get turned away before we even get out of the car."

Wait here," I said, jumping out. "I'll be right back." Before anyone could stop me, I plunged into the crowd. A few minutes later I came back with Bob, a man many times more important than the President of the United States. Bob was the security guard who decided who got in and who did not, and Bob thought that dancing identical twins would be great on *American Bandstand*.

Before anyone could say "Cinderella," Bob asked Franny Giordano, one of the well-known regular dancers on the show, to take us into the studio. She very sweetly led us through a side door into a hot, dazzlingly bright little room. Inside were three sets of grandstands, a map of the United States, and the podium where the star Dick Clark stood, all behind a red line drawn across the floor. Three enormous TV cameras occupied most of the rest of the space.

"It's so small," I thought. "How are we ever going to do so much dancing on this postage stamp floor?"

But somehow or other Priscilla and I did, along with sixty or so other teens, that afternoon and many, many other times over the course of three years.

After Priscilla and I had been on a few shows, the regular bandstand dancers started to welcome us as regulars too. Soon people began to recognize us on the street. Even some of the mean parents and kids from high school began giving us their attention. It was such a big change.

They'd stop us on the street and say, "Are you the Dancing Twins on television?" And we would say, quite sweetly and graciously, "Why yes, as a matter of fact, we are." It was the stuff that dreams are made on. *American Bandstand* marked the end of our suffering era, and we began to emerge somehow as deserving individuals. People from outside our area liked us and accepted us. Regulars on the show like Kenny Rossi, Arlene Sullivan, and Frankie Branchaccio, who had fans all over the United States and got bags of fan mail every week, became our friends. We could relax and have fun with them without being gossiped about and criticized the way we were back in Ridgewood. Dick Clark, the show's star and all-around Emperor of Teen TV, knew us by name. We met just about all the rising rock'n'roll royalty of the day –– Frankie Avalon, Fabian, Sam Cooke, Jerry Lee Lewis, Chubby Checker, Chuck Berry, Paul Anka, Pat Boone, Connie Francis, Frankie Valli, and Annette Funicello. *American Bandstand* was a gift from Heaven. What an eye-opener! What a relief to learn that Ridgewood, New Jersey, was not the center of the universe.

One Saturday night in the early spring of 1958, after a Dick Clark show in Atlantic City, we were invited to a party hosted by Pop Singer, who owned the delicatessen next door to the Bandstand studio in Philadelphia. Frankie Valli, Danny and the Juniors, Lou Monte, and Janice Harper were there, along with Dick and some of the Bandstand regulars. I was feeling especially shy and awkward because I didn't know many people there. I went to the back of the room to get some punch, and I saw an especially handsome boy reaching for a chocolate chip cookie on the table. His eyes were deep and kind looking, and his hair looked so soft and wavy that I was tempted to run my fingers through it. My breath was catching in my throat, and I was afraid I would sound like a frog if I said anything. At last I mastered my fear enough to produce some words in something like my normal voice.

"Hello," I said. "You're new to the group here, aren't you?"

"Yes, I'm a guest of Dick's. My name's Bobby Darin, and I've just recorded several new songs. I was hoping Dick would play one on his show next week. It's called *Queen of the Hop*. This guy named Woody Harris and I wrote it." He looked at me for a minute. "Say, aren't you one of the twins on the show?"

Yes, my name's Beth."

"I really like the show," Bobby said. "My favorite's Justine Carelli, the beautiful blonde."

My heart, which had been flying up near the ceiling on pink frosting wings, crashed to the floor and tried to hide under the table.

The song's about her," Bobby said. "It talks about tuning into *American Bandstand* and watching Justine dance. 'She's the queen of the hop. Sweet little Justine, yeah, she's my queen.'"

"Great," I said. "Can't wait to hear it." This was not entirely a lie. There was still hope. He hadn't said that he was engaged to Justine or anything. Besides, everyone in the world knew that she was dating her dancing partner Bob Clayton. "What's the beat?"

"Oh, it's a jive song. You know a lot about music?"

Music! How I knew music. I could tell you the name of any popular song or show tune on the first three notes and then sing all the words. "Yes, I've studied music all my life. I have a wonderful record collection, and I take voice lessons too."

"You sing?" he smiled.

"Not very well. My twin is much better," I said, looking down.

"Okay, but what about dancing? Guess that's your talent. I know because I've watched you. You even won the Spotlight Dance recently."

I felt my cheeks and ears turn red. "I love to do all the new dance styles."

"Well," Bobby said, "Let's try a few." My heart took up its previous position on the ceiling.

At the time, I never realized how shy Bobby Darin was and how difficult it was for him to meet girls. Later I found out that he rarely went to a party or a dance because he was always working on his writing or singing. When he did get out, he always stayed in the back of the room because he didn't know anyone. He never seemed that reticent to me. Maybe it was because he sensed that I was even shyer than he was.

It was a slow dance, and I was enjoying the lightness of his step and, of course, his wonderful sense of rhythm.

"I have a feeling your record will do well," I said.

That's good to hear. I've got to make it and soon, before the age of twenty-five."

Why?" I asked.

Because," Bobby hesitated, "because I have a bad heart. I had rheumatic fever when I was a kid, and it messed up my heart."

We danced silently for a while. Then, in the middle of the floor, we stopped and did something more daring than I would ever have thought possible. We gazed into each other's eyes. I was only fifteen, and it was the first time I had ever felt someone's energy completely penetrate my body. I actually started to swoon. Bobby had to catch me.

His voice came to me from far away. "Are you okay?" he smiled and his dimples were overwhelming.

Oh, yes, I was okay.

"You know, you dance really great. You float like a feather. Where did you learn to follow like that? It's like you know my mind as well as I do."

"My Uncle Fred teaches me," I said.

"Well, I owe your Uncle Fred a debt of gratitude."

I didn't tell Bobby that being psychic doesn't hurt either. It makes it easier to zero in on what your partner wants to do, and it helps you avoid getting your toes stepped on.

"By the way," Bobby said, "what kind of song do you think would make it big on the charts?"

"Well, I'm not really sure. Perhaps it's like the way it is with books. Romance novels are a dime a dozen, but a classic is timeless. Have you ever thought about recording a classic song, maybe from one of the Broadway shows?"

"No, I haven't, but I'll keep that in mind for the future."

"Bobby, I just know you're going to make it. You'll make it big, and your music will be everywhere, even overseas."

"Thanks, Dreamboat," he grinned. "Say, when can I see you again? Where do you live?"

I was taken aback and a bit frightened. What would my father think? "I live in Ridgewood, New Jersey," I heard myself say.

"Whew," he whistled. "That's a fancy place. I live in the Bronx. You ever been to the Bronx?"

"Not really. I've passed through it, though, when we go to Yankee Stadium."

"I've seen Ridgewood, too, but just from a distance," Bobby said. "But you know, the two places aren't really that far apart. Why don't you give me your phone number?"

Again, I was worried about my father's reaction to him. I was fifteen. I had almost no experience dating boys. Bobby was six years older than I was, from the Bronx, and Italian. "Father will never let me go out with him," I thought.

"So, where are you staying in Atlantic City?" Bobby asked.

"Oh, we're not staying here overnight. My parents are coming to pick my sister and me up in a little while."

"Aw shucks," Bobby said. (Yes, he really did say, "Aw shucks.") "I thought I'd get to walk you to your hotel in the moonlight. Can I have a rain check?"

My parents showed up a few minutes later, and I had to leave. Bobby walked me to the stairs to say goodbye, his arm around my waist. He gave me a tight squeeze and winked. "I'm sure glad we met, Beth, and I'll call you soon. I have a meeting with Dick Clark after this party. Wish me luck. I've just got to get this record played on *Bandstand*."

"You will," I said. "Believe me, you will." At that moment I had a vision of all the regulars on the show dancing to Bobby's music. I didn't tell him, though. I had learned to be cautious about telling anyone about my visions of the future.

"Who was that guy?" whispered my twin when we got into the car.

"His name's Bobby," I whispered back.

"He's kinda cute, but isn't he Italian? And that means Catholic, too, I bet. Dad will never let him into the house."

"I know. Anyway, he probably won't call. He likes Justine."

"Don't they all," Priscilla said, chuckling.

"Even if I never see him again," I thought, "I did get to dance with him. I just know he's going to make it big. His name will be known all over the world. Sure do wish I could have heard that song, *Queen of the Hop*."

Early one Saturday afternoon, two weeks later, Bobby called. Only another fifteen-year-old girl could possibly understand how excruciating those two weeks had been. "Hi, Dreamboat," he said, "what are you doing? Need some company?"

My heart started its aeronautics again. "When?" I asked.

"How about an hour?" he said.

Shaking with happiness and fear, I ran to ask my mother whether Bobby could stop by. "Oh, what will your father think?" she said. "Well, all right, but make sure it's after dinner.

Your father is out at a meeting, so we can't eat until three o'clock."

I ran back to the phone. "Make it four o'clock," I said.

"I have a real clunker of a Chevy, and I only hope it will make it across the bridge. Don't be upset if I'm a little late. I'm leaving in a few minutes so I'll get to see your pretty face before dark."

Dad got home late, and we sat down to dinner at three-thirty. Ten minutes into the meal, the doorbell rang. "Who's at the door this time of day?" my father growled. Mother hadn't told him that Bobby was coming. Dad, scowling, went to the door and ushered Bobby into the living room.

When Dad came back to the table, I asked why he didn't invite Bobby to come in and sit with us. He leaned over, looked at me, and said in a voice Bobby couldn't help hearing, "That kid will never be good enough to sit at our table."

"Really, dear," Mother said, "that's so rude of you to say."

I don't care," Dad said. "He doesn't belong here, and he's too dumb to know about rudeness. He's Italian and from the Bronx. What kind of education or manners could he possibly have?"

I wanted to crawl under the table. Dad ate slowly, lingering over the meal until I was squirming. Finally Mother said, "Go in and see your young man now, Betty Ann, but you cannot go out with him in that car. We don't know what kind of driver he is."

Quietly, with my head bowed, I went into the living room, and Bobby rose from his chair. "Hello, Beth," he said. "Thanks for letting me come by. You sure do have a nice home." He held out an unwrapped box. "I brought you this because you told me you collected Storybook Dolls. It's the one from Spain. I picked her out because I liked the colors of her outfit."

Hurt and embarrassed, I didn't know what to do for a moment. Bobby looked so vulnerable standing there and holding the doll he had bought for me. "Hi, Bobby," I finally said. "Were my directions okay?"

"Great," he said. "I came to your house like a beacon light."

Suddenly Bobby walked into the dining room. "Mr. Reich," he said. "May I take your daughter for a walk? We'll just be outside, walking around the house. I won't take her off your property."

"Fine," my father answered, not looking at him.

We went out the front door, and Bobby took my hand. "Look, Beth, I would never, never cause you any harm. I know I'm older than you are and all that, but how can I see you? You're great, and I'd like to get to know you. You seem to know so much about music. I promise I'll never harm a hair on that pretty head. You'll learn that you can trust me. I believe in honesty and being direct. I hate the games they play in show business."

"I'd like to see you too," I answered, "but you saw what my father just did."

"Why don't you come in to New York?" Bobby asked. "I know you don't drive, but there must be a train or a bus around here someplace. So let's make a plan. You come to New York, we can find a place to have lunch, and I'll have you back by sunset. How's that? Can you come in next Sunday?"

"I'll try."

Bobby and I walked around the yard for a while in the early spring air. We talked about his plans for his career and my dreams of acting in the theater. He lifted my chin and looked into my eyes. "You are so beautiful," he said. "Don't let your family stop your dreams. I'll call you this week to set a time and place for us to meet in the city." With that, Bobby drove off, his car sputtering and spurting its way down the street. I prayed he would get back to the Bronx safely. That was the only time Bobby Darin ever came to my house.

I met Bobby in the city many times. Sometimes we just went to a restaurant and sat around talking with singers and musicians like Connie Francis, Frankie Valli, or some of Bobby's other friends. The most common topic of conversation seemed to be getting big breaks: whether they would ever come, when they would come, how we could get them to come, how we could recognize them when they came, what we would do when they came, and how other entertainers got them.

In the fall of 1958, Bobby called and told me he was working on a new song. "I'm writing it about you, Dreamboat," Bobby said, "and I've got a really good feeling about it. The tempo is kind of like a cha-cha or the new calypso dance you're doing on Bandstand. Every time you hear it, I want you to think about me thinking about you." Then he began to sing:

> *Every night I hope and pray*
> *A dream lover will come my way.*
> *A girl to hold in my arms and*
> *Know the magic of her charms,*
> *Because, I want a girl to call my own.*
> *I want a dream lover, so*
> *I don't have to dream alone.*

The following February Bobby played the demonstration recording of "Dream Lover" to me over the phone. He was doing his own piano accompaniment, although Neil Sedaka played on the version that was finally released. The demo was imperfect and rough, but it was marvelous. I still remember it clearly, and I prefer it to the smoother, more technically perfect final version. *Dream Lover* was released in March, 1959. It was an instant hit. My vision of seeing the kids on Bandstand dance to his music came true over and over again as Bobby's star rose.

I went along to some of his recording sessions. He would ask me what I thought about his work, and he actually listened to what I had to say. His voice, how can I describe it? He made it seem easy, that voice that could go from a whisper to a shout so deftly, that ability to sing almost any kind of music. He could enter into a song and find its heart. As time went on, I kept after him to do an album of classic standards. "I think it would be something good for you, a new direction. I sense it would be a good move since you're so versatile."

In September I got another call from Bobby. "Guess who I just met," he said excitedly.

"Elvis?"

"No, Dreamboat, George Burns."

"George Burns? What does he have to do with music?"

"He doesn't, but he wants to take me to Vegas."

"Las Vegas? Night club work?" I asked, surprised. "Do you think you can keep up with the pace? Is it what you really want?"

"I need to stop doing so much teen stuff and break into the adult music market."

"Oh, my Bobby, I'll miss you." It took me a little while to collect myself. Then I teased, "Have you begun to choose the songs for your new album of standards?"

"What do you think of *That's All*?"

"A Sinatra song? They'll think you're a wanna-be. I know you can do a fine job with it, though. Anything else? Anything with a beat?"

"Well, I've been practicing a few. Do you know anything from the *Threepenny Opera*? It's originally from Germany, but an English version is playing Off-Broadway."

"Now you're talking. Yes, I know the *Threepenny Opera*."

"What's your favorite song from the show?"

"*Mack the Knife*," I said immediately, "but you could never do a song about a murderer."

"You know," Bobby said, "you're a funny kid. You've got a sixth sense. I've learned that about you. I've decided I'm going to do that standards album. I'm even writing a new song for it called *That's the Way Love Is*. But I've decided that *Mack the Knife* will be the first song on the album. Remember that, Dreamboat. I just hope I don't lose my record contract because of it. If I can get that album done before December twenty-fifth, consider it my Christmas gift to you. Gotta run now. Take care of your-self and know that a part of you is always with me."

Bobby Darin went to Vegas with George Burns, and Burns became a sort of father figure to him for the rest of his life. Bobby had never known his own father, and it makes me happy to think that he finally found someone who could at least partly fill that void.

The album Bobby and I talked about, titled *That's All*, was recorded a few days before Christmas, 1958, and was released in the spring of 1959. Just as Bobby had promised me, *Mack the Knife* was the first track. No one thought the song would be a hit. His producers tried to talk him out of doing it, and Bobby was nervous about it too. No one expected the fire-works of popularity and praise that it engendered when the album hit the streets; nor the two Grammies Bobby got, one for Best New Artist and the other for Best Record of the Year. No one except a teenager from New Jersey, who had seen it even before the song had been officially chosen.

It was four years before I saw Bobby again. The calls still came, but not as often. He had married the actress Sandra Dee in 1960, and after that he spent most of his time on the West Coast. He did, however, play the Copacabana nightclub in New York several times a year. I went to see him on a Saturday night in 1963. The place was packed, and my seat was in the top ring of tables. I thought he'd never see me in such a crowd, so I left my name backstage, hoping I could catch him after the show.

The lights were just beginning to dim as we were seated. When Bobby came out in his tuxedo dancing to the tune of *Mack the Knife*, he had a mischievous smile on his face. I was laughing and enjoying the moment and feeling proud to know him. Then I realized that he was walking toward me. Up the steps he came, first ring, second ring, then up to my table, where he held out his hand to me, all the while singing, *"...Oh, the line forms to the right, babe, when ol' Mack is back in town."*

Tears streaming down my face, my knees almost buckling out from under me, I took his hand and walked into the spotlight and down the steps with him to the stage. Still singing, he motioned for me to have a seat. After the first set, he introduced me as a dear friend as well as one of the twins from *American Bandstand*. He even had me take a bow. That was the last time I saw him.

In one of the last telephone conversations I had with Bobby, he asked me to promise him something. "I want you always to remind Paul Anka and Dick Clark how much they mean to me. Dick gave me more than one break, and he's a wonderful friend. Paul and his creativity have always inspired me. When you see them, Dreamboat, say 'Hi' for me." I gave him my word, and to this day I always do tell them "Hi" from Bobby. It was in 1973 that he died, following heart surgery.

Bobby believed that he would never see his twenty-fifth birthday. I think he felt forever rushed, pushed, as if he had to accomplish all the things he wanted to do in a hurry. His desire to achieve all he could, his great energy, and his talent carried him twelve precious years past his expectations.

Our relationship was laughably innocent by today's standards: some kisses, some dancing, many long talks, and, of course, some looking deeply into each others' eyes. I miss him still. Whenever I am walking along a beach in the moonlight, if I listen for a while, I can hear Bobby's voice on the night breeze. At first faintly, then clearer and clearer, the familiar words come back:

> *Somewhere beyond the sea,*
> *Somewhere waiting for me,*
> *My true love stands on golden sands*
> *And watches the ships that go sailing.*

> —Beyond the Sea,
> Charles Trenet and Jack Lawrence

Those three and a half years on American Bandstand were wonderful times. None of us knew, even the artists, that we would be a part of the new era of Rock and Roll, but as Danny and the Juniors sang, with a great beat, *Rock and Roll is Here to Stay.*

CHAPTER 4

Brenda and Joe

THE TEARS FELL AS THE drums rolled. Standing in the tower entrance of Ridgewood High School, the entire class of 1960 began the march down to the football field to the orchestra playing *The War March of the Priests.* Dressed in our finery. The girls in long white evening gowns, carried red roses, and the boys wore black and white tuxedos with a red rose in the lapel. Here I was, finally, standing in a state of fear, not wanting to take this walk. I was surprised by my feelings of anxiousness.

From the time I was able to look out the window, every year I would watch the seniors walk down our street, Brookside Avenue for commencement. I felt such joy, excitement, and anticipation. One day it would be my turn. Sometimes I would close my eyes and visualize the line of slowly marching seniors, to cheer myself up. I knew my day would come.

I often wondered why the school always played that sad music, but today I understood completely. With every step, I was begging God for one more year. "I am having my personal inner battle with the priests," I thought. I needed one more year to "be ready." Ready for what I could never imagine. My transition into adulthood and self-responsibility came quickly, like a slap across the face.

Bobby had wanted me to move into New York City and to follow an acting and singing career. "You can live with a roommate in the Village and waitress until a part comes along," he explained.

My parents had different thoughts. My older sisters had gone to a secretarial school in New York City instead of college. They graduated five years ahead of us, and were now married. That's what mother wanted for us—to work until we found husbands to take care of us.

Our parents always forced Chris and I to do things together. If I was invited to a party, they expected her to be invited too. However, her upsetting behavior meant this was not the case. People did not want to be around Chris.

Chris and I applied for college in the early spring of our senior year. I wanted to be in New England, and we applied to Green Mountain College in Poultney, Vermont. I was accepted and Chris wasn't. I was thrilled because eleven girls from our class were also going to Green Mountain, including two I had grown close to, Kathy Nolan and Amy Lou Robinson.

In my senior year, I began to like Ridgewood, my classmates, and school. I was in the Senior Play, but my sister wasn't because of her grades. I was on honor roll, but my twin was flunking out. The other girls were beginning to recognize us as separate individuals. They were nice to me, we shared, and I began to find *myself* for the first time.

The play was an enlightenment for me as well as my fellow students. I got to know the others in the play and they saw the real me. One of the girls, who I thought very highly of, Betts Saunders, had been in my homeroom for the last three years. We hardly spoke. However, in this play, *The Crucible*, Betts had the lead. Sharing this experience brought us closer and we remain friends to this day.

As we walked toward commencement along with the tears, my arm was bruised and throbbing because my twin grabbed my arm hard, and yanked me over to the inside of the line. She had to walk on the outside. She had to be seen, and I had to be erased again. The tears began and I could not stop them.

Adulthood began in chaos. I only went to college for the first semester. My firstborn son arrived when I was ten days nineteen. It was not an easy path. I was married, had two children, divorced, remarried and widowed before I was thirty-five. It was my second marriage, to Joe, that began my path of awakening and self-knowledge.

I'm not sure when the dream began. A terrifying dream, more vivid than any I ever had. This dream was three dimensional, with bright colors, and vividly real. I saw an explosion. I saw a house, rather ramshackle, with brown clapboard siding. I saw a woman's body flung out the roof. I was aware of an oil well and a trailer park near by. I knew somehow that the front screen door on the house was hanging by one hinge, and it was banging in the wind. I saw ivy climbing up the left side of the house.

"She's in Houston, Texas. Your Aunt Claramay died. She's in Houston, Texas." The words were repeated again and again until I woke up. I wanted to reach over to my husband, Joe, to have him reassure me and help me go back to sleep. But then I remembered that I would never see Joe again. He had passed away suddenly the month before. Ronnie, Joe's son, had been murdered by three teenage boys the previous fall. His body had just been located in a shallow grave at Teterboro Airport. I lost both loved ones in a period of six months. The emotional strain I was under was beyond belief

On Thanksgiving Day 1977, my husband Joe and I sat down at the table. We had been discussing Ronnie's disappearance. Ronnie had been gone since September 27th. Had Ronnie run away from home or was he dead? It was a mystery, and his mother, Nancy, was suffering. Joe and I were suffering too.

"I've been having this dream about Ronnie," I said. "I can't tell you how distressing it is. Every night, as I'm falling asleep, I see Ronnie lying inside a dirt pit and staring up at the sky The brown leaves are blowing across his nose. I can't shake the feeling that the pit is his grave."

"My God," Joe said, taking my hands. "It sounds horrible."

53

"That's not all of it," I said. "After I see Ronnie in the pit, I always get this kind of flashback. I see Ronnie walking toward his girlfriend's house. Then some of his friends call over to him, and they all got into a car and drive off. Three boys and Ronnie are in a blue car. Then I see the grave again. I can see it as clearly as can be, but no matter how hard I try, I can't figure out where it is. I do sense that his body won't be found for six months."

"Beth," Joe said, "I've been getting the feeling that something terrible has happened to Ronnie too. Sometimes it just about drives me out of my mind. The police say their investigation has come to a dead end, and I haven't been able to find out anything on my own either. I hate to say it, but I think your dream is probably right. Ronnie is probably dead.

"I'm pretty sure that Nancy will make the police find out what happened to Ronnie," Joe continued. "She's his mother and won't rest until Ronnie comes home, dead or alive." My psychic powers were burning me up. I was too close to the situation. I could almost see the face of Ronnie's killer. Joe tried to comfort me and get me to relax. He recognized my gift but also knew that his ex-wife would never listen to me. He would have to work it out another way. He told me then that Nancy was hoping that a famous psychic by the name of Dorothy Allison would come in and work on the case. I felt relieved to know that someone else had these strange powers and would be of help. I was exhausted. I asked him to please tell Ms. Allison about my dreams. He promised that he would.

We sat in silence for a while. Then Joe spoke again. "This might sound peculiar, but I've had my own psychic experience recently too." His hand shook a little a he took a drag on his cigarette. "I had this dream, and Honey, I don't know the best way to say this, but the dream told me I'm going to die, and it's going to be soon."

Joe had severe plaque on his arteries from smoking. It was only a matter of time before a clot could kill him. There was nothing medicine could do. The technology for the surgery that could have saved his life had not yet been discovered. His father had died from the same ailment at fifty-one. Joe was forty-seven. "You know," he said, "I have a feeling that you will begin to use your psychic powers professionally soon." I asked him why he thought that. I knew about gypsies and crystal balls, but I wasn't familiar with psychic readings or tarot cards. I felt no different from I ever had.

"I know you have the ability to foresee the future for others," he said.

Then Joe became quite serious. "You were born with a gift. You know things about other people, things about their lives that someone without your psychic abilities couldn't possibly know. It's unexplainable. Don't you see, that's why your friends love talking to you on the phone. You tell them what's going to happen, and then it does. You have a true gift of insight. It can't be faked, and it can't be learned.

"I am going to die, Beth, but you will go on." Joe said. "You have to educate Jeffrey and watch over your other son, Vance. Jeffrey is gifted with a high IQ and has a bright future. He will go to college and perhaps become a doctor. You have to put him through school, and you will. You will pay for Jeff's education by giving psychic readings and become well known in this region. You were born with the *Gift of Knowledge* as spoken about in the New Testament. Don't be afraid of this, as it's like being chosen. You have powers you have not yet tapped into. Powers you don't know even exist. These are natural to you, and you don't need a tool like tarot cards or a crystal ball, to know. You just know! As you develop this gift, you will begin to reach out to the world."

Grammie Hemphill told me I had this *Gift of Knowledge*. No one had ever said these things to me since I spent my eighth year at her house. Now Joe was saying the same thing. At that time I did not take him seriously.

Joe died of a sudden heart attack in February, and my stepson Ronnie's body was found in March of 1978. He had been knifed to death by three teenage boys. After six months of keeping quiet, they finally admitted the crime. It was then I realized that Joe and I were soul mates. I would always know when he was driving up the street, or when he came into a room. We were so attuned that I could feel his touch before he actually touched me and almost hear his thoughts. He passed away on a Friday afternoon. I was walking down a hallway at work, and stopped dead in my tracks. I felt something yank out of my heart, and I knew it was Joe's spirit. Bowing my head in tears, I whispered, "Joe, I will miss you."

After Joe passed, I was frightened and spiritually drained. Feeling the loss, empty and deserted, I thought I was losing all control. Then something strange began to happen. I began to have another dream. This dream was very real, almost three-dimensional. I had the dream every night for three weeks. It was always the same dream; the feeling of immediacy and reality, the brown house, the explosion, the woman exploding out of the roof, the voice repeating that my aunt had died in Texas. Needless to say, I was more and more terrified as those three weeks went by. This may sound strange, but all the time I was afraid, I also felt puzzled. My family comes from New Hampshire, not Texas. My Aunt Claramay was very much alive and living in Concord, New Hampshire. Why was this dream coming to me, and why would I hear that my aunt was in Houston? I tried to think of someone who might help me understand the riddle.

Finally I went to see Brenda Hayes, a social worker I knew. She had helped me with my boys after my divorce from their father. I told her that I thought I might be suffering from some emotional problems or even more, that I had really "lost it!"

"Tell me about this dream," she said in her soothing voice. Immediately I felt myself relax a little. I was confident that she would give my story a thoughtful and compassionate hearing. My boys and I had visited her a few years before when we were having some family problems, and I had come to trust and admire her. In a kind and non-accusatory way, she had skillfully guided me and my children to understand ourselves better and to discover for ourselves how to work out our problems.

Brenda listened intently to my dream. Her face turned pale as I described what I had seen. When I was done, she sat silent for a moment, looking shocked. Then she said, "Elizabeth, you don't know this, but my family lives in Houston. I grew up there. I have only been living on the

East Coast for about five years. My aunt is missing from an explosion that happened at her home in Houston a week ago. Her name is Ivy Beasley, and I feel your dream is describing her death." We stared at each other in awe. "There was a gas pipeline explosion and fire on her property on May twenty-first," Brenda explained. "Her home was entirely destroyed, and the police found the bodies of five other people nearby. But they couldn't find Aunt Ivy's body. We all want to know what has happened to her." She began to tell me about the area where the explosion had occurred, but I interrupted.

"No, wait, Brenda. I'll draw it for you." To Brenda's surprise, I drew an exact picture, locating the oil wells, the trailer park, a nearby weedy area, and the little brown house. The clincher was the screen door, hanging off its hinge.

"That's what it looks like at my aunt's house," Brenda said. "There are only two differences that I can see. One is that you've drawn the whole thing completely backwards. You made a perfect mirror image of the place. The other one is that you show ivy growing up the side of her house. In Brazoria County, it's too hot and dusty for anything like ivy to grow."

"Brenda," I said, comprehension dawning on me, "Your aunt's name is Ivy. The ivy vines on the house are a symbol for her name."

At that moment Brenda asked me if she could use the phone. She called a childhood friend who lived near her aunt's house. He contacted the sheriff's investigators, who were still searching for Mrs. Beasley's body, and explained to them what I had envisioned. Then Brenda phoned the man in charge of the investigation, County Deputy Benny Clifton. Later, Deputy Clifton remembered both calls. "When Brenda Hayes told me what her friend from New Jersey had dreamed, she described things that hadn't been in the papers, things she would have no way of knowing."

The next day, Deputy Clifton asked his captain for permission to conduct a wider search for Mrs. Beasley's body beyond the immediate vicinity of her house. "The captain was pretty skeptical," the deputy recalled. "He made it extremely clear to me that he didn't want anything about those phone calls in my formal report." In spite of this, the search was authorized, and early that afternoon Clifton's search party found the woman's body five hundred thirty-four feet from her house, completely hidden in the tall grass, just the way the body in my dream had been hidden. It appeared that Ivy had been running away from the fire, even though my dream showed her flying out from the roof.

Both Brenda and I were quite shaken about the phenomena we had experienced. One had had a dream, the other a close life connection to this dream. What could it mean? Could certain dreams be a kind of key to understanding something about human existence? Could dreams be a way for a person to pull information from his subconscious or someone else's? If this were true, did that mean that there might be some sort of collective unconscious that can be tapped into, one in which all people might share basic knowledge?

"How can we learn about this," Brenda asked me, still in a state of disbelief.

"I'm not sure," I said. I felt as if I were standing at the beginning of a new road with a great, mysterious and unfamiliar territory stretched out before me.

This was the beginning of a lifelong friendship with Brenda Hayes. We talked on the phone everyday for more than twenty-five years. She became my best friend and confidant. I knew I could trust her. We developed a strong, sister like bond. Something I had been desperately missing in my own life despite having three sisters, Meeting this kind, loving, and patient woman was my first step towards actively pursuing my own spiritual growth.

CHAPTER 5

Jeffrey
My First Out-of-Body Experience

MY BODY STIFFENED AT MY son's terrified cry. "Mom, Mom, watch out!" As I was driving, I was blinded by approaching headlights, sudden and huge, shining through my car's windshield. I realized with horror that the vehicle was headed right toward Jeffrey. I threw my right arm off the steering wheel, trying to protect my son. At the same instant I heard an enormous crash, and, wrapped together, Jeff and I were flying forward. The top of his head hit the rearview mirror just as the left side of my head slammed into the windshield. I heard a thud, and the world shattered into white fireworks. Then, all at once, everything stopped. There was nothing but silence. My arms were still tight around my son. I looked down and saw a red stain forming where his head lay on my shoulder.

It was eight in the evening on November 30, 1979. My car was stopped at the top of an infamously steep hill on Lake Street in Saddle River, New Jersey. I was taking my fourteen-year- old son Jeff to a party at his friend Eddy's house. In the back seat was Mike, another friend who was coming along with Jeff. Our car was just about to turn left into Lomas Lane, where Eddie lived. Jeff and Mike were waving out the car windows to their friends, and they all were whooping and laughing the way only boys can at that age. We'd get to the party in less than a minute, I thought. But a drunk driver saw to it that we never arrived.

"Mike, go get help," I whispered, trying to turn my head toward the back seat. A sharp pain began at my left shoulder and tore across my back. "Go get help!"

Both cars were in terrible shape. The white BMW had slammed into my Oldsmobile Cutlass with such force that its engine was pushed into our front passenger's door. The door was so mangled that it looked impossible to pry open. But as Mike lunged forward in his fear to get out, a figure appeared inside the car. It looked like an extraordinarily beautiful being all aglow with pure white light. Whatever this thing was, it was nothing like a dream or a vision. The entity was really there, I was sure, just as much as the boys and I were. The entity reached out its hand and touched the mutilated door, and immediately it swung open. Mike, dazed and unaware of anything but his terror, shot outside and began running up the street to Eddy's house. Shocked beyond pain, Jeff and I sat in the car and waited for the ambulance. There was more and more blood on my coat. Oh, God, I thought, how badly is Jeff hurt?

Less than five minutes before we had been laughing and talking about the party, and now a deep hole inside me had opened up, and hideous fears were flying out every which way, uncontrolled. He's hit his head so hard, I thought. Is my son going to die? Dear Lord, please, please send help as fast as you can, I prayed as the bright stain grew bigger. I began to rock Jeff back and forth in my arms.

"Jeff," I murmured, "why are you bleeding?"

"I don't know," he whimpered, uncomprehending what had just happened.

The fears were coming at me like attacking creatures. I recalled the odd, worried look on my mother's face as we were leaving the house. "Drive very carefully, dear," she said. "I have a funny feeling about your going. Perhaps Dad should drive the kids ... No? Well, be sure to watch out, dear."

I began to feel myself floating upward. I realized I was still sitting behind the wheel, but I also knew that, at the same time, I was hovering in a place just above my body. Before I had the chance to think about the strangeness of the feeling, I found myself hurrying down the street toward Eddy's house. I rushed through the front door. "Jeffrey's been hurt," I told Eddy's father. "Somebody hit our car, and Jeff's head is injured. Please hurry."

A strange awareness came over me as I realized I spoke not with my voice, but with my thoughts. To my amazement, Eddy's father could neither see nor hear me, and he passed right through me, running outside toward the tangled vehicles. I saw other people on the block running down the street too. I stood there alone, feeling confused and helpless.

Slowly I made my way through the dimness, back down the street to the tangled cars. I saw people milling around and heard their confused talking. Several of the boys were crying. There were sirens. Men were hurrying to the car. I watched them from a distance as they pried the driver's door open and dragged my body out. Copious blood stained my coat and slacks. "Keep her head straight," someone said. "Be careful of her back." I saw the men lay me onto a gurney and then lift me inside the back of an ambulance.

Eddy's father, his face ashen and sweating, asked to ride in the ambulance with us, but the emergency medical technician wouldn't let him in. "It's too crowded with both of them in there," the technician explained.

My son called out to Eddy's father, "Call my grandmother. She's at our house." The emergency medical technician asked Jeff, "Which hospital should we take you to? Valley or Good Samaritan?"

"Valley," Jeff answered.

With that, the EMT stepped up into the ambulance, shut the doors, and with sirens screaming, we began the fifteen-mile drive towards Ridgewood. Two medics were working on my body. One was administering CPR and the other was giving me oxygen. "Her heart's stopped!" one of them exclaimed.

Suddenly worldly feelings faded away. Jeff, the car crash, the terror, the blood, Mike running to get help; everything was gone. I began floating upwards, higher and higher. Up I went, up out of the top of my head. I realized I was reaching out, reaching, reaching. What was I reaching for? I felt myself floating towards a tunnel, while being drawn into a bright light. With an awareness of great relief, I felt the lifting of a heavy burden of pain and fear, as I traveled.

My internal world of thought was still clearing as the bright light swirled toward the perimeters of my subconscious. I began to remember the headlights, those headlights racing right toward my son ... the BMW coming over the hill so fast ... the crunching sound that could be both heard and felt at the same time ... the impact ... the slow but inexorable force shoving me past any sound or awareness of pain into this void. I tried to gain control of my hearing. Why was it so quiet? Where was the screaming that had ripped through my senses a moment ago? Or was it really only a moment ago? Time seemed to have disappeared.

I struggled to shake myself back into consciousness. Fear gripped my heart in the darkness as I struggled to shake myself back into physical consciousness. Something was wrong with me. Something was very different. My body was enormously different. I realized that the body I was in felt transparent, weightless. A deeper fear gripped my returning awareness. Had I been killed? Was I dead? I had often wondered what it would be like to die, to pass beyond the boundaries of space and time.

Gravitational forces were suspended. Space and time seemed blotted out. Again I was aware of the sensation of weightless movement. I was rising, escaping. It was like the first plunge on a roller coaster, but a roller coaster turned upside down; it was like falling upward.

Doubts and fears hit me like stones thrown against a windowpane. Was there an afterlife? A Heaven? My beloved Grammie Hemphill had promised me that a loving, all-powerful God truly existed. There simply was no doubt about it. It's so easy to believe when you're little and walking hand-in-hand with your grandmother through the woods or sitting close to her by the fire. But was there really such a thing as life after death, I wondered, all the while helplessly flying through the tunnel. My eyes widened. Did I still have eyes, or was this just an illusion? What if death really were a dark, heavy door banging shut, and after that final slam there was nothing, nothing at all?

Right at the moment I felt more like a piece of nothingness than I ever had before. But I was still not completely nothing. I was aware of myself. I was still thinking. That was something. I started the mantra, *I think, therefore I am, I think, therefore I am,* because I couldn't imagine nothingness. There was no category in my mind or experience for such a notion. Nothingness conflicted with all my training and instincts. Nothingness as the final state of life would make a mockery of humanity, I thought. Either human beings have souls, or they dream them up to avoid the dread of an endless void. One cannot live without hope, even if it is a false hope. Still, I realized with a shock of joy and relief, I was continuing to think and feel. *I existed!*

Slivers of recollection zoomed past and I numbly grappled with them before they slipped away. Try to remember. I had heard someone saying something of great significance. What was it? Try, try, try to call it back. The words came again, like dancing, prismatic lights. With great effort my mind reached out and grasped them. It had been a man speaking. "We're losing her; quick, we're losing her!" Then a female voice had shouted, "What a mess. Stop the bleeding! Stop it!" Then there were other voices too, but a mist rolled over them and they disappeared. Half-formed shapes faded in and out of view. I struggled to focus.

Suddenly I heard another voice, the familiar voice of a boy, "No, no, please, no. Oh, God, no." Then a wail, "Oh my God, I can't believe it. Mom, Mom, wake up. No, God no. She can't really be ... " Then the voice was crying. Mental shapes slowly crept into view beyond the bounds of my awareness. I struggled to focus, to comprehend. They were darker than the rest, harder to grapple with, yet I must.

So, I thought, I am dead after all. I died, and now I am in the middle of the great mystery. I had waited all my life to know the truth about

God. I tried to raise my head to see, but everything was dark. Should I be afraid? I was afraid, that was certain, but should I be? At least I was still feeling something. If life ended in nothingness, I wouldn't be feeling anything. I wouldn't BE at all. So I rejoiced in my fear. I wanted to jump up and down with joy because of my fear. Fear was something. Even darkness was something. Darkness and fear -- these two things gave me hope as I continued my upward flight. I had the distinct impression that time no longer existed; neither did space. Yet, paradoxically, my thoughts still flowed in something like a time sequence, and I felt like I was moving somewhere.

Yes, I still existed, and that was good. Or was it? It all depended on the nature of this new kind of being. What if this dark tunnel went on and on forever? Would I be pulled into the darkness forever with this upward rush? My heart pounded in my chest. (Did I still have a heart, a chest?) I remembered stories my mother and grandmother had told me, accounts of Heaven and Hell and the afterlife. I wished that I had paid more attention. Why had I always been so busy with life's trivialities? The day before the accident I thought it was life-shatteringly important to get the grocery shopping done. I remembered the urgency I had felt to get to the A&P so I could find just the right things to fix for my visiting parents. Now it all seemed a million, million miles away. A few nights earlier, I had briefly looked up through the chilly air to the stars. For a moment I marveled at the size of the universe and pondered the meaning of existence. I remembered how small I had felt then, smaller than a dot on the eye of the smallest ant.

Maybe I should have taken time, gone to church more, studied more and opened my eyes to the real essentials of life. But there had always been more immediate distractions instead, day-to-day questions like what I should wear and whether I should fix roast beef or fish for dinner, what was good on TV, whether my sons would come down with chicken-pox, how to make enough money to keep going, or whether I would look good in a new hairstyle.

Panic seized me again. What if this wretched darkness went on forever? What would I do then? I tried to force myself to move farther along
the tunnel, hoping to get closer to the bright light beaming from far away
at the other end. My mind kept up its zigzag dance from molecules to
universes and anything in between. Some of my friends had taken their
beliefs from Eastern religions, I thought. For them, all things were part of
the Cosmic Unconscious. Everything was God and God was everything.
God was impersonal, a life-force, the unknowable principle behind the
curtain. Life is fulfilled only as each one of us loses his or her individual identity and sinks back, disappearing into the "nothingness of what
is." I hadn't been impressed with what seemed to be an Americanized,
homogenized version of paganism, Hinduism and Buddhism. It seemed
everyone was desperate to find meaning behind their hurried pace of
life. In their desperation they had created many varieties of gods *in their
own image*. The ego ruled in many cases. I decided to set aside the other
jumbling thoughts crowding for attention

I had to make sense out of all this craziness. I needed to find a definite reason and was thinking as fast as possible, while I still had time. I
believed strongly in the Lord God Jehovah of the Bible. I had heard the
Bible stories during my lifetime, from my Mother and Grandmother, as
well as my Aunt Claramay. I was brought up with a strong New England
Baptist background. I knew I had received The Lord's blessings many
times. After all, hadn't He brought me my boys and everyone else I loved?

The sensation of acceleration brought me out of my thoughts. I was
rapidly speeding toward the bright light. On my left and right I started to
notice flashes of light and patches of a deeply disturbing kind of darkness
that was somehow darker than pure black. Ebony. It was all rushing around
with a speed that made me dizzy and nauseated. "Stop, stop!" came the
piercing scream. I didn't realize it at first, but it was my own voice. I ached
to go back to the familiar world, my home, my mother, my children, my
daily routine. I wanted to watch the news with my father, hug my boys, eat
dinner, and sleep in my own bed. But all that was impossible now.

My mind reeled back to the question of religion. Not only had I known atheists and so-called New Age people, but I had also come across those who spoke about God as though they knew everything about Him, right down to the color of His beard. And, of course, the Almighty was without doubt a Him, so there was no question that He had a beard. These people knew for sure that there was life after death. The Bible said so. These deluded simpletons were stuffy, hypocritical, and always attacking everyone who questioned their beliefs. These people thought they had the only valid tickets to Heaven. Everyone else was headed for a place where there was a lot of suffering and emotional turmoil. How could such bigoted people have the real information about the afterlife? Oh, God, I hope they're not right.

The surrounding darkness was changing into a rosy-colored hue as I continued to search for answers. How many possible ways were there to explain existence? Reality demands an explanation. Whenever I read the Sunday paper, I was always amused by the religion page, with its little boxed-up advertisements for all sorts of places of worship, each one with its own particular little set of rules and beliefs, its tidy little collection of "do's" and "don'ts." There must be hundreds of explanations of what God is, what He does, and why He does it.

I longed for the Universe to explain itself. Had it existed forever, or did it have a beginning sometime in the past? Every machine or work of art has a creator, someone who thought of it and then made it. After all, grandfather clocks and Mona Lisa's and houses, even very little houses, don't suddenly appear out of nowhere. So how could something as enormous and complex, as beautifully ordered as the Universe just appear out of nothing? I didn't think it could. Well then, who made it? How did it get here? And, for that matter, what would explain the unique qualities of human beings, their personalities, their creativity, their ability to think abstractly, and, especially, their capacity for unselfishness and love?

Again the darkness deepened. I was certain now that I had burst through the barrier of time and had entered a strange sort of new existence. My body felt very different. It became light and transparent. Then terror again seized my thoughts. What if this continual, wretched darkness is forever? What would I do then? I tried to force myself deeper into the tunnel, where a bright light was beaming from the center. I made out two indistinct forms of light a little way ahead of me. A silvery blue light was on the right, and an orange-red light was on the left. Their brilliant radiance obscured their shapes. First I thought they might be angels. Did human-like creatures with wings exist anywhere outside fantasy and imagination? Perhaps the idea of angels was silly, outrageous, and foolish. But until the car crash, I would have thought everything I was experiencing right now was silly, outrageous, and foolish. I remembered that a light being had opened the door of the car to let Mike out. Could that have been an angel?

Things seemed clearer in this new environment; my mind felt more lucid and agile than it had before the car crash. I was thinking faster, much faster. I was analyzing multiple reasons for human existence so quickly that it seemed I was thinking three or four thoughts all at the same time. Suddenly everything came into focus. It was simple, I realized. The possible reasons for how and why we came to exist were not endless. There were only three. All the religious, philosophical, and scientific theories I could think of boiled down to three basic solutions.

I was spinning again, twisting and turning upward and outward, struggling to keep my center and not be pulled out of myself. What was I thinking about? Concentrate! If I stop thinking, I will be pulled into the blackness. *I think, therefore I am; I think, therefore I am.* If I stop thinking, I will stop existing. If I stop thinking, I will fall backward into the darkness. I can feel it pulling me toward a bad place; there is a black emptiness that wants to envelop me. I can feel the bright light too, drawing me forward. I think I want to go that way, but does the light want to devour me? Does it want to eradicate me in its bright flames? I must get my thoughts in order. It's the only way I can stop spinning out of control.

Where was I? What had I been thinking? About the origin of the Universe and the idea that there were only three possible solutions to the riddle life and of how we got here. The first explanation was that the whole Universe just appeared, alakazam and presto-change-o, out of nothing. I rejected that idea instantly. It didn't make sense; it seemed to go in one brain cell and out another. That left only two possibilities, either a personal beginning or an impersonal beginning. The Universe was ultimately the result of either impersonal "matter" configured by time plus chance, or it could be that the Universe was created by a purposeful, thinking entity. That's it, pure and simple: random process or a living creator - "A" or "B."

On an earthly scale, every action has a reaction; every choice has a consequence. What if, oh God, what if our choices and actions on the earth somehow impact this strange afterlife, or our next life, if any? I wish I'd thought more about consequences. Then it occurred to me that maybe earthly life, which I suddenly realized was very short, could be a kind of preparation for an ultimate union with this creator. Oh, God, I might be in big trouble.

The two figures of light ahead of me were glowing brighter now. I tried to dismiss the suspicion that they were angels. Probably they were just some kind of cosmic glare, or maybe my eyes were just dazzled. No, the two entities were still there, their blue and orange lights getting brighter all the time. They kept traveling along, always right ahead of me, almost like escorts. Oh, Lord, what if they were escorts? What were they taking me to? Did I really want to go wherever that was? Did I have a choice? The mist was dispersing. I was drawing near to something important, but what it was I didn't know.

The glowing, almost-like-escorts ahead of me were now joined by others. Some were like the original pair, made of various colored lights. But there were others too, and they had no light at all. They were like the shadows of shadows, like darkness intensified, like the opposite of matter. If there were such things as black holes, then that's what these things were. They seemed ominous and full of treachery. If I drew too close to these dark voids I would be swallowed up by their darkness, canceled out. As I looked, the dark objects began to far outnumber the bright ones.

Think, think, come on think! Memories of the car crash kept intruding like a bad dream. The sounds of crunching metal and words of death still rang in my ears like clashing cymbals. The darkness continued to brighten and the mist gradually dispersed. I had the distinct impression I was drawing near something important, but what it was I didn't know.

My heart was beating fast. I had to prepare. Prepare for what? Oh, I wish I had paid more attention when I had time to pay attention! Where was I? The world came into being in one of two possible ways, there's just no way around it: a) personal and b) impersonal. Since reality cannot have emerged out of absolute nothingness, something has to be eternal, either matter or a personal being. So, what are the implications of each? One would tend to have moral, ethical, and relational overtones, whereas the other would not. Was God truly a personal God? I was terrified. I felt as if I were running out of time to think. I must remember to think!

Without warning, I was back in the ambulance. I felt as though I had fallen from the top of a high building and landed flat on my back on the sidewalk. The shock was enormous. The pain in my chest was close to unbearable. How heavy and helpless I felt, like a rag doll stuffed with buckshot. Somewhere above me, something was shrieking out, "Hurry, hurry, danger, danger," but without words. It must be the siren, I thought. I felt my body slide to the left as the ambulance flew around a corner. Where was Jeff?

"Mom, are you okay?" Jeff asked.

I saw him lying next to me, safe. Someone had wiped the blood away from his face, and the nurse was tending to the gash in his scalp. I began to relax. My son was going to be just fine. I closed my eyes in relief, and then I was floating away again. I left the pain behind in the ambulance. Out I went, reaching upward.

The light grew brighter and brighter. This time, to my delight, all of the horrible black fearsome shapes were gone. There was no fear. It had fallen away like an old, dirty coat that you take off and throw into the trash. I could smell flowers. They were roses, my favorite. I was enveloped with the sound of beautiful music.

"Her heart's stopped again." The medical technician's voice floated up to me from far away. I didn't look back. I wanted to know what was ahead. The two forms of light came softly back into view. Now I saw human figures looking at me from within the radiance. Did I know them, or was it my imagination? Could it possibly be Joe in the center of the red-orange light and Ronnie in the center of the silver-blue?

Joe, my darling, my husband, had died the year before, just a few months after we lost my stepson, Ronnie. Yet there they were, speaking to me without words. It seemed as if they were placing thoughts into my mind. The colors were vivid now, and I felt pure love beaming down on me from within the light. I reached forward harder, determined to get to that place.

I heard a woman speaking from far, far away. I slowly realized that it was the nurse inside the ambulance, and I knew she was talking to my son. "Call to your mother, Jeffrey," she said. "Take her hand and hold onto it."

"Mom, Mom," came the cry. "Please wake up. I love you so much." I was jerked back into my body as the nurse put my hand into my son's.

I love you too, darling, I thought, but there is something wonderful I have to get back to. I don't want this heaviness and pain. I'm going to the place where Joe and Ronnie are.

Quickly, I floated back out. The light was so bright, and its attraction was irresistible. Then I heard, "Go back, you must go back. It's not your time to join us," Joe and Ronnie called in unison. It felt like they were placing their thoughts directly into my head, directly into my being. "Go back, go back. There is work left that you still have to do. You must write. There are things waiting for you to learn and discover, and there are things you must write about." I didn't know whether the words were separate from me or within me. Wherever they were, I didn't want to hear them. I began to realize that my body was changed. As I reached forward, I saw light glowing through my hand and arm. I felt weightless. There were no physical limitations. I was made of light, and I could see light passing through me. My thoughts were clear.

I was aware that my new body was the double of my ordinary body, but it wasn't made of any physical material. This body was transparent light. Any sense of time or distance was obliterated. I knew absolutely that I was one with all things. Rain and sunlight could pass through me, but I wouldn't feel them, and they wouldn't be able to affect me. I felt as if the molecular structure of my body had melted like a patch of snow in the spring sunlight.

Just as movement is unimpeded in this spiritual state, so, I discovered, is thought. I could feel ideas and images flying out of my mind, faster and faster. My thoughts became clear and effortless. They instantaneously shot outward, and the replies from Ronnie and Joe came back to me just as quickly. "Go back, you must go back. You must write, they echoed in unison." The telepathic message from Ronnie and Joe was coming directly into my being. Within the glow of the soft orange and blue light, they were holding their arms out, as if to stop me from coming any closer. I felt desperate. Please don't send me back, I thought to them, I love you so much.

Yet even as the two figures gestured for me to go, a brilliant yellow light behind them was drawing me forward. The force of love from that yellow light was immensely powerful, unlike any I had ever felt before. It was a desire that filled my entire being and went beyond me, filling the tunnel and all space behind me and before me. I felt as if I were returning to a very familiar place, one I recognized, longed for and loved.

I hung suspended, lost in timelessness, as the light blinded me for a moment. Then I surrendered to it. I received my answer in the brightness of that experience. I knew the angels and God were real and ever present. My faith had been renewed and restored. My teaching and lifetime training became an active part of my being. At that moment, all I wanted was to be completely immersed in the light and be filled with the great love that was there. I wanted to realize and receive more and more knowledge. I had been given the golden key. What was I to do with it?

"Mom! Mom!" came the plea from Jeffrey. With a powerful jolt, back into my body I came, this time to stay. We had just reached the emergency room entrance of Valley Hospital in Ridgewood, New Jersey.

For the next ten days I lay in the hospital on an air mattress with my neck tightly fitted into a brace so I couldn't turn my head. The doctors told me I had received a severe concussion to the left side of my head, especially affecting the left frontal lobe of my brain. Because I had grabbed Jeff, he had avoided going through the windshield and only hit the rearview mirror. Since Jeff hadn't gone through the windshield, his body had prevented me from hitting the glass much, much harder. "It looks like that hug of yours saved you both," one of the doctors said. "You saved his life, and he saved yours."

My car, a heavy Oldsmobile sedan, was totally wrecked, as was the BMW that had hit us. The other driver, so drunk he didn't know exactly what had happened, walked away without any injuries. He never, then or later, asked whether the people in the car he had hit were alive or dead. Mike, thank Heaven, was fine.

When Jeff came to see me the next morning, his poor head was swollen, and there was such a thickness of bandages wrapped around his head and jaw that he looked like a walking pumpkin. The doctors had put sixteen stitches in his scalp and forehead. But for all that, he was fine except for a minor concussion. He was preparing to go home. "Are you ready, Mom?" He asked.

"I'm afraid I'm not going with you just now, Jeff," I responded. "Grandma and Pop-Pop are here and will take care of you and Vance. I have to stay in the hospital and rest."

"When are you coming home?" Jeff asked, surprised.

"I'm not sure," I said, trying to look away as I answered. I didn't want him to see my tears.

As soon as he left, I was filled with fear and despair. Yes, my son and I had been spared. Yes, I had seen and felt something of amazing beauty and ecstasy. Yes, I had been given a vision of two dearly beloved people whom I thought I would never see again. I shared thoughts with them. But none of that made much difference at the moment. I felt alone and in pain. The concussion I suffered caused my ears to ring and my head to pound. I could not move without help. Because my neck was in a brace, I could not turn my head in any direction. The fever caused me to feel nauseous, and the IV made me drowsy. I was completely helpless. The peace and the bliss were gone. There was a hollowness within me now. A long parade of dismal and frightening thoughts marched through my mind.

My son and I had experienced a grievous wrong. I didn't know how long it would be before I recovered. I was lying in a hospital, having to endure the embarrassment of sponge baths and bedpans. I was forced to stare perpetually at the monotonous cream-colored ceiling. My only food was tea, spoon-fed to me by an orderly. Friends telephoned and sent flowers and cards, but only my parents were allowed to visit. I was acutely sensitive to sound and light. The headaches were almost unbearable, and the blinds were always kept closed. As if all this weren't enough, my personal, built-in doom machine began reminding me that the horizons of my fear and pain stretched much, much farther than the car crash.

For the past ten years, I had been in the hospital about every six months, fighting severe kidney infections and other illnesses. Closely following that came the horror of discovering I had ovarian cancer. Then came my total hysterectomy. After the cancer surgery, my husband and stepson had died. Then I lost my home. I didn't have any money left, and I didn't know how I was going to get any more. I didn't have much faith left, and I didn't know how I was going to get any more of that, either. I had no idea what to do next.

Mother had brought us up with a strong Christian faith. Where was that strength now? The world seemed to be nothing but a storm of injustice and chaos. Everything we love is taken from us. Tragedy can come at any moment, and there is nothing we can do. If God is real, He either doesn't care about us or He can't help us. I was filled with fear and despair. "Please, please," I prayed, although I wasn't sure anyone was listening. "Help me find a way out of this emptiness."

Strangely, when I slept, the hollowness and terror faded away. Asleep, I reveled in the memory of my experiences in the spiritual world. I would close my eyes, and recollections of my unexplainable journey into happiness and love would flood back to me. Every time I thought about that place, the feelings returned. I felt enveloped in light. The sights, the freedom from my body, the fragrances, the music, the message, the awareness, the passage through fear and doubt, the renewal of faith, they were all there. They were inside of me. Even though I had never heard of what is now commonly called a near-death experience, I never doubted the reality of what had happened. What meaning would this whole thing have? Would I have? What direction was next for me?

Once each day in the hospital, while I lay sleeping, a wave of tingling and chills would wash over me. It was as if the energy from the tunnel had found its way back to me and was pouring through my body like a river of golden light. I felt nourished and strengthened. In the months to come, I would need to draw on every bit of that strength and every ounce of that remembered glory.

CHAPTER 6

Meg Stettner
When the Student is Ready the Teacher Appears

Could it be? Yes, it could.
Something's coming, something good,
If I can wait!

Maybe just by holding still
It'll be there.
The air is humming,
And something great is coming...

—*S. SONDHEIM*

A GNAWING, FERVENT DESIRE FOR a spiritual teacher grew within me. Life seemed to be all questions and no answers. My clairvoyant experiences weren't making things any easier. On the contrary, my mind was a whirling kaleidoscope of confusion and doubt.

Why was I having prophetic dreams? Why did vivid pictures appear unbidden before me: these angels, lights, sounds, these visions of people who had died? Where was all this coming from? What was I supposed to do about it? Sometimes I wondered whether I could use this clairvoyant ability to help myself and those around me. Other times I worried that all of this psychic stuff might be dangerous and nothing to fool around with.

I knew I was more dismayed over never being permitted to "be me" than I was over the misery from the domination and the continual undeserved punishments. Simultaneously, another part of my mind constantly played an especially dreary and depressing game of "what if." I longed to know what sort of person I would have been if I weren't a twin, if my parents had been different, if I had been born strong instead of sickly. What if my parents had allowed me to be the person I was meant to be, if they had listened to me, trusted me, believed in me, encouraged me?

Their desire to mold me into something I was not hurt me even more than their continual and undeserved abuse. Still, throughout my entire, desolate childhood and early adulthood, during the times of deepest despair and moments when I thought it might be impossible to go on, I would recall my year with Grammie Hemphill in the Mink Hills of New Hampshire. I would visualize her smile and remember that, at sometime in the past, *someone* had loved me.

After the car crash I knew that someday I would write. While floating out-of-body, I had received my assignment as I reached up to Joe and Ronnie. A destiny was resting upon me that was far greater than I because I felt as if I was born without talents, wealth or position. Others had taken over my life so definitely from the beginning that I had not been able to find out what my own inclinations were.

Dimly in the back of my mind I was also aware that this ability would not be given to me until I had found my real, genuine self and chosen my own pathway. I had a lot ahead of me, and my prayer was that if I ever did write, my pen might be dipped in the golden inkwell of the Divine. I knew my voice might remain unheard. I was the least of all, the last born, the weakest in the family. How was I ever going to write anything that anyone would read, much less about a subject that I knew almost nothing about? I did know one thing: Grammie had her hand on my shoulder and would lead the way.

"I think what we both need is a good teacher," Brenda told me. "I understand a little about your internal struggle. I think I may have some psychic abilities also, even though they are not as active as yours. These special gifts of are raw, and we need a good cook," Brenda teased, laughing.

"You're so right, but where in the world can we find someone like that to help us?"

Of course we had heard about clairvoyants like Jeane Dixon, the famous seer who was quoted in books and newspapers all over the world, but people like her seemed as inaccessible as the moon. We wanted to find someone nearby who was willing and able to teach rank beginners. This teacher would have to be strictly honest and knowledgeable. So where were we going to find such a paragon? We didn't even know anyone who admitted to experiencing a psychic occurrence of any kind.

There is an old spiritual saying: *When the student is ready, the teacher appears.* Within the month, Brenda gave me a call. "I just met the most wonderful woman," she said, her voice high with excitement. "Her name is Meg Stettner, and she's a clairvoyant from Ossining, New York. I found her ad in the local *Penny Saver* newspaper," and I thought, 'what the heck, I'll give her a try.' So I got in touch with her, and she gave me a psychic reading. And guess what? It was absolutely amazing."

"You've got to tell me what happened," I said. "What did this woman say? What did she do?"

"Well, Meg uses astrology along with Tarot cards," Brenda said.

All I could picture was someone simultaneously looking through a telescope and dealing out cards for bridge. "I don't think I understand what you mean," I said. "How did the reading work, exactly?"

"First I gave Meg the time and date of my birthday," Brenda said, "and she did some figuring on a chart to find out the positions of the planets and stars at the time of my birth. She looked in an Ephemeris, which is a volume about the size of a phone book, filled with completely indecipherable stuff about astrology. Then she got out her deck of Tarot cards."

"And what are Tarot cards?" I asked.

"They're a deck of cards larger than the regular cards," Brenda answered, "but these cards are definitely not for playing games. Meg says they can tell you about your overall destiny, or your karma, as Meg called it. The Tarot can tell you about happenings in your everyday life too. Instead of fifty-two cards like there are in a regular deck, the Tarot has seventy-eight, and they each show a different picture: queens, kings, knights, wands, cups, a tower, a skeleton, a fool, a magician, the sun, the moon, stars, all kinds of things, so many I can't remember. Each one has a different meaning, and the patterns they make when they fall influences that meaning. Meg shuffled the cards first; then she had me cut the deck twice, making three piles. She laid the cards on the table in a certain way - I can't remember exactly how - and then she told me what they meant." Brenda giggled. "It's so strange to see how they fall during a reading.

"At first I thought the whole thing was pretty far-fetched," Brenda continued, "but when Meg started to talk, she was right on the money. She told me I was going to move somewhere in New York State within the year. She knew, without my telling her, that I have two children, a boy and a girl, and she knew that they're both blonde and that my son is the older one. She also said that my son is very bright. Of course, I didn't contradict her there," Brenda laughed.

"I'm so glad I went. I almost turned back several times on the way out to Meg's house. I felt apprehensive, and it almost seemed like something was trying to prevent me from getting there. I kept losing my way. I felt strange. My car even spun out of control on the Taconic Parkway, but I finally made it, even though I was late."

My stomach started doing acrobatics. "When can I have a reading?" I said.

"Call her, Elizabeth. I'll give you her number."

At the sound of Meg's voice over the telephone, tears gathered in my eyes. I felt shaken, as if I were remembering an old, dear friend. I couldn't wait to meet her. We made an appointment for the following Saturday afternoon.

Driving up to Ossining, New York, seemed to take an eternity, although it was only about thirty-five minutes from Allendale, New Jersey, where I lived. I was afraid I'd get lost on all the strange roads, but the directions were good. As I turned into the long drive leading to the large white house on a hill, I felt as if I were coming home.

Meg answered the door, and a cry came out of me from deep within my soul. "Mom!" I gasped, not quite understanding what was happening. If by chance a stranger had seen and heard me just then, he might have wondered what was going on. There I was: a tall, fair-skinned, auburn haired, suburban Protestant matron; and there was Meg: a tiny, dark-haired, Jewish lady. I felt as if I could fly into her arms for a big hug, which was surprising because she was just a little over half my size, but then so was my mother. At the same time, in a way I still can't describe, her presence seemed taller than I was. I think I must have looked confused and frightened because I didn't know whether to stay or run away.

"Hello, dear," she said, smiling her adorable, crooked smile. "I knew exactly what you would look like. For some time now I've had the feeling that we were going to meet, and now here you are. I have been told that I'm supposed to teach you about the invisible powers, the real powers that are available to all of us. I'm so glad you found the courage to come."

Smiling, Meg motioned me to come into the living room and sit down. Her eyes were brown and penetrating. "The spiritual gift to humankind is invisible power: we are born with power and dominion over all created things and also power over our own minds, our bodies, and our affairs. Most human unhappiness comes from lack of spiritual power. Human beings imagine that they are weak and victims of circumstances. When we fail, we claim that the failure was caused by conditions beyond our control. Now it's true that by ourselves we are indeed victims of circumstance, but when we are linked with the God-power, or the Blessed Higher Self, anything is possible.

"Let me show you an example of this power. When is your birth date?" Meg asked, picking up a pen and a paper.

"March sixteenth," I said.

"So, let's take a look at who you are and why you have come to this planet to live this lifetime. Hmm, do you have a sister?" she mused.

"Yes, three," I said hesitantly. "I'm one of two sets of twins."

"You and your twin don't get along too well, do you? Does her name begin with a 'C' or a 'P'?"

"Priscilla," I said, "but everyone calls her Chris now. She was named after my mother. No, we don't get along, even though we are identical twins. We never did."

"Oh, I see you've lost a husband by death, as well as a child," Meg continued. "I'm sorry you've had so much pain in your life. Two marriages? Two children? Boys? They are so different, like night and day. I also see other children around you, children from a different country. Who are they?"

I was flabbergasted. How could this strange woman know all these things? We had just met. "I take care of two Swedish children, Nilas and Caroline, most of the time now. They live with their father in Allendale, but they're at my house a lot because their father works twelve to fourteen hours a day. You're right about my family, too," I said. "I have had two marriages, one divorce, and now I am a widow. My second husband died of a heart attack. I lost a daughter at birth, and my stepson was murdered in 1977."

Meg continued on with the reading for over an hour. She used astrology and the Tarot, just as Brenda had described. I took page after page of notes. When it was over, I had learned a lot about my karma as well as what might lie ahead for me. I was delighted to hear that Meg taught classes on psychic awareness. She handed me the class outline and said that classes would begin in two weeks on Tuesday evenings in her home.

"I think Brenda and I will take these classes," I said.

"Good," said Meg. "You'll need them. You have a lot ahead of you, and you will need to develop your psychic powers to help with bringing up those boys. I am here to help you. Call me to confirm, and I'll hold spaces for both you and Brenda."

Reluctantly, I got up to leave. I began to feel extremely tired and drained on the way home. What, really, had just happened? I had gone to a strange house that somehow felt like my home. I met a woman who somehow was and was not my mother. This woman knew all sorts of things about me even though I had never told her any of them. She said that I had unlimited power from an infinite energy source. I had no idea how she knew these things. I had no idea how she was able to use strange-looking cards and calculations about the positions of planets to find things out about my life.

When I got home, I went to bed immediately and slept for twelve hours straight. It was as if my body were drinking in the sleep and absorbing the information given at Meg's reading. At the same time, I was gathering strength for what was to come.

The classes began two weeks later. I have always loved learning, and the time I spent studying with Meg was the most exciting and eye-opening education I had received since my year with Grammie Hemphill. One by one, Meg opened the curtains over the windows of my mind. The course lasted eight weeks, and it was nothing less than an overall tour of the psychic world.

Meg taught us first about something called *White Light*, an unseen, spiritual light that contains a powerful, universal energy available to all. Then we learned about the hidden energy centers of the body, called *Chakras*, how they work, and how we can learn to use them. Meg taught us about astrology, telepathy, intuition, and how to understand the meanings of dreams. She showed us how every action creates a reaction and how the laws of Karma work in each life. We learned how much of our lives are planned before we are born and why it is that certain people come into our lives. We experimented with mental telepathy. I peppered her with questions about everything. I took seas of notes. I wonder whether I exhausted her sometimes with my constant need to know more and more.

"Tonight I will be teaching you about scrying," Meg announced to the class one Tuesday night. "It's an ancient art, dating back at least to early Egyptian and Arabic peoples, and it is practiced all over the world."

I didn't know what in the world she was talking about. I had a fleeting mental image of the prototypical gypsy fortuneteller with her crystal ball, and I wondered whether the image had any connection to what Meg was going to tell us. "The term *'scry'* comes from the English word *'descry,'* which means to discern or to see dimly," Meg continued. "Scryers try to look into the future to answer questions, solve problems, or see the face of a lover or soul mate. You can also use scrying to find things like lost people, pets or valuable objects. Scrying has even been used to find criminals."

Meg went on to explain that the tool scryers use, called a speculum, can be all sorts of different things. Most specula have a reflective, shiny surface. Other than that general guideline, it's anybody's game. The most important thing about any speculum is that the scryer can use it easily and is comfortable with it. The scryer gazes into the speculum until she or he sees visions. The oldest and most common object used for scrying is calm, still water. It can be in a lake, a pond, or even a dark bowl. Some cultures, such as the Egyptians, use blood or ink. The French physician and astrologer Nostradamus scried with a bowl of water set upon a glass tripod. His preparatory ritual consisted of dipping a wand into the water and anointing himself with a few drops. Then he gazed into the bowl until he saw visions.

Other specula include mirrors; spherical glass fishing floats; polished metals and stones; and precious gems such as diamonds, emeralds, and rubies. Spanish and Mexican gypsy fortunetellers use crystal balls, and the popular image of the gypsy peering into her crystal ball has made that item the stereotype for all specula. (Aha! I'd been right when I'd mentally connected the word "scry" with an image of a gypsy.) Noted American psychic Jeane Dixon used a crystal ball. John Dee, the royal magician to Queen Elizabeth I, used a crystal egg and a black obsidian mirror. Witches of Germany and Spain use curved mirrors, the convex side painted black, or they use small cauldrons painted a shiny black inside and filled with water. In Arab countries, scryers use their own polished thumbnails.

Each scryer develops his or her own technique for inducing visions. Some who use crystals focus on points of light on the crystal's surface. Others enter an altered state of consciousness and allow images to float into their awareness. Some images come disguised as symbols, which the scryer must learn to interpret.

"When scryers see visions, it is because their third eyes have opened," Meg said. "The third eye is an invisible energy center in your head, just a little above and between your two outward eyes. It is a center for psychic powers." Meg taught us how to open the third eye by looking into a candle flame. We practiced staring at the flame for about twenty minutes, then looking up at a light-colored wall. To my delight, images appeared on the pale surface. They were fuzzy and I didn't understand completely what they were, but Meg said the visions would get clearer if I practiced. And was I going to practice? Just let someone try and stop me.

We also learned how to use a mirror or a crystal ball, first putting a drop of sandalwood on the third eye, then, gazing into the reflective object. Meg explained that patience and persistence are necessary to learn the art of scrying. Paramount to success is the ability to relax both the mind and the body, and to put the mind into a passive, unfocused state while blanking out all conscious thought.

I found that I naturally took to this kind of divination. I especially loved to practice on the New Moon, the one day in the month when there's no moon at all. In ancient times, people believed that when you are scrying on the energies of the New Moon, the messages you receive reveal the events coming in the next month. In my experience with the art of scrying, this old belief is exactly correct. The only exception is on New Year's Eve, when the events shown are what will be coming up in the new year. At that time, I found that I needed to make notes of the foreseen events and the order they appear to me, because that is the order of how the events will materialize throughout the coming year.

As I developed my skill with scrying, using the candle flame, I found that I would first see a mist that then slowly evolved into a circle, first black, then dark green. A deep red dot would appear through the center of the circle. The red dot grew until it took up most of the circle, with the black-green color still vibrating around the edge. After a time, the inner rose-colored circle would become white and look much like a movie screen. Then the pictures would come, always in black and white. As I became more skilled, the shapes began to sharpen and reveal discernible objects, people, faces, and symbols. I would sit at my kitchen table and stare into the candle flame for about twenty minutes. Then I would gaze up at the wall until the black-green circle would begin to form. At times I would gaze back at the candle to get some more juice.

"You know, Elizabeth," Meg said to me one day in her beautiful New York accent, "you were born with remarkably advanced psychic abilities. You just soak these things up like a sponge. You said your grandmother told you that you were born with the gift of prophecy, and I agree. But now I want to add something more to what your grandmother said. I think you brought a great deal of psychic information with you from your past lives. I'm convinced that you lived one of your lives in Egypt at the time of the dynasty of Isis. Remember, dear, that scrying was performed with great skill then. It may even have originated there."

As I practiced scrying, it seemed that whatever I saw in that candle flame was sure to happen. One of my early visions revealed that my father was going to suffer a serious illness. About a week before my parents arrived for their annual Thanksgiving-Christmas visit in 1981, I was practicing my scrying when a deeply disturbing scene opened up to me. In the flame I saw my niece Patricia, who was then a volunteer nurses' aid at Kingston Hospital in Wilkes-Barre, Pennsylvania. She was standing by a hospital bed and holding someone's hand, but I couldn't see whose hand it was. I saw people come to visit the patient: my mother, my aunt and uncle, my sisters. Then I realized that I hadn't seen my father come in. With a sinking heart, I knew that he must be the person in the bed. I began to pray for him. There w as nothing more I could do except wait for further information.

After my parents arrived for the holidays, Dad and I went shopping for the Thanksgiving feast. We were in the Allendale A&P when, all of a sudden, a shot of energy went through my body, and I began to cry softly. There was a dull pain at my heart. It felt like I had a fist punching my chest. I knew without a doubt that this would be the last Thanksgiving dinner I would share with my parents. I watched Dad walk his slow walk. He was stooped over with age, shuffling along and holding onto the shopping cart handle. Overwhelmed, I stood still. Suddenly I was so very thankful for all the years he had given to the family. My Dad had mellowed in his old age and fervently tried to make up to all of his daughters for any past wrongdoing. He had been harsh, critical, and fearsome, even violent, and he had a quick temper, but at that moment there in the supermarket he was only an old man getting older. I realized that he no longer held any power over me. I was the strong one now. I wanted to be of help to him as he moved toward the last days of his life.

"I'm just fascinated with this new talent of yours," my mother said as she helped herself to the cranberry sauce at the Thanksgiving dinner. "I never knew that people could make money just by reading cards. Of course I've always known you are especially intuitive, Betty Ann, but this is amazing. Do you think you could give your father and me a reading while we're here?"

I gave both readings separately and privately in a room off the kitchen. When I read my dad, most of the cards that fell were swords. My father had a great sense for cards. He had played and taught Contract Bridge all his adult life and co-authored the bridge column for *The New York Times* for many years. When he saw all the swords, which he appropriately related to spades in the regular deck, he knew something of great importance was coming into his life soon.

The reading I gave to my father that day was probably one of the most powerful I have ever given. It was certainly the most difficult. I clearly saw the pattern of his life begin, evolve, and finally come to its end. The entire experience was overpowering. I saw that the following April my father would return to my home again and that while there he would catch what he would think was a cold. Then, not realizing the seriousness of the illness, he would return home to New Hampshire, where he would suffer a stroke. I saw that he would go to the hospital and never again be back to normal. I also saw that he would be cared for in Pennsylvania where my older sister Nancy lived. The reading matched the vision in the candle several months before, when I had seen Nancy's daughter Patricia standing at a hospital bed and comforting someone.

My head began to pound and I felt sick to my stomach. How could I explain to him what I was seeing? Meg always said that I should be scrupulously honest in my readings and that I should try to warn people if misfortune was threatening. I wanted to be truthful with my father, but if I told him everything I saw in the cards, I knew he wouldn't believe me. Besides, it was a prediction of things that might happen, not things that positively were going to happen. No prediction is written in stone. "A prediction is only a possibility of an outcome and does not become real until the action occurs," Meg had taught us carefully. I did not want my father to become ill, yet felt that's where he was headed. I silently prayed for the insight to say the right things. Then I looked him in the eyes.

"Dad," I said, "you've got to be very, very careful about your health in the coming months. Promise me you'll see the doctor immediately if ever you aren't feeling well. Take any symptoms you have seriously, and make sure you do something about them right away."

"I guess it's like that old tune, *'Button up your overcoat when the wind blows free; Take good care of yourself, you belong to me,'* " he said.

"I really mean it," I said.

"Okay, Betty Ann. I'll be careful." He said, smiling weakly and patting my hand. Perhaps he sensed something.

My father took sick the next spring, just as I had seen in the candle flame and the cards. He suffered a stroke in New Hampshire and was later placed into Leader Nursing Homes in Wilkes Barre, Pennsylvania, where Nancy's husband was Chaplain. Patricia indeed watched over him early on. Mother moved in with Nancy to be near my father and remained with her for two years.

It was way, way too early on that March 1984 Saturday morning. I didn't want to wake up, but the bed kept shaking so there wasn't any choice. Slowly I realized that I wasn't in my bedroom any more. I found myself going down a hallway, and I knew that I was in Kingston, Pennsylvania, in the nursing home where my father was a patient.

As soon as I walked into his room, I felt a rush of fear flowing from Dad. Although neither of us spoke, I sensed that he was having a difficult time trying to leave his body because of that fear. Within myself I kept hearing, "Go to Pennsylvania! Go to Pennsylvania!"

A few minutes later I opened my eyes with a start and realized that it was 7:30 am. I dressed, had breakfast, called Nancy to tell her I was coming, and began the drive from Allendale, New Jersey to Wilkes-Barre, Pennsylvania. When I arrived at my sister's home, my mother was waiting to go with me to the nursing home. I had to marvel at her. She had been at my father's bedside every day for two years. Her determination and her strong faith in God and The Christ had kept her going all that time.

I had not been able to see my father for a few months, and I didn't realize how much his condition had deteriorated. It was a shock to see how thin and pale he had become. His aura was like a light from a little gray lamp just about ready to go out. Using prayer and a healing method that came natural to me, I worked to clear his aura and dispel all the negative energies I sensed around him. Then I drew him up close to me and put his chest against mine. Our hearts were beating simultaneously. "Dad, Dad, do you know who I am?" I whispered.

"They keep telling me to come with them, but I won't go," he finally said.

Very softly I explained to him that it was all right to go with the beings who were calling him. "They are God's messengers, and they want to take you to a safe and beautiful place. You don't need to be afraid any more." I felt his body relax. "Are you strong enough to say my name?" I asked.

"Betty Ann, Betty Ann," he whispered.

"Remember, Daddy, whenever you call my name again, I will come." Silently, I set a condition to the Universe that when my father called me again, I would come to him instantaneously to help him cross over. "Don't forget, Dad," I said, "You are safe, and you are loved." The room filled with a great, beneficent power. A feeling of deep love embraced everyone. My mother, my sister Nancy, and the nurses who were there all felt it

Then Mom was in tears. "It wasn't until this very moment that I realized Walter is really going to die soon," she said. "You know I've been hearing a voice inside me saying that I would be back home in New Hampshire in April. Up until now, I thought Dad would get well and go back with me, but I can see now that he won't be there."

I took her out to dinner, and I tried to calm her fears and answer her many questions. Later that evening I drove back to New Jersey.

Early the following Sunday, April 8, 1984, as I slept in bed, my consciousness abruptly was taken back to Dad's nursing home in Pennsylvania. I was floating near the ceiling and looking down at my father. He was curled up in the fetal position. Suddenly a golden cloud mushroomed out of the center of his body. It lifted upwards. Then I saw my mother dressed in black. I knew my father was ready to rise up and cross over that day.

Joy filled my soul when I awoke. I knew my Dad would finally be free from his suffering. I decided to stay at home until I heard from my family. At noontime my sister Nancy called and told me that Dad was having a difficult time breathing and was being carefully watched over. I told her of my love for her, and I told her to be at peace within. I knew she would be fine.

My twin called from New York City. "I'm going to Pennsylvania as soon as I can get a flight from LaGuardia. I want you to join me and go

out to see Dad. I just know he'll wait for me. He won't go until I'm there."
I was afraid that she was mentally trying to hang onto him and keep him
from dying until she could see him again. I warned her that he might
not be alive when she arrived.

"Promise to send your love to him while you're still on the plane," I
said, over and over.

"He will wait for me. Please don't say that. He will wait for me. I know
he will wait." Priscilla cried.

"I'm completely at peace with my father and I don't need to rush out
there. Nancy has her hands full already." I explained to Priscilla. "I'll
stay here and continue my prayers."

"You always have your head in the clouds," she responded, and hung
up, sounding very disgruntled.

Dad was already gone when Priscilla arrived at the nursing home.
He had passed away about a half hour before she arrived, just as her
plane was landing in Wilkes Barre.

I was alone and watching television at seven that evening. The classic movie *The Best Years of Our Lives* was on. It had been a family favorite.
My father had especially loved it. All of a sudden, I heard the sound of
a pair of hands clapping. Startled and thinking someone might be playing a joke, I checked around the house to make sure no one was there.
I satisfied myself that I was quite alone and settled in front of the TV
again. The clapping returned, several times. Then I felt my father's presence in the room with me. "I wonder whether Daddy has passed?" I said
to myself. Within minutes the phone rang, and Nancy told me that Dad
had died about a half hour before.

I felt a peace and serenity deep within. Despite all the upsets and sorrows when I was growing up, despite all the disputes and the abuse and
the misunderstandings, my father and I had come to deeply love each
other at the end. I have missed him, and I'm so grateful for the experiences we shared toward the end of his life. They have not only strengthened my faith, they also eased my own fear of death.

As I continued studying and practicing scrying, I became fascinated with the idea that it was possible to see the face of your soul mate if you looked into a mirror on Halloween Night. I didn't exactly know what the term *soul mate* meant, but it sounded wonderful. I imagined that it was something like a perfect lover, the one ideal person who would always understand you, always be kind to you, and never turn into a skunk or a snake the way ordinary men usually do. I wanted to meet my next soul mate. All my sorrows and troubles would probably float away on clouds of ecstasy if I could just get a look at his face and figure out a way to bring him into my life. Of course perfect soul mates existed, my fevered reasoning told me. Why would the term "soul mate" be in the English Language if there really weren't any soul mates? I had called Joe my soul mate. I asked Meg whether it was possible to scry yourself up a soul mate on Halloween or New Year's Eve.

"Well, dear heart," she said, "the first thing I've got to tell you is that nobody seems to know exactly what a soul mate is. There's a whole barrelful of conflicting opinions on the subject. Nobody knows where the term started, although Socrates speaks of a theory that true lovers are like two halves of the same circle. It's my personal opinion that 'soul mate' became a popular term to throw around at parties and such during the nineteen-sixties and -seventies. I don't think most people had a clear notion of what it meant, though.

"But to get back to Socrates' ideas," Meg continued. This broken-circle theory, and it's still popular today, says that soul mates were formed in ancient times when a cleavage in human physical and spiritual nature occurred, leaving each soul imperfect and searching for its other half. According to *The Platonist Doctrine of Compliments*, man could find in woman the virtues that he himself lacked. According to this theory, a soul may be reincarnated many times before it finally finds its mate. At last they join together and fulfill their purpose and are mysteriously melded together in perfect love and bliss, much like the union of the Hindu deities Krishna and Rahada.

"There are plenty of other theories too. Some say that soul mates have to be of opposite sexes, others say they do not. Some say they must be spouses or lovers, others say they can be friends, business associates, parents, even neighbors. Another viewpoint is that soul mates are beings who have shared many past lives to help each other reach their highest potential. They are completely in tune with each other and can communicate without words. Identical twins can be like this.

"Some people believe that you can have only one soul mate; others take the attitude of 'the more the merrier.' According to the great clairvoyant Edgar Cayce, the ultimate soul mate is always God or the Christ, the universal consciousness of which every soul is a part."

I was scribbling notes as fast as I could, trying to get everything down. Meg paused and smiled at me. "Didn't you think you had found yours in Joe? You want to know more about this kettle of fish?" she asked. "Or are you getting to the point where you're learning more than you care to about the subject?"

"Meg, what do you believe a soul mate really is?" I asked.

"I believe that soul mates come in three basic varieties, sort of like three flavors of ice cream. There's the twin soul or counterpart, then there's the lover or companion, and finally there's the karmic soul mate who comes into a person's life to teach her hard karmic lessons." Right then and there I knew that my identical twin was my karmic soul mate.

"So how do I think you can find your soul mate? You have to program yourself mentally, physically, and spiritually. First, I always tell people, get it on paper. Create a vision board with a picture of the handsome stranger, someone you find attractive. Cut a photo out of a magazine and paste it on cardboard. Gaze at it often. Then, make a list of all the characteristics you want in a life mate. Then read the list every morning when you get up and every evening when you go to bed. This way, you may meet your soul mate during the day or see him or her in your dreams."

After mulling over what Meg had said and doing some extra studying on my own, I came up with my own plan to try to see and meet my true soul mate. I decided that I would scry into a mirror on New Year's Eve. Tenacious thing that I am, I did it every year for ten years. I always made sure that the room was very dim and that there was a black background behind me. I would light two white candles and place one on either side of me, letting the flames glow in the mirror. For at least twenty minutes, I stared into the mirror while romantic, soft music was playing. I concentrated on allowing my third eye to open. Often a face appeared to me, sometimes more than one face. I learned a great deal from this procedure, but I don't think it ever revealed a soul mate to me.

On New Year's Day 1984, I saw the face of a man in the mirror, along with a string of other people. The man's face was the last one I saw that night, and I met him in December of that year. We were very close for a while, but then he chose to walk away from the relationship.

In 1985 I clearly saw the face of another man in the New Year's Eve mirror. A few months later he appeared in my life and helped me through a bad car accident. He is still my friend, but he's not my soul mate. However, each face you see when you scry will have some kind of action to share with you, and it usually is dramatic and important in some way.

So what do I think of this soul mate business now? Have I come up with my own definition of a true soul mate? I have learned over the years that two kinds of deep affinity are essential for a close, balanced, and healthy destined love relationship. The first is the heart connection. It's that feeling of desire and unspoken closeness that we feel most vividly when we are falling in love.

A reliable indication of a heart connection is the sense of warmth, nourishment, and wholeness we feel when we are in the beloved's presence. A heart connection is possible in many types of love relationships. It's a universal kind of affection. We can feel it with a close friend, a child, our parents and siblings, or anyone we are open to, even a passing stranger. This heart connection, however, isn't the same as the special attraction we feel toward certain people with whom we sense a deep, unexplained resonance, causing the sensation that we want to be with them all the time, to live with them, to know them, to love them and become an intrinsic part of their lives. This unnamable feeling is like a drawing or pulling together of you and your beloved. You both feel powerless to fight it and the feeling is both scary and wonderment. It is the sign of another type of affinity commonly called recognizing your soul mate.

When two destined souls connect, there is a vibration set up between them. They can see beyond the outer personality straight into each other's beauty. They can choose to connect their true selves together on the deepest kind of level. It is a kind of mutual recognition, almost as if both had been together sometime and somewhere before, perhaps in a past life. It feels like destiny brought both souls together. Endless songs, books, and poems have been written about this kind of coming together. It is a sacred alliance. It is part of a timeless human experience where both partners can discover and realize their deepest potentials and possibilities. It is what the Sufi poet Rumi wrote about fifteen hundred years ago:

True lovers don't meet somewhere.
They are in each other all along.

Where a heart connection allows us to appreciate those whom we love just as they are, a soul mate connection opens us up to more than that. Both members see each other as they could be at their very best and also for the person they could become with the help of the other. The power of their mutual love helps both partners to become more fully who they really are. These twin souls know deep inside that they are stronger together and can do more with their lives than if they were apart. To become separated causes them great pain.

Someone who loves us on a soul mate level can see our soul's potential more clearly than we can ourselves. This unique vision creates a catalytic effect; it encourages dormant parts of us to come forward and find expression. Then we feel the blossoming of our inner fulfillment and gratitude. We are most often attracted to lovers who we sense will make us live our lives more intensely rather than just make us feel good.

Soul mates recognize each other immediately and form an unspoken bonding to the very depths of their beings. A soul mate connection not only inspires us to expand ourselves, but it also forces us to confront our personal demons and anything else that stands in the way of that expansion. All emotional blocks fall away, and we embrace life and each other. The soul mate, the awaited lifetime in unified love, creates a unique way for the Divine to manifest itself within us. It brings about a match of souls profound consciousness of inwardness, completion, and depth. It is the joy we feel when we see goodness, the tears we cry over injustice, an ever-expanding, growing awareness of ourselves, and all that we are a part of.

Whenever we see ourselves as having some rigid, fixed identity, whenever we define ourselves by saying, "I am a happy person," or, "I am a sad person," or even, "I am a spiritual seeker," we experience ourselves indirectly, through our self-image. This is the *false self*, a mental construction based on past experiences. But during moments when we are in touch with our soul, such as during meditation, we experience ourselves with fresh eyes, alive and without restrictions. This is the being who is alive in this moment. It is our true individuality, a special way of being, that allows us to connect with another person's inner vibration. We fall completely into the purified *State of Being*.

When our hearts are open, we can love each other equally. When our souls are joined in this experience, we love fully, as we have never loved before. When two lovers meet on this level, their false identities float away like smoke, and the lovers become energized in the present, as I and Thou. They realize they are a complete unit, with greater potential for fulfillment than if they had not met and united.

The soul's longing is always a double yearning, the individual and the universal. We want to feel the meaning and beauty of our individual lives, and we also want to connect with the larger, universal currents of life flowing through us. As the great Yogi teacher Paramahansa Yogananda said, *"I am a bubble, make me the sea. As a bubble, I become a part of the sea. Therefore, the sea is me, and I Am!"*

Our greatest challenge as human beings is to live fully in both of these worlds. We are not just the body and mind; we are also a being with awareness and presence infinitely bigger than our individual physical forms. In the same way, we are not just this body, but also this greater, formless being. Each of us is an individual being as well, living in this particular place and at this particular time. Soul work is the most important part of a lifetime. It involves breaking open the tough hulls of our conditioned personalities that constrict our potential for growth. It allows us to plow the fields of our deepest humanity so seeds can blossom and bear fruit. This kind of cultivation takes time, patience, dedication, and perseverance.

When we are youngsters, our soul richness shines forth in a simple, spontaneous way. Babies simply are what they are. As we grow older and get caught within the confines of our false self, we isolate ourselves from our Higher Self. We are separated from the vast place of power, of unlimited possibilities and potentiality that is our birthright. Our soul stops developing, and we experience the painful consequences of that loss: loneliness, alienation, separation, disempowerment, meaninglessness, and the inability to trust and love deeply. Our soul suffers this loss, but it also finds the inner strength to see us through and spur us on in search of our lost birthright. Our soul recognizes those who can help it along in its search, and it cries out to them.

The more we tap our deepest potentials, the richer our souls become. Our responsiveness to our lives and to others becomes greater. Each of us has special qualities and unique aptitudes. Every soul possesses its own individual, jewel-like character, its own richness. We each have our unique path of soul-work, the personal direction we need to follow in order to find our deepest potential and life purpose. Two lovers with a soul mate connection recognize that they can help each other move forward along the way.

When the classes finished, I realized that I still had lots more to learn from Meg. I had taken the grand tour of the psychic world, and now I wanted to visit each place again so I could stay longer and understand more. I asked Meg to teach me the Tarot and astrology in depth. We worked together for several years, meeting two Saturdays a month.

It took me two years of daily work to learn how to penetrate the secrets of the Tarot, but I finally became an expert. I read book after book on the subject and experimented with all sorts of different card layouts. Every morning for those two years, I gave myself a reading and wrote the card layout down. Before I went to bed each night, I would compare the happenings of that day with what I had read from the cards in the morning. If you go with the belief that everything happens for a reason and nothing happens by accident, then it is only logical that the cards fall every day as they are supposed to fall. I discovered that you cannot control a reading, although at first I sure did try. Alas, I couldn't make the cards say I was going to win the lottery or that a magnificent European nobleman would cover my kitchen table with rubies and my bed with emeralds.

I got to know those cards as if they were my family. I learned the special and distinct identity of each card. More than that, I gradually began to see not only that each card had its own meaning, but also that particular combinations of cards had particular meanings. Ten years later, on video cassettes, I recorded my knowledge and discoveries using my own devised set of Tarot card combinations and this detailed teaching later became a CD.

I was working with Meg for about three months when she told me I was ready to give my first reading. She instructed me to go carefully and not to hurt anyone. "Now don't be afraid to charge for your reading, Meg instructed. "Remember, you're worth it. Think of the reading as an exchange of energy. We pay to turn on our electric lights. We also pay people like scientists and doctors for their expert opinions. It is the same with giving a reading. I have found over the years that if I don't charge something for a reading, the message is not appreciated. It took me awhile, but I am very comfortable with the understanding that time is energy and energy has a price." With much trepidation, I put a small advertisement in the local paper.

Elaine, my first client, came to see me on a Wednesday afternoon at around two. If I seemed confident and calm to her, it was more due to my acting ability than anything else. Inside I was about as steady as a serving of jello. We talked for a while, I answered her questions, and then I laid out the cards and explained to her what they meant. When the reading was over, she said she was very pleased and told me I was a good reader.

"You sure are accurate," she said. I'm going to pass your name around to my friends. She took out a ten-dollar bill, laid it on my kitchen table, and left with a smile on her face. It was all I could do to keep my mouth from dropping open. Wow, ten dollars! It might as well have been a hundred. I got paid for what I said to her. Who ever would have thought it?

I called Meg as soon as the reading was over. I couldn't believe that I had actually pleased someone with a reading. "Meg, Meg, it's just so inconceivable," I babbled into the phone.

Meg laughed. "Now maybe you are beginning to see how you can help other people and put Jeffrey through college at the same time."

"I feel like I've just gone through a rite of passage," I said.

"You have, my darling girl," Meg said, laughing.

"You actualize what you visualize," Meg told the class over and over again, and I was learning to believe it.

I was continuing my studies with Meg and working at Atlantic Aviation in Teterboro, New Jersey, when I decided I needed a new car. My Oldsmobile was running out of steam. One day during lunch I drove over to Bergen Buick on Route 17, where I fell in love with a dark blue Buick Skylark, trimmed in white, much like my business suit. I put down a hundred dollars as a deposit.

I had no idea how I was going to come up with the rest of the money, but I decided to practice Meg's teaching about visualizing what you want to actualize. Every night when I came home from work, I sat down at the table, cleared my mind, and visualized that skylark in my garage. I got so good at it that I could even hear the motor running. The only problem was that whenever I closed my eyes to see the car, all I could make out was a dark, indistinct shadow, not a clear image of the Buick. This perplexed me, so I asked Meg about it.

"Be careful, darling," she said. "Perhaps this isn't the car for you."

I didn't understand. I believed I was strong enough to visualize and bring in my desire. Meg told me to be cautious. She thought there might be a reason that I was not getting that car. "Perhaps there's a serious problem with it," Meg cautioned.

How could there be anything wrong? It was clearly the car for me, for heaven's sake, and I loved it. It took me more than three weeks to get credit approval. When I called back the Buick place to explain, they had already sold my car. I was furious. The General Manager told me that a man, whom I'll call Mr. Williams, had come in and put cash down on the table and said he wanted my Skylark right away. Mr. Williams was the manager of a New Jersey football team and a regular customer. I asked the General Manager if I would receive my deposit back, and he told me I would not. I had to get my lawyer to write him a letter before the dealership returned my money.

I was discouraged about the entire process and gave up. Three months later, in May of 1983, I met John Iozia, a delightful, intelligent man who kept his airplane at Teterboro Airport. One day he asked whether I was looking to buy a new car. I told him the story about the blue Buick. He laughed and told me he was General Manager of Brogan Cadillac/Oldsmobile in Totowa, New Jersey. He invited me to come down and look at their new Cutlass Supreme SL sports coupe. He said he would get the car at a great price because I worked at Atlantic Aviation, and he could also arrange for the loan through my credit union. Who could say no to that?

I called Meg and told her what happened. She explained that according to Natural Law, there is always a valid reason when you don't get what you want the first time, and Spirit will always bring you something better. "Patience, child," Meg said. "Patience. Just go down and look at the cars and see what happens."

The very next Saturday I was there on Route 46 at Brogan. "Go on out and walk the lot," John said. "If you see a car you want, come back and ask me for the keys."

Using my sixth sense, I walked up and down the rows of cars. Suddenly I felt strongly drawn to a silver and blue Oldsmobile Cutlass Supreme SL. As I climbed in behind the steering wheel, a piece of paper fell into my lap. It was a description of the car, pricing all the extras on it and giving the date when the car was completed, March 14, 1983. A thrill went through me. March 14th was the date of my son Jeff's birth. I took this to be a sign that I should buy the car. Skylark, shmylark, this Oldsmobile was the car for me. Within three days. I had the loan from the Credit Union and drove the car off the lot.

Meg explained that things like this happen when the energies support you. If something is supposed to happen, it will, with little or no effort on your part. "What did I tell you? When it's right, it's right," Meg said and smiled one of her beautiful crooked smiles.

Oh, but this story doesn't end there. After all, whatever happened to the Blue Buick, the car I was prevented from buying by the *powers that be*? In June of 1983, Mr. Williams, the owner of the New Jersey football team, stomped into my boss's office, steaming mad. I knew he was the one who had bought the Buick. His face was a most unbecoming shade of red. He told my boss that he had been driving along Route 46 the Sunday before, when his new car began to swerve. He pulled over to the side of the road just as the engine dropped out of the car.

Tears filled my eyes as I realized that Spirit had been protecting me all the time. What if I had been driving that car? Would I have been able to make it to the side of the road, or would there have been an accident? Who would have taken care of my boys if I had been injured? Even if no one had gotten hurt, I could never have sustained such a financial loss at that time. That experience would have been devastating. Filled with gratitude, I ran into the Ladies Room to say a prayer of thanks. I knew I had been blessed and saved by the *Law of Grace*. It was just as Meg taught me. If you cannot manifest a desire the way you wish, something better will come along. Surprise! It could turn out that the something better could even cost five thousand dollars less than the item you originally wanted. That is *Natural Law* and that's the way it worked out with my new car.

CHAPTER 7

Shirley and the Psychic Fairs

IN THE EARLY SPRING OF 1981, Shirley Tabatnik, the owner of the Psychic Fairs Network, asked Meg whether she knew anyone who was qualified to teach adult evening school. The New Milford, New Jersey school system's Adult School's Program was going to offer a series of courses in a new category, Alternative Medicine and Stress Relief. They wanted someone to teach self-hypnosis.

About a week later, Meg called me and said she had spoken to a woman by the name of Shirley Tabatnick. Shirley and her husband had established an organization called *The Psychic Fairs*, headquartered in Little Falls, New Jersey. The fairs were held at shopping malls and hotels in New York and New Jersey. People would come to the fairs, choose a psychic, and get a fifteen-minute reading. The money was divided between Shirley and the reader. Meg wasn't interested in giving readings there herself. The money wasn't enough for a reader of her standing and experience. Also, Meg's readings lasted for an hour or more, and Psychic Fair readings were only fifteen minutes. But Meg had told Shirley about me, and she told me it might be good for me to sign up.

"It will be very good practice for you," she said, "and the money won't hurt either. You can begin to build your reputation as a reader and get yourself some steady clients."

Without hesitation, I signed up for two Sundays a month, one day at the Howard Johnson's Motor Lodge in Saddle Brook, New Jersey; the other day at the White Plains Hotel in White Plains, New York. I found a little blue suitcase, packed my Tarot cards with my astrological data inside, and declared myself ready to go.

I couldn't help giving a little gasp when I walked into my first Psychic Fair. "Fair" was the right word for it, I thought, as I looked at the other readers, each at his or her own table. Turbans, hoop earrings, wild makeup, silk embroidered gowns, feathers, capes, thousand-foot ropes of imitation pearls and rubies, all this and more seemed to be the general style. I was wearing a conservative dark-blue business suit with a white blouse, set off with small gold earrings, and I carried nothing but my little blue suitcase.

Oh well, I thought. This is what I feel comfortable wearing. Maybe my suit will make potential clients feel more at ease with me, as they sit at my table. Maybe I'll appeal to levelheaded types, business people and such. I sat down and waited to see what would happen. In a little while, a level-headed-looking businessman actually did approach and ask for a reading. Thus began a twenty-year association with the Psychic Fairs. I always did my best to give clear, honest readings.

I always wore a conservative suit, and I always carried my little blue suitcase. I estimated that the little blue suitcase earned me enough to put my son through college and kept bread on our table for many, many years. I felt a sense of sadness and loss when I finally had to throw the little blue suitcase out. I felt like I was losing a familiar companion.

"Elizabeth, I think this is the perfect thing for you," Meg said.

"But I don't know anything about hypnosis," I protested. "I'd rather teach the psychic work that you teach. I've never been hypnotized!"

"Yes, you have," Meg said, laughing. "You know how you sing and study your voice lessons? You memorize the words to new songs almost immediately. Well, that's self-hypnosis right there. When you practice your scrying, you are putting yourself into a type of hypnotic state. Think about it. Haven't you ever concentrated so completely on reading something that you lost track of everything else around you? The truth is, any time you focus clearly and intently on one specific thing for a significant length of time and remember it afterwards, that's self-hypnosis. You do it all the time, Elizabeth. You know all about hypnosis -- you just don't know that you know. Since you are very capable, you would make an excellent teacher and would be learning while you teach.

"Look," Meg continued, "just give Shirley a call and see what you can work out. I am sure the both of you can find a way to make this happen. I think you should offer to teach a class in psychic awareness, too. It's related to hypnosis because they both have to do with the thought process, and you certainly shouldn't have any doubts about teaching psychic awareness. If anybody is psychically aware, it's you. I am sure both you and Shirley can find a way to make this happen. It's time for you to start teaching others now Elizabeth," Meg reassured me. "That's one of the reasons you were placed here on earth. Now, I want you to come up to my house on Saturday. Come for lunch. I have something for you and it's very important that you come."

As soon as I could, I contacted Shirley Tabatnik. She offered me the job of teaching two courses, Self-Hypnosis and Psychic Sensitivity, at the New Milford Adult School. "Just offer the Psychic class and see what happens," Shirley said. "If no one registers, there won't be a class in either case."

"Shirley, how can I teach a hypnosis class? I know nothing about the subject." I felt very hesitant with this new idea.

"Hmmm," Shirley said. "I know someone who may be willing to help you. His name is Mel Phillips and he has a hypnosis clinic in Wayne, New Jersey. He and his assistant Howard Stanton, travel all over the world teaching the Silva Mind Control Course, and they've written extensively on self-hypnosis and altered states of consciousness. They're very successful. Their books and tapes have helped thousands of people. Mel is a good friend of mine, and I'll ask him to teach you the important basic skills and concepts of hypnotism before you begin the adult school classes."

"Okay, Shirley," I responded, feeling very apprehensive, "I'll give it a try."

The following Saturday I arrived at Meg's about eleven-thirty in the morning. "Hello, darling," Meg said, smiling from ear to ear. I wondered what she was up to. "I have such a surprise for you today and such a gift for your future. Come into the dining room." Meg said as she beckoned me forward.

"Oh my, what's this?" I stopped short, gaping at the long dining room table there were at least twenty piles of papers. The piles were thick and I could see the chakra instruction sheet, the aura drawings as well as the energy exercise diagram we had learned in class. "Elizabeth, what you see here is all the information I use in my classes," Meg explained. "It has taken me over twenty years of discovery, practice, study, and organizing to put all this together. So here it is: beginners meditation, White Light, the chakra system, the laws of Karma, clairvoyance, telepathy, intuition, dream-interpretation, tarot reading, scrying, everything."

She walked around the table, putting her hand on the piles one by one, as if she were touching her favorite children on their heads. "I've put everything down as clearly and honestly as I could. I want you to take it all and begin to use it. Teaching the Psychic Awareness course will be your first step. You need the work and many people will be helped by this information. The best part is, you will never be too old to teach this course. You have a son to educate and college isn't cheap."

I looked at Meg with tears in my eyes. I wanted to protest that I wasn't ready, that I wasn't worthy of such a gift, but there was such a big lump in my throat, I couldn't speak. Meg put her hand up. "Now don't say anything, Elizabeth, my darling. I'm absolutely determined about this. You're going to need the work. You know you will. You're a single parent with a limited income. I want better than that for you, but you're going to have to work for it. Remember now, you're not being selfish. Many, many people will be helped by this information. You should keep in mind that it's perfectly all right to earn money from this kind of work. If you didn't, you would starve, or you'd have to spend your energy doing something you weren't meant to do. That wouldn't be good for anybody -- yourself, your family, or the people you could have helped but didn't because you were typing memos or calculating numbers for a bank or something. Of course there's nothing wrong with things like typing memos or accounting. They are honorable occupations. Perhaps you're skilled at that kind of work, but they are not the things you were meant to do in this lifetime.

"We have gone about as far as we can together. I have nothing more to teach you. You've learned it all and you've learned it well. Now you must apply your knowledge and allow others to have their eyes opened to the field of metaphysics. I love you like a daughter, dear one, and am always your friend. Please take this step and show me that you have faith in yourself. This is a courageous new road that will change your life."

I looked at Meg with tears in my eyes. Never before had I felt such love and support from anyone. Meg was handing me a part of her life. The gratitude I felt was beyond words.

"I have divided up this material into eight class sessions," Meg said. "So make the Adult School course eight weeks long for both classes and teach them on the same evening each week, back to back. Begin the hypnosis course at six-thirty and the psychic classes at eight. I sense you will do very well. There is an awakening that will take place in the 1980's, and it will be a time when you will be both teaching and learning. Over the next decade, people's hearts will begin to soften and open up, as if rousing from a long sleep. Many books about clairvoyance and other psychic issues are going to come out in the near future, and all kinds of classes will appear all over the country. I have a feeling you are going to find a new teacher, someone who will help show you other aspects of your inner self.

"Now," Meg said with her eyes shining bright, "Let's have lunch. I made you a great salad from my garden. Sit down, relax and don't look so worried."

When I returned home I received a call from Mel. "Hello Elizabeth," he said. "My name is Mel Phillips. Shirley Tabatnick asked me to give you a call. She told me you were about to teach a hypnosis class. What can I do to help you?" I explained to Mel that I had never experienced a formal hypnosis session and had no idea how to teach the subject. I told him that I wanted to teach the psychic classes, but the school wanted me to teach a self-hypnosis class, too. Mel laughed. He had a light and infectious laugh, and his voice sounded warm and reassuring. "Come to my office tomorrow, and I'll try to help you."

When I arrived at Mel's office, he and Howard introduced themselves. I almost gasped aloud. Why hadn't Shirley prepared me for this? Mel was absolutely gorgeous – he stood about five feet, ten inches, dark haired and handsome face, lithe but muscular body, good clothes, good shoes, good haircut, with an easy, self-assured manner. His aura shone out around him like a peacock's tail. Mel gave me a general guidebook he had written about self-hypnosis and also a book he had co-authored about what was then called *Silva Mind Control*. (It is now simply called *The Silva Method*.) He told me to make outlines for each of the eight classes, showed me the basics of how to self-induce hypnosis, and told me that class members should be able to experience hypnosis each week.

"Don't worry, Elizabeth," Mel said. "You can do this. In fact, self-hypnosis is so simple that you'll find that people do it for themselves. The class will wind up benefiting everyone. That includes you, too. I'll call you once a week the day before you teach, and we will go over the next night's class. I'm here to support you, and I wish you only the best with this experience. Once you go through your first eight weeks, you will be teaching this class forever. I'm sure you will grow in the process."

Smiling half-heartedly, I left with an armful of books and papers to read and organize. Much to my surprise, the classes filled up immediately. The Adult School was very pleased. I had twenty students in the Psychic Awareness class and eight students in the Self-Hypnosis class. Every Tuesday Mel called me around four in the afternoon and gave me detailed information about what I was going to teach the following evening. The classes went very well for the first five weeks. My students were intelligent and cooperative. All the hypnosis class members were able to induce light to medium trance states within themselves. I had always loved acting, even though I was shy, and I enjoyed speaking before people. Teaching others felt powerful and I enjoyed the students' questioning eyes. Of course it wasn't the same as singing and dancing in a summer stock production of *Oklahoma*, which I had done a few years before, but teaching was fun in its own way. Besides, I was able to prove the old teachers' saying, *"As long as you keep one lesson ahead of your students, you'll be okay"*.

Howard, Mel's assistant, telephoned me on the Sunday afternoon before my sixth class. He told me that Mel had been called out of town for the next week and had asked him to give me the material I would need for the next self-hypnosis lesson. Howard asked me if I could come up to the office that afternoon. He explained that he wanted to show me some new techniques that would help me with the class. Although I was disappointed about not working with Mel, I agreed and arrived around four o'clock.

"Hello, Elizabeth," Howard greeted me. The place seemed entirely different with only Howard there. It was as though Mel had rolled up the atmosphere of friendliness and welcome, stuck it under his arm, and taken it with him when he left. I hadn't paid much attention to Howard before, but now I took a good look. He was a short man with intense eyes. His hair was dark brown and thinning. There was dirt under his finger nails and his tan slacks were very wrinkled. He seemed creepy. He certainly did not have Mel's charisma. At least he wore a suit, I thought. Somehow I did not feel relaxed in his presence. I felt like turning and running, but that would have been ridiculous, I told myself. Howard was Mel's trusted assistant, and I respected Mel's integrity and judgment.

"I can't stay very long," I said instinctively. "My son is coming home soon and I have to get back to make dinner."

"Don't worry," Howard said, "This won't take long. It won't take long at all." He made an attempt at a smile. "Come and lie down on the couch so I can put you under."

"What are we going to do?"

"Just a simple technique to help you relax and gain control of your heartbeat, so you can reduce stress," Howard was patting the side of the couch.

Oh, why had I ever agreed to this? Reluctantly, I lay down. Howard began the induction, and all seemed to be going along painlessly. He was working in the air over my stomach, waving his hands and chanting something. I had never seen such behavior and didn't know what to do or what to say. Oh, well, I thought, trying to relax and unclench my fingers, he's not even touching me, so what harm can this possibly do? I'll just go along with it and see whether I can learn something. Mel's going to be back next week so I won't ever have to deal with this guy again.

Suddenly, something happened! It was like someone picked up reality like a tablecloth and gave it a violent shake. I must have gone into a trance without realizing it, and a beautiful woman, surrounded by dazzling white light, seemed to explode out from the center of my being. She had long, blonde hair and was dressed in a light blue draped garment with a gold belt. She was fine-featured, almost like a Greek goddess. She pointed her long finger at Howard. "Don't touch this woman," she said. If a female cougar could speak, I think its voice would have some of the power and authority of this woman's voice, but not with its honey smoothness and timbre. "You cannot have her. She is a high priestess and belongs to the realms of God."

Could Howard see her too? Was he hearing her speak? Suddenly he was lifted up and flung, surrounded by a ball of light, across the room. His head banged into the wall and he slid down to the floor, stunned. For a few minutes he sat there, dazed. Then he struggled up and stood with his hand on the wall for support. He looked at me like a drunken man, bent over and swaying. "Get out of here," he shouted, "Just get out!"

I shot up from the couch, ran as fast as I could to my car, and drove off. I didn't look back. I don't even remember the winding ride home along Ramapo Ridge Road. I was shaken to the bones and still in a semi-trance.

About four days later, Mel gave me a call. "What did you do to Howard?" he asked.

"Well, he had a heart attack and almost died," Mel said. "Howard told me you had been to the office for a hypnosis lesson, and he was muttering something else, but I didn't understand. He collapsed last Sunday night and was rushed to the hospital. He's just come home and looks thin and pale. He can't work and will not talk about what happened between the two of you."

"I can't say too much, Mel." I said. "I really don't understand what happened. Howard fell and then he asked me to leave. I thought he was feeling all right, but I left quickly. I had to get home to my son."

About three months later, as I was giving Psychic Fair readings at the Livingston Mall in New Jersey, I looked up and saw Howard. I almost didn't recognize him. He was pale and thin and could hardly walk. I was very surprised to see him.

"Why are you here?" I asked. "Maybe you had better get a reading from someone else."

No, Elizabeth," Howard said. "I don't want to see anyone else because I came to see you. I don't want a reading either, I just want to explain something to you."

"What?"

"I want to explain what happened the day you came to see me," Howard said. "It is very important that I tell you this today."

"Okay," I said as he took a chair at my table.

"I know you may find this surprising and almost unbelievable, but perhaps over the years you will understand." Howard began. "I am a devil worshipper and always have been. All my work is for Satan. Yes, Elizabeth, there is a devil. He is as real as your God. My mission on this planet is to bring Satan new souls. I wanted your soul. I thought it would be quite a prize to offer my master. I had every intention of taking it the day you came to the office to work with me. That had been the game plan, and this was the work I was doing every day."

Howard stopped. He was choking his words and began to sob deep, guttural wails. "I didn't know! I didn't know," he repeated over and over again, shaking his head and looking down. "The woman who came out of your center. Do you know her?" Howard asked.

I was stunned and could hardly respond. My heart was beating fiercely.

"Not really," I said. "I saw her once before when I became pregnant with my second son, Jeffrey. I had suffered several miscarriages and she came to reassure me that the baby I was carrying at the time would survive."

"Well, her name is Isis and she is a High Priestess from Egypt," Howard explained. "She is your guide and protector. Do you know of her legend?"

"No," I said. "My teacher had mentioned this Goddess in class. I don't know much about Egypt, but feel I may go there someday."

Howard laid four small blue books on the table. "These are for you. When you get a chance, I hope you will read them." I read the titles: *The Kybalion, The Secret Doctrine of the Rosicrucians, The Art and Science of Personal Magnetism*, and *Mental Therapeutics*. Each book was imprinted with gold and had a gold pyramid on the binding.

"I have been a student of the history of occultism and esoteric teachings," Howard continued. "These books are valuable and precious and I hope you will never allow them out of your sight. Please guard them well." "Have you ever heard of the fallen ancient Atlantis?" He continued.

"No," I said.

"Well, maybe you could find out about Edgar Cayce, the sleeping prophet. Cayce explains about the lost Atlantis and some mysteries regarding Egypt as well." He said. "I have been instructed to give these books to you for your education and use, I'm not going to need them any more."

"What do you mean?" I asked.

Howard looked at me long and hard. "Please forgive me, Elizabeth," he said weakly.

"For what?"

"For trying to take your soul. You are a High Priestess and you have great work to do on this planet. Please forgive me. Please forgive me."

I felt embarrassed. I did not know what to say. As far as I knew, Howard had achieved nothing and could not harm me. It was much later, in Maui, Hawaii, that I would learn of the intense invisible battle that had been warred against me and of the great protective forces that had saved me. "Of course I forgive you, Howard," I said. "No harm done. But you had better stop taking souls or you could come to harm."

Howard smiled at me in my ignorance. "I will, Elizabeth," he said. "I can no longer continue, because once a servant of Satan fails, as I have with you, the penalty is always death."

Of course I didn't believe what he was saying. He was clearly mentally ill. Three days later, Howard had another heart attack and died. I told myself, Satan hadn't come and whisked him away to Hell. It was just a heart attack. People have heart attacks every day. It's a physical process that happens to the body, the result of purely physical things like high cholesterol or blood clots or defective arteries, that's all. When Mel called to tell me of Howard's death, I felt an inner sense of relief and was not surprised.

It was three months later when I had the dream. Ever since I can remember, I have had all kinds of vivid dreams, several times a week. This particular dream, however, was the most vivid of them all. It was not a living dream, like an appearance, but the colors were so bright that I can close my eyes now, thirty years later, and see the glorious imprint which that dream left on my mind. I was praying in a church, much like St. Patrick's Cathedral in New York City, and there before me was an enormous, round, stained glass window. The colors were stunning. I could see them clearly as the sunlight shone through, with colorful rays falling on me, and all around me in kaleidoscopic shapes of light. The window portrayed the Peace Dove holding an olive branch.

As I gazed at it, I became aware that there was something different about the bottom right hand side. It alone, out of the whole window, was in black and white, just pieces of clear glass held together by black lead strips. For a moment I wondered what the significance of this vision might be. Then it came to me. It was as if I were looking at a perfected soul that had just a little way to go before it was entirely self-realized. A message came with the dream. "Go to Hackensack and open *Visions of Reality.*"

"What in the world does that mean?" I wondered, still half asleep. I didn't know much about Hackensack, New Jersey, except that it was the county seat and I was born there. All the lawyers seemed to work there, which I didn't think had anything to do with me. And what was this "Visions of Reality" thing? I was completely stumped.

For some reason, I thought to call Bill Urban, a banker friend of mine. He asked me if Hackensack was the Bergen County Seat (I was living in Bergen County at the time), and I said yes. Bill told me that he didn't exactly know why, but he thought the message in the dream meant that it would be a wise move for me to have my psychic work become an official small business. He said I should go to the County Courthouse in Hackensack and look up the name Visions of Reality in their registry of small businesses. If it were not listed, then I would be able to open a business under that name for about thirty-five dollars, and I could then establish a business bank account. It would benefit me in many ways, including my annual tax return. I did just that, and *Visions of Reality* was born on May 18, 1981.

My psychic powers were growing stronger and stronger as I worked with the Psychic Fairs and saw increasing numbers of private clients. Every morning I did a card layout, and I became a little more adept with each one. Life was busy. I had begun teaching psychic classes in my living room, and I continued with my work at the Adult School. In the spring of 1982 I began a meditation group.

My phone never stopped ringing. My reputation for having psychic powers grew, and I was nicknamed "the brain" at the airport, where I still had a full-time job in addition to all my psychic work.

One afternoon I was walking through the airport hangar at Atlantic Aviation where I worked as administrative assistant to the ground services manager, Hank Esposito. I ran into Mike, one of the aircraft mechanics for Colgate-Palmolive Company.

"Come and take a look at our new aircraft," he said. "It's a beaut."

"Wow," I said, "a G-IV. It is beautiful."

The new G-IV was one of the largest aircraft I had seen in a long time. The new company plane was almost as long as a Boeing 747, it could carry between thirty-five to fifty people. It had wall-to-wall carpeting; leather seats, each one with its own television set, VCR and telephone; a bar; a dining area; and two private rooms that could be used either as bedrooms or conference rooms.

"It's about to make it is maiden voyage, and it's going to fly completely around the world over the next six weeks. They're planning to make business stops in major cities on every continent except Antarctica."

"That's great," I said. "Wish I could go along."

Mike asked me to put my hand on the plane to bless it and also tell him how the trip would go. *I did not want to do this* because Hank, my boss, had told me he would fire me if I ever tried to do any of that weird psychic stuff at the airport. But Mike kept after me and wouldn't let me leave the hangar. He told me he kind of believed in psychic powers. He seemed so earnest, and, beside that, he was very, very adorable in his pleading, so I reluctantly gave in and touched the plane with my left hand. Suddenly a rush of power went through me like silent lightning, and a vista opened up in my third eye. This was a very familiar feeling, and I knew I was about to answer his question.

I saw the aircraft having engine trouble as it approached Tokyo, Japan. I saw a fire in the engine on the left side and advised Mike to tell the pilot not to be afraid. It would be a small fire and not serious, but some parts of the great G-IV might be damaged. I saw the plane landing safely, but there would be a three-day delay because it would be difficult to find a replacement part. I added that there would be some small mechanical failures in Germany, Denmark and Ireland, but otherwise all would go well. Mike was shocked. He had never seen me work before.

I slowly walked back to my office, and a short time later my boss Hank came in. He sounded angry and his voice became very authoritarian. "I just received a call from George at Colgate and he wants to see you right away. What's going on? He sounded anxious."

"I don't know. By the way, how do you get to the Colgate offices? I've never had to go there?"

It's in the new hangar," Hank said. "Don't be long, I need to get some letters out."

I was shaking as I approached George's office. "Hello Elizabeth," George said. "Please sit down. I need to ask you a few questions." He was a short man with brown, wavy hair, in his early forties. He looks as strong as a front-end runner on a football team. He looked puzzled. "Mike was just here and told me what you did with our new G-IV."

"Oh, George," I said. "I didn't mean any harm!"

"Well, I have an important question to ask you, Elizabeth, and it's quite serious," George said sternly. "How did you know the itinerary of this upcoming flight?"

"What?" I asked.

"How did you know the itinerary?" George asked again.

"I'm not sure, I just touched the plane and gave Mike the message that came through my mind."

"Are you certain of that? Are you very sure you didn't see a list or something that would have this itinerary written on it?"

"No," I answered, shaking in my chair. "Why do you ask?"

"Because Colgate has had some problems of late and the president's life was threatened. We are under top security with this trip. He and I are the only two people who know the itinerary."

I closed my eyes. "This is it," I thought. "Goodbye, job."

"How long have you been with Atlantic Aviation, Elizabeth? This is the first time we've met and I am baffled at your insight. My mother was psychic to a certain degree," George continued, "so I have some understanding of these things, but this is amazing, just amazing. I've made notes of your predictions, and I assure you, I'll pay attention to them. Somehow, I believe you."

"Please don't tell Hank. He hates the fact that I'm psychic and believes that it doesn't belong at an airport. Funny, but I just might agree with him after today."

"Okay," George said, laughing. "Got you covered. Just to make sure he doesn't wonder why I called you over here, I'll tell him my girl is out, and I need you to do a few letters for me. So, get out your pad and we'll make it look official." I breathed a sign of relief.

Two months later George called Hank again and asked whether he could spare me for a few minutes. I went over to the Colgate office, curious as to why George wanted to see me. He beckoned me to sit down. "We're back from the trip."

"How did it go for you?" I asked.

"I just don't know what to say," he responded, smiling. "It all went exactly as you predicted: the breakdown in Japan; the three-day wait for the parts; the mechanical problems in Germany, Denmark and Ireland. It all happened."

I felt overwhelmed and the look on my face must have said so. "Elizabeth, don't worry. You are very gifted," George said, sensing my discomfort. "You were quite helpful to me. It was terrifying when our wing caught fire. Since I'd been warned ahead of time, I could calm passengers down by assuring them that it was only a surface fire. We landed safely. If I hadn't listened to what you said, who knows what might have happened? I really appreciate what you did, and you have made a believer out of me. Thank you." I was flabbergasted.

A few weeks later, I had another dream connected with Teterboro Airport. In the dream, I saw the "N" Number of an aircraft, and, at the same time, I had a strong impression that the plane was going to crash. ("N" Numbers are to aircraft what license plates are to cars. No two "N" Numbers are alike.) I woke in a cold sweat, and I wrote the number down so I wouldn't forget it. That morning, against my better judgment, I told my boss Hank about the dream. Of course, he was angry.

"Hank, you have to do something," I said. "This plane is going down. Perhaps I had the dream to prevent this from happening."

A red flush, starting at his forehead, was spreading downward into his neck, never a good sign with him. "I told you before never to mention anything about that crackpot hoodoo stuff anywhere in this airport. What can I do? People will think I'm crazy. No, they'll know I'm crazy."

"But that plane is going down unless someone steps in to prevent it. I know it as sure as I know anything. I think I had the dream as a warning." My eyes were filling with tears.

"Okay, I'll see what I can do. Don't tell anybody about why I'm doing it, though, or it'll be your job." With a sharp thump, he pounded his fist on the desk.

My heart went out to Hank. He was so loved and respected at the airport. It didn't seem as though this man, with the build and the attitude of an affable bulldog, could be afraid of anything. Yet he deeply feared my clairvoyant abilities.

By the end of the week, Hank had an answer from the tower. There was, indeed, an aircraft with that "N" Number, and it was housed at Teterboro. Hank knew Tom Harrison, the owner, and asked him whether the plane was in good repair. Of course he didn't mention anything about my dream. Tom was a little surprised at the question and said that he had been postponing its annual checkup. Hank asked him to get the plane gone over immediately. The mechanics found something wrong with the engine, as well as a few other problems that could have caused trouble in the future. Tom, of course, ordered the plane repaired right away. Hank and I were both relieved, although I heard him mutter something that sounded like "It's got to be just a coincidence."

There was a man who stored his plane at the airport named Roccos. No one liked him. He was loud, rude and belligerent. The girls warned me that he would give me a hard time. He thought nothing of using profanity or teasing the girls in a sexual manner. In those days, not much could be done about it. He was a customer, not an employee.

Roccos had never been into my office. One day, he entered, took one look at me, and stopped in his tracks. He smiled, said hello very graciously, and walked on to see Hank. "Where did you get this angel?" Roccos asked Hank. "She is from heaven."

Hank did not know what to say. Roccos never used profanity in my presence. When I would walk through the hangar in the morning, he would wave to me from wherever he was and shout, "Hello, Elizabeth, how's the angel today?" I got a big kick out of it, and the girls were shocked. At times I wondered if he could see auras, as his behavior was baffling.

Tom was good friends with Roccos, who also cared for Tom's plane while it was at Teterboro Airport. Sometimes Roccos would fly Tom to his house in Harrisburg, Pennsylvania, and then return by himself to Teterboro. One day, after Roccos had flown Tom home, he decided to practice some stunt flying on his way back to New Jersey. He misjudged an angle, and the wind sent him crashing into a tree. Roccos was killed instantly. He had been flying Tom's plane, the one with the "N" Number I had dreamed about three months before.

Teterboro airport is a busy place. It is located in Little Ferry, New Jersey, only ten miles from New York City, and services private corporate jets and turbo-props. A lot of people haven't heard of it, but it's the second largest airport in the New York City area, next to Kennedy. Robert Redford, Diana Ross, Liza Minelli, Elizabeth Taylor, Christopher Reeves, John Denver, and Cliff Robertson, all came by at one time or another. Statesmen came in as well. I remember often seeing Bob and Liddy Dole as well as Richard Nixon, who lived nearby. I used to sit in Mr. Nixon's limo, waiting for Jimmy Carter and Gerald Ford to arrive for meetings schedules in the Woodcliff Lake Hilton, not far away.

I was administrative assistant for a day to the then-Vice President George Bush, several astronauts, and all sorts of world-class dignitaries. Arthur Godfrey, Kurt Douglas, Johnny Travolta, and John-John

Kennedy flew out of Teterboro often. But the person who made the greatest impression on me at the airport wasn't part of the glitterati at all.

One day, as I went into the ladies' room, I happened to see a girl in her early twenties combing her hair at the sink. She had a bright, celestial kind of glow all around her. For a moment I just stood still and stared. Then, before I could stop myself, I blurted out, "You're an angel, you really are. What is your name? Are you new here?"

Laughing she said, "Thanks for thinking I'm an angel, but I'm just Evelyn. Yes, I work here, near the airport museum. I'm an artist, and I design the inside of aircraft. And yes, I am new here. By the way, can you see auras?"

"Why do you ask?" I said.

"Because of your comment," Evelyn said. "You're not so bad yourself, you know."

Surprised, I said, "Yes. What do you know about auras?"

Evelyn smiled and beautiful, deep dimples appeared. Her hair was very curly, and I thought she looked like Shirley Temple. "Oh, a bit." She answered.

"Let's have lunch soon," I suggested.

"Okay," Evelyn said. "Then you can tell me how you got the reputation of being psychic." Blushing, I laughed and we became instant friends. I did not know at that time how much we would affect each other's future.

I was doing more and more readings at the Psychic Fairs, and I began to do psychic work at several shopping malls as the Psychic Fairs expanded. It was a warm June day at a mall in Paramus, New Jersey, when a quiet, rather nervous woman in her late forties slid into the chair facing me. She told me her name was Ann. She didn't look me directly in the eye, so I spoke softly to her, trying to calm her down.

"I don't know why I came here," she said "I never do this kind of thing, but as I was passing by I saw you sitting here. No one else spoke to me. I don't know you, of course, but all of a sudden I got the feeling that you have a message for me. I'm just a little worried about what it may be."

Smiling, I asked for her birth information and began the reading. I told her that she had two children, a boy and a girl. I knew she was divorced and that she taught school. When I do a reading for a new client, I usually tell them a few simple, basic things I see about them first, mainly to reassure the person that my psychic abilities are genuine. Then I move on to the more important information. What I saw for Ann was not good.

"Is your ex-husband well?" I asked.

"I am concerned about him," Ann said, "Why do you ask?"

Does he live near you?"

"Yes," she answered. "Just on the other side of town."

I see a problem coming. It seems that your son may be involved. I see, on November eleventh, that your son is talking with his father when a tragedy happens. That is all that is being shown to me right now, I'm afraid. I feel your husband is depressed and may come to harm."

"I also see your son affected by this event and he will want to drop out of school for a year," I continued. "This may be the best thing for him. In time he will be all right and lead a productive life, but will need a lot of understanding and perhaps some short-term therapy."

"What can I do?" asked Ann.

"Watch on that day, and if anything suspicious happens, take immediate action," I advised.

Ann picked up her purse and hurried away, a worried look on her face. I never enjoy telling someone that trouble may be coming. It's not pleasant at all to warn someone of impending danger or loss. It's tempting to tell someone that their dreams will all come true and life will be nothing but roses, roses all the way. But Meg had taught me that it's always best to be honest and tell what you see, not what the client wishes you see.

I didn't hear from Ann again until after November eleventh, the date I warned her about. It seems she had pushed the reading to the back of her mind and forgotten about what I had predicted. November eleventh fell on a Saturday that year, and Ann went food shopping in the late morning. When she got to the Grand Union, she realized that she had left her checkbook and money at home. She drove back to the house, walked into the kitchen, and heard her son sobbing in anguish. He was on the phone.

"Why, Dad?" he cried. "What do you mean I won't see you anymore? What's going on? Dad, Dad..."

In a flash, Ann remembered everything in the reading. She ran next door to borrow the phone and called the police, sending them to her ex-husband's address. Then she got in her car and drove across town to his apartment. She arrived just after the police.

Do you know who lives here?" the Sergeant asked.

Yes," Ann responded. "My ex-husband."

"Well, he's dead," said the Sergeant. "Shot himself in the head with a rifle. Are you the one who called the police?"

Yes."

"Why, what made you call the cops?" the Sergeant demanded.

"I was at home, and I heard my son talking to his father on the phone," Ann said. "My son was crying and saying over and over, 'Don't do it, Dad, don't do it,' and I knew right away that something was terribly wrong. I called the police and drove over here."

"Well, you're lucky you did that," The Sergeant said. "If your ex-husband's body had been found in a day or so instead of now, it might have been a different situation altogether. You or your son might have been a murder suspect. But now there's no doubt that this man killed himself."

This is only one example of what can happen during a psychic reading. The psychic reader cannot stop the events from happening. Some people think that a psychic can magically prevent things from occurring. This just is not so. We are guides and helpers, and the main function of a reading is to give information to help a client find his or her own way. If a psychic tries to force a decision on you during a reading, get up and walk away.

Ann and I are still in touch, and she has the original paper I gave her at that reading, where I wrote many notes concerning the up-coming events. I never used a tape recorder at the fairs because there just wasn't enough time. Also, the readings were short and incomplete. The client was supposed to book a full reading later if he wanted complete information. Many times I went over the official time allowance of fifteen minutes anyway because the readings were intense, and I couldn't stop in the middle. Shirley was always upset about this and sometimes would yell across the room for me to hurry up.

After many years, the fairs got tiring for me. It had always been hard for me to confine my readings to fifteen minutes. It wasn't enough time for me to get into the depth of information that many of the clients needed. The Psychic Fairs were supposed to introduce psychics to new clients, and the readings short samples of their work. A truly adequate reading always seems to take an hour at the very least. Also, we weren't paid enough money, since the fairs were only on weekends, and readers were never guaranteed any clients at all.

On top of that, I was beginning to have a kind of longing, a feeling that I wanted something else in my life. I sensed that it was time for me to move forward into something else, but I didn't have the faintest idea of what that something else might be. I began to pray for enlightenment, and, of course, *the prayer was answered.*

CHAPTER 8

Indira and the Clear Light Group

SOMETIMES I THINK THERE IS nothing so lonely as walking through an empty house in the thin, cold air at three a.m. My younger son Jeffrey and my foster son Nilas, had both left home to begin college. Caroline was in California with her mother, attending Pepperdine in Malibu. Vance was living with his dad. The house was emptier and quieter than it had ever been before. More and more nights found me sleepless, lying in bed staring at the alarm clock: Calculating in my head. "It's two-thirty, so if I go to sleep now, I'll have four full hours before I have to get up. ... Now it's three-ten, and I'll have almost three and a half hours. ... Now it's four fifteen...." Sometimes I would just give up on sleeping and wander from room to room as if I were looking for something, but I didn't know what that something was.

I looked at Jeffrey's and Nilas' empty rooms, with their banners and posters and assorted high- school boy paraphernalia on the walls, and I knew that all my mothering days were over. I went into the kitchen to make some chamomile tea. Everything was just as I had left it the evening before. There was no one around to change anything. I headed back to my room, but the sight of the empty bed repelled me. My first husband Dick and I divorced years ago. My second husband, Joe died and left me, and now I didn't know whether I would ever again share any real, lasting love with a man.

123

I went into the bathroom to get an aspirin. As I turned on the glaring light over the medicine chest I flinched. When I looked into the mirror, I realized that I didn't really like the woman I saw. It wasn't just the pale, washed-out skin and the sleep-disarrayed hair that distressed me, nor the signs of incipient wrinkles, it was more.

"You act like you're pretty hot stuff, my girl," I said to myself. "Big-time psychic clairvoyant who knows all and sees all. People come to you from miles around just so you can tell them how to run their lives and fix their problems, and most of the time you don't know what the hell you're doing in your own life. You act like you know the great mysteries of life. Well, let me tell you, sweetie, you don't even know the first letter of the very first word."

I shook as I took the aspirin. I went back to bed again, but still couldn't sleep. The voice inside my head kept going on and on. "You want people to think you're a combination of Career Girl of the Year, Oz the Great and Powerful, and Miss America. You want yourself to believe it too. Deep down, though, you know it's all a lie. What you are is a woman whose husband and children are gone, and you don't have anything left to do. You pretend that you're the master of your life, but you're nothing but a dilettante at best. You work at an airport, you do a little modeling on the side, and you read Tarot cards. There is absolutely nothing in your life that has any meaning or significance to you or anybody else."

"Oh, just shut up," I said. "I'm not listening to you." But I was. My stomach was in a tight knot, and my head ached. Fear engulfed me. It was in the very air I breathed.

Jeff came home from college during winter break. Frank, a dear family friend, invited us to come up to his place in Mt. Snow, Vermont, for New Year's. Jeff jumped at the chance. His friend Mike's father had a condo in Dover, Vermont, and they were going there. Jeff liked Frank and he also loved skiing. When we got there, Frank took Jeff out on the slopes while I went to scout somewhere to go for New Year's Eve. I drove along Dover Road and finally stopped at a restaurant that looked like it might work. It was dark inside, with a long bar in the back, tables in front, and three or four television sets mounted on the ceiling so patrons could watch sports.

I was waiting at the bar to speak with the manager when a tall, gray-haired man came up to me and started a conversation. "I know this person," I thought. "He looks so familiar. I'm sure I've seen him before, but I can't remember where." Then it came to me. I had seen him several months earlier in my kitchen, at my own kitchen table, as I scried into a candle. His face had appeared in the flame. "I guess I was destined to meet this guy," I thought. "I wonder why."

His name was Richard, and he asked me out for that evening. I accepted. We spent almost every moment of the next three days together. I felt as if I had unexpectedly stepped onto one of those moving walkways they have at airports, except this one was going about a hundred miles an hour, and I couldn't see where it ended.

The man seemed to understand instinctively how to charm me, how to delight me. He sang into my ear while we danced. He knew, without being told, the exact place to kiss on my neck. He said he admired my intelligence and enthusiasm. My son Jeff, my friend Frank, skiing, New Year's Eve, Mt. Snow, everything receded. The only thing I could clearly see in that moment was Richard. As it turned out, we spent New Year's Eve at Frank's condo, invited Richard to join us, and ordered in. It was simple, intimate, and very enjoyable.

I went back to New Jersey, and Richard began calling me every day. Every time I heard his, "Hello, Beautiful, it's me," over the phone, all my feelings of failure and weakness dropped away. I began to believe -- no -- I knew that I was beautiful. We saw each other on weekends. The drive was only 185 miles, but soon it seemed entirely too long a distance. He proposed. I accepted. We were married six weeks after we first met. It didn't occur to me then that I had taken more time than that to decide on living room carpet.

My son begged me not to marry Richard. "Mom," he said, "you haven't given the relationship enough time."

"I know all I need to know," I said. "I've lived a lot longer than you have, Jeffrey, and sometimes a quick decision is the right decision. Besides, if worst comes to worst, I think I can handle just about any problem that could emerge. At this time in my life I just don't see any point in putting off happiness if one can have it right now."

The union was an eight-month-long disaster, a bitterly destructive love affair. Practically before the ring was all the way on my finger, Richard's personality became the negative image of itself. Before the marriage, he had instinctively known how to enrapture and delight me. Now he just as deftly sought out my fears and weaknesses, and, with a master's hand, rubbed them raw. He seemed to gain more strength every time he insulted me or put me down. If my new husband had lived in the nineteenth century, Robert Louis Stevenson could have used him as a model for Dr. Jeckyl and Mr. Hyde.

"Richard would say to me, "Now this girl I used to know, Veronique, when she smiled, it would light up her whole face. She was so natural and spontaneous. She was natural and spontaneous in a lot of other ways, too, that woman. Like the way she made love. She knew how to please a man a hundred times better than you'll ever know. As a matter of fact, I've been thinking about looking her up again. Anything to get a break from being with you all the time. Asian girls are the ones to marry. They know how to cater to a man. You're a New York girl and way too independent for a Vermont man."

I never knew how to act with him, never knew how to keep him from getting angry. If I was silent, he would accuse me of being uncommunicative. If I spoke, he told me that what I was saying was stupid. He laughed at me when I said I wanted a monogamous marriage. I hated his promiscuousness and the way he exploited women.

"I'm going to let you in on a little secret," my bridegroom told me one evening as we lay in bed. "I married you because I wanted to make my old girlfriend jealous. She deserved it, too. I hope she's really hurting. Maybe after this she'll appreciate me more."

My new husband refused to pay the bills or let me have any money for basic necessities. I drove back to New Jersey on weekends to work at the Psychic Fairs.

Luckily, I discovered a marvelous health food store, The Klara Simpla, in Wilmington, Vermont, near where we lived. The Klara Simpla had a room available where I could teach courses in psychic awareness and development, and soon I had several classes filled. Richard looked disgusted when I told him where I was working. "Only crazy people go into that store," he said. "Weirdos with bandannas on their heads, guys with long ponytails." I laughed and kept on teaching.

The store was my little patch of calm in a stormy sea. It was a plain gray building that was once a farmer's barn. There wasn't even a sign out front, just a number "10" on the door. Everything inside was arranged in a plain and simple way. A dazzling variety of grains and beans were kept in barrels and boxes on the scrubbed pine floor. Hundreds of books about health and spirituality filled an alcove off to the right. The air smelled of herbs and spices. Something else was in the atmosphere too. It was the warmth and kindness of the owner Faye Hollander and her two daughters who helped Faye run the store.

One day when I was at The Klara Simpla, I noticed an old Volkswagen van with New Mexico plates parked in the driveway. I was walking up the back stairs to my classroom, wondering whom the van belonged to, when I heard singing:

> *Let me never forget Thee,*
> *Let me never forget Thee.*
> *Fill my heart with undying love.*
> *Show me, show me the way.*

I peeked into the room where the music was coming from. There were about twenty people sitting on cushions on the floor, singing. Their faces were radiant. My heart ached to join them. Tears filled my eyes, and I could not speak. The bitterness and horror of the last few months flashed in front of me, and I felt helpless and dazed. I stood still, draw-ing energy from their presence. After the group finished and the people were getting ready to go, I shyly walked into the room and approached a pleasant-looking woman in her mid-twenties. "Excuse me," I said, "but I couldn't help listening to the singing. I've never heard anything like it before. It's beautiful. What kind of music is it?"

The girl turned to me and smiled. "It's called chanting. It's an ancient way of singing, but people in our culture don't do too much of it any more. I've just recently learned to chant myself. It's not all that hard." She went on to tell me that her name was Maria. "We're all here because we want to study with Indira and the Clear Light Group. Indira is this wonderful teacher and healer from New Mexico. She's going to be here for three weeks, teaching a course in some-thing called Clear Light Therapy and giving people healing sessions. There's going to be an open meditation Friday night. You can come if you want to. If you liked the chanting, I'm sure you'll enjoy the open meditation."

"I'll be there for sure," I said. "The course in Clear Light Therapy sounds interesting too. How much does it cost?"

"It's a three week course and costs fifteen hundred dollars," Maria answered.

"Ouch," I said. "That's pretty much out of the question right now. I'm still looking forward to Friday, though. I've never meditated with a group before."

The singing had already begun when I came into the room that Friday evening. Maria smiled at me, moved over to make room, and motioned for me to sit down next to her. We all began swaying to the beat of the music. The words were in a language I couldn't understand, but I did my best to follow along. *"Om nemah Sheva, Om nemah Sheva, Sheva om nemah."* The room was pleasantly warm, and the voices of the other people seemed to support me. The words weren't hard to learn; there were only a few of them, repeated over and over again. I didn't have the faintest idea of their meaning, but they made me feel wonderful. My head began to spin. Strong pulsations started to beat in my forehead; then I felt like I was getting lighter and lighter. It seemed like I was flying: a dandelion seed riding in the wind. "Whatever is going on," I said to myself, "I wish it could last forever."

Eventually, however, the music stopped. The lights in the room turned up, and I opened my eyes. How long had we been singing? It could have been fifteen minutes. It could have been three hours. I had no idea. I took a quick look at my watch. The meditation had started at seven o'clock. Now it was almost eight. In fifty minutes I had taken what felt like a thousand-mile journey into an unknown, wondrous place.

A woman at the front of the room began talking. She wore a navy blue, flowing garment and a glorious violet and light blue scarf draped over her shoulders. In her forties she was around five feet two, if that, with short, brown hair and the look of someone who met things head-on with great assurance. Her rather plain face was without makeup, but it glowed with intelligence and calmness. She had a strong charismatic, compelling demeanor. It was as if she said, "Listen to me, I have the answers you seek."

"Good evening," she said in a soothing, sweet voice. "I'm Indira. I've come here to be with you and teach you something about the art and science of meditation and how you can use it to enrich your lives. I know many of you may be new to meditation, so before we proceed any further, feel free to ask any questions that come to mind."

"What is this singing?" I heard myself saying. "I really don't know what's going on. I feel so funny, sort of light and dizzy. I've sung together with a group lots of times before, like at school and in church, but I never felt anything close to the way I do now."

"That's marvelous," Indira said. "It's just possible that you might be having a real spiritual breakthrough." I wasn't sure what she meant.

She must have noticed my blank, perplexed look. "Let me back up and explain a bit about chanting," she said. "Chanting, as I'm sure you realize by now, is the continuous recitation of a sacred word or phrase.

Tonight, we've been chanting in the ancient language of Sanskrit. The phrase, 'Om, Nemah Sheva' means 'Please remove my negative blocks.' The origins of chanting date back thousands of years. People from virtually every spiritual tradition all over the world practice chanting. It's a powerful, mystical technique.".

"There are many ways people perform this powerful technique. Sometimes people chant unaccompanied, sometimes with musical instruments. Sometimes they clap, sway, dance, or whirl around. Sometimes people use strings of prayer beads, like rosaries or malas, to help them keep their attention on the chant. Sometimes chanting is done to a simple melody, sometimes it is done in a monotone. There's no such thing as a one and only right way to chant.

"Chanting can help you reach an altered state of consciousness, where you are thinking and feeling things outside your normal range of consciousness. Chanting opens up the heart center in your body. It destroys energy blocks that can make you 'stuck' and unable to move on with your life. It offers you ecstasy and communion with the Divine. It can summon up healing. Its rhythm and music help create a pattern of energy and power.

"Group chanting raises consciousness more strongly than chanting alone because the movement and energies of the group come together, and the space around them becomes powerfully charged. It's something like the difference between water pouring out of a pitcher and water crashing down Niagara Falls.

"This combined energy can help the group reach a specific objective. That's why, before we began chanting tonight, we set an intention that the energy blocks to the third eye opening be lifted so all of you can come into a state of bliss. Have some patience, keep going, and allow your body to flow with these energies. Trust yourself. Try to quiet your mind. Don't think of so many questions.

"Right now, I want each person here to focus his or her attention on an important problem or concern. Then, as we begin chanting again, trust the Divine, and see what the Higher Forces have in store for you."

I began to think about my son, Jeffrey. "I've really let him down," I left our home in New Jersey and came chasing up here to marry Richard. Jeffrey must have felt like I was deserting him. I've made a fool out of myself in his eyes because he begged me to be more careful, and I didn't pay attention. I resigned from my job at Atlantic Aviation and I don't have any money left for Jeff's college tuition. I'm sure that his dad isn't going to help. I don't think my son is ever going to forgive me. I'm afraid he'll never finish his education either." A wave of guilt washed over me, "I really messed up this time."

The lights dimmed, and we began to chant again. *"Om nemah Sheva, Om nemah Sheva, Om nemah Sheva, Sheva om nemah."* All at once I felt a sharpness pierce my skull. A wide, glowing space opened before my vision, and I went into a swoon. I'd never experienced anything like it before. It was like going downhill on the Palisades Park roller coaster, magnified about a thousand times. A large, white cloud appeared to my closed eyes. I concentrated on the cloud and watched as it parted and revealed a glowing figure. Briefly I noticed that the chant had changed *to "Lord Jesus Christ, have mercy on me."*

I gladly participated in chanting the old, familiar phrase. With a smile I lay back onto the floor and watched the vision. I felt and saw Christ coming toward me from the cloud. He came closer and closer until, suddenly, a white light shot out from his forehead and pierced my third eye. There was no pain, just a feeling of warmth and overwhelming love. Then, He told me not to worry about my son. There would be enough money for Jeffrey to finish his education, and he would go on to work for the benefit of humankind. As the vision faded, I felt a peaceful bliss. I soared inside. It was as if my body was so transparent that the wind could blow right through it.

When I came out of my reverie, I told Indira what happened to me during the meditation. I had never, ever had an experience as powerful as that one before.

"This is very, very good," she said. "It's amazing that you had such a powerful experience the first time you meditated with a group. I want to urge you to accept the reality of what you heard. I'm sure you experienced a genuine vision of the Lord."

"I don't know whether I believe it or not."

"Accept it, Elizabeth," Indira said. "What the Lord told you is going to happen."

I talked to Indira for quite a while that night and told her about my wretched marriage and feelings of guilt and depression. "I just don't know what to do now. I can't see any point to my life. I keep making mistakes and messing things up. I marry the wrong men and do the wrong things. I'm supposed to be clairvoyant, but don't know anything much at all about anything. My life is just a bundle of rags and scraps."

"Elizabeth, I'm worried about you," Indira said. "I'm concerned about your marriage and your mental and physical health. Why don't you make an appointment with me for a session of Clear Light Therapy? It might be just what you need right now. I can see you tomorrow afternoon if you like."

"Okay," I agreed, not at all sure whether this woman would be able to do anything to help me.

I hesitated for a couple of heartbeats before I entered the space upstairs at The Klara Simpla that Indira called her Healing Room. Did I really want to go through a Clear Light session, whatever that was? Indira had assured me that the procedure would help unblock and balance the flow of energy within and around my body. This clearing was supposed to somehow assist my body and mind to heal themselves. I'd never heard of such a thing.

Meg, dear Meg, who had helped me learn to use my psychic abilities, never mentioned anything about chanting or healing with energy. Just about the only thing I knew about healing was that when you were sick, you went to a doctor, who would give you medicine or schedule an operation. That was how you got healed.

I thought about making a quick retreat. The six-year-old inside me was silently howling "I wanna go hooooome!" A picture of Howard came into my mind. What if Indira turned out to be a Satanist like Howard?

Would she try to steal my soul the minute I relaxed and let down my guard? The place was small, quiet, and pleasantly warm. There were only a few chairs and a long, narrow table. Bright sunlight poured through the windows along the two walls. I didn't sense anything like the creepy feeling I had gotten from my encounter with Howard, but I was still fearful. Then I thought, "Well, what if she does try to do something evil? The woman with the long, flowing hair will just jump out of my midsection and throw Indira across the room." That idea suddenly struck me as oddly funny, and I began to laugh. I decided to trust Indira, at least a little bit.

Indira was gentle but firm. She was in command and there was no doubt about it. She told me to lie down on the body table, relax, and close my eyes. "Now," she said, "I'm going to ask your body where it needs help. I sense that your body is crying out for help, even though your rational mind doesn't know what's wrong. For the most part, I will be working in the energy field around your body, and for this I won't be touching you much, if at all. I am also going to use a technique called muscle testing. Don't worry; it's really very simple. I will press on your forearm a number of times, and you will resist that pressure each time. With each pressure, I will ask your body a question, and your body will reply with either a strong or a weak resistance. It's nothing you have to do consciously. Just concentrate on relaxing."

"Close your eyes and relax now," Indira instructed, "breathe deeply."

It all seemed confusing, and I soon gave up trying to figure out what was going on. All I remembered afterward about the muscle testing was that sometimes my arm went down when Indira pushed on it, and sometimes it didn't. At other times I could sense her hands moving close to my body. Sometimes I could feel heat underneath the spot her hand hovered over. At last Indira made an announcement. "You need to go through a past-life regression, Elizabeth. We have to find the reason why you married Richard Joyce so quickly."

"What's that?" I asked, bewildered. "How does a person do something like that?"

"Just keep relaxing with your eyes closed," she said, "and concentrate on connecting with your Higher Self. I am going to blend my energies with yours, and we'll see what we can find out."

I closed my eyes again, and Indira began to hold her hand over my body, beginning at my hips, moving upwards systematically, going from one energy center to the next. Meg had taught me about the chakras.

She taught me that there are seven major chakras, each spinning and radiating a different color of spiritual light and each controlling a different aspect of the body and its energies. I never knew you could use them, balance and work with them for physical, mental, and emotional healing. Now I was experiencing it. What Indira was doing was checking each chakra for blockages. Suddenly I realized I was trembling.

All at once, I felt like I was moving swiftly backwards, butt first, my body formed the shaped of a horseshoe. My legs and arms were stretched out before me. Then my feet landed on the ground, and as I looked around me, I realized I was on an island in the South Pacific. The island was familiar, and I realized that I had seen it in a childhood dream. A woman was clutching a small baby and pleading with a man who, I felt, was her husband.

"What is happening?" Indira asked.

"The woman is crying. She's begging her husband not to kill her son. The boy was born deformed, with a red rash over his face. Now the man jerks the baby away from the woman and drowns him in the ocean. I can see the husband bent over in the water, his hands holding the tiny little thing down under the waves. It doesn't take long. The woman is devastated. She feels like knife blades are piercing her heart. I can feel it too." I began to sob uncontrollably.

"Keep watching, Elizabeth," Indira said. "You need to see the outcome of this relationship."

"Oh, now the man is telling her that she's old, and he has other wives, younger wives. The woman is banned from his side and his bed. He won't even look at her. Now he's calling someone else to him, a beautiful girl of about sixteen. He takes the young girl's chin in his fingers and turns her face toward the older woman, as if to show the girl off. He strokes the girl's hair. He embraces her and laughs.

"Some time has passed now. The woman is dying, embittered and with a broken heart. She has lost all her faith."

"I thought we'd find something like that," Indira said. "This man Richard has deep karma with you. He married you during your present lifetime to give himself the opportunity to pay back his debt to you. Obviously he hasn't done any better this time than he did in the past. He owes something to Jeffrey as well, but he has refused to pay it back in his current lifetime. He will suffer greatly."

A strong knowing flowed through my body. I knew that what Indira was saying was true; the awareness that came from deep within. When someone speaks the truth, the body knows it subconsciously.

"When you go home tonight," Indira continued, "I suggest that you look Richard right in the eye and tell him you recognize him. Say you know who he is. Stand your ground. See what he does with it. This action will set you free."

I did just that, as soon as I walked in the door. Richard's blue eyes turned hazy. Despite his swagger and the nasty grin on his face, I knew he was shaken. He looked at me for a few seconds. Then he said, "You don't please me at all. I know I have a really good future with someone, but it's not you." He didn't ever deny anything I told him about our past life together on the island in the tropics.

I left for New Jersey the next day. I had a class scheduled at *Quiet Decisions Institute* in New York City with Dick Summer. I was finally taking the hypnosis classes taught by the celebrity and story teller; classes that I should have taken before I ever tried to teach the course a few years before.

Dick taught us how to use relaxation and dreaming, to change our inner belief systems, and modify behavior. "Self Help" relaxation systems require work and concentration. Quiet Decisions was all about being comfortable in our own skin, using exercises for relaxation, visualization, and fun. The traditional approach of advice giving was replaced by reflective listening.

The Quiet Decisions material was defined as, *"a directive, client-centered counseling style for eliciting behavior modification and change by helping clients explore and resolve ambivalence"*. At first, it was used to motivate patients who were mentally or physically abused and perhaps used alcohol, to modify their thinking and drinking behaviors.

Initially, it was developed to assist people who abused alcohol to change unhealthy behaviors. It became evident that benefits of the program extended far beyond this population. The Quiet Decisions program helped students identify and change risky behaviors that could lead to health problems or prevent management of a chronic condition. The techniques helped women who needed to improve their self-image. There were eight classes in all, each one focused on different aspects of self-esteem building. Boy, did I feel that I needed adjustment in my life.

These classes were mainstream. The program created stages of readiness to change risky or unhealthy behaviors using motivational hypnosis. Participants had a safe space to allow fears to surface, known as triggers, and explore them reaching a deeper understanding of one's self. Although not necessarily spiritual, I found the inner work invaluable.

Dick Summer showed me the value of present-life regression work. Hypnosis work is a technique that can break through resistances to achieve behavior change.

Dick Summer's classes gave me the strength and confidence I had been missing up to that point in life. Today, I still use some of the techniques in my healing work.

Every time I take three deep breaths, rub my thumb across the tips of my fingers, and think of my name, being said with respect, I can hear Dick's famous voice running through my mind, as I take the time to relax and calm down. I can always smile., and can feel *my inner smile* as well.

Dick was a crackerjack at imagery, and meticulous in his work. I felt he really cared about others' development and wellbeing. These classes really changed my life because for the first time, I associated practical action with my new spiritual beliefs. I am still in contact with Dick today, and will always treasure the gifts I received in those few classes.

After the classes ended, I went to Raritan, New Jersey to visit my older sister Claramay. I always turned to her when I needed strength and comfort. She had a strong Christian belief, and I thought she might be able to help me figure out why my life was so chaotic. I ached to know more about how God works in the lives of human beings.

Richard called while I was there. "I am personally evicting you from my house!" he yelled. "I'm going to take all your clothes and things, and I'm going to bring them to New Jersey and dump them on your sister's front lawn."

After that dramatic performance, I knew I had to go back to Vermont and settle things. Faye at The Klara Simpla very graciously said that I could stay with her for a few days until I could find a more permanent place to live.

I had a vivid dream on my first night at Faye's. I'd been praying fervently to be shown a pathway through the mess I was in. The dream was about a person named David. "Don't worry, child, David will help you," I heard a voice say.

The next day I discovered that Richard had taken my clothes and dumped them in a rundown motel nearby. I called my lawyer, and he told me to see a judge in Brattleboro. What Richard had done was against the law in the state of Vermont. While I was waiting to see the judge at the courthouse, I picked up a newspaper someone had left on the bench. "Might as well look for a place to live while I'm sitting here," I muttered.

Nothing in the paper caught my eye except for one name: Dale Everett. It seemed to pop up wherever I looked in the Real Estate section. I called Mr. Everett's number, and he told me to come right over after court.

Still waiting for the judge, I decided to give Meg a quick call. "Meg," I said, "what kind of place do you think I should look for?"

"Don't worry, darling," she said warmly. "Everything's going to turn out just fine. You're going to move into a very nice green house with a front porch. This man Dale Everett will help you a great deal. Oh, and in case you're wondering, you're going to find a good job soon."

Finally I got in to see the judge. He gave me a court order that said Richard had to leave the premises and allow me to move out all my things. As soon as I received the order, I drove to Dale Everett's office. He was a charming e real estate man. "You used to work at Teterboro airport?" he asked. "I keep a private plane there myself." We soon realized we knew many of the same people at the airport.

Dale showed me a few apartments, but I didn't care for any of them. "Let's try this place over on the other side of town," he said. As we were going down the street, I saw a row of green condominium apartments. Only one of them had a front porch.

"Is the condo with the porch the one that's for rent?" I asked.

"How did you know?" he said. "I haven't even had time to put a sign on it yet."

Thinking of Meg, I just smiled.

The next morning at the Klara Simpla I was on the phone calling every mover in town. I couldn't get through to anyone. Frustrated, I slammed down the phone just as a young family walked in the door. The husband had come to visit the chiropractor who had his office on the second floor. The wife and her two children sat near me while the husband had his appointment. The three of them looked hungry, as if they had left home too early to have any breakfast.

"Would you like me to fix you a little something to eat while you're waiting?" I asked impulsively.

The woman smiled. "My name is Nancy, and this is Vinnie and Dana, and we'd love some breakfast, thank you."

I made them a good breakfast of eggs, toast, juice, and fruit. They ate as if they hadn't had anything for days. When the father came out of the session, he sat down with us, and we visited for a bit. I asked him what kind of work he did.

"I do odd jobs—cleaning, painting, hauling, stuff like that."

"Well, what do you know," I said. "I need to have my furniture and things moved out of my husband's house and into a new apartment. I've been calling moving companies all morning, and I haven't turned up a thing."

"I think we could rent a U-Haul truck and do the job ourselves," the man said.

"There's an awful lot to move," I said.

"I don't think that'll be a problem," he said. "The people here at The Klara Simpla will help us. I'll make some calls and everyone can come in shifts until the job is done."

"I'm so grateful. I'll see about renting the truck, and you let me know when everyone's ready." I held out my hand. "Thank you —Oh, my gosh, I just realized something. I don't even know your name."

Reaching out his hand, the man smiled, "I'm sorry. My name is David."

David. The name I had dreamed two nights before. The voice in the dream said David would help me. I was speechless.

Two days later the Wilmington police evicted Richard from his house at 7:30 a.m., and we began the move at 9:00 a.m. It was a carefully orchestrated miracle. I wasn't used to having so much loving support. Working in shifts, two new people came every hour or so to help. It took all day to load the truck. Richard sat across the street in his car, watching us like a malevolent gargoyle.

I was in the green condo with the front porch the very next morning. From the time I had come back to The Klara Simpla from New Jersey, it had taken only four days to move. The phone rang; my first call in the new place. "Hello, my name is Bill McCarty. Dale Everett gave me your resume. I need someone to manage my law office in Brattleboro. Can you come in for an interview? Dale recommended you highly."

I thought back to my conversation with Meg, and how she had told me Dale would help me and through him, I would find a new job soon. Once again I was stunned into silence. My amazement was becoming a habit.

My divorce became final in August, 1985. Looking back on the marriage, I felt like I had been sucked up by an eight-month-long tornado and had lived to tell the tale. What shape had the experience left me in?

I was a little smarter, for one thing. I had learned that just because you see someone's face in a candle flame, you may have some karma with them, but it doesn't necessarily mean you have to marry them. I learned that just because your children are younger than you are, it doesn't mean that they can't give you valuable advice.

Also, without Richard's influence, I might never have moved to Vermont, and I never would have met Indira or all the wonderful people associated with her. I would not have found out about energy healing, nor would I have learned about my past life in the South Pacific and how it affected me during my present existence. Finally, it occurred to me that I never would have taken the last name of Joyce. Much as I disliked Richard, I liked his last name. The name Joyce put joy into my life and it suited me. I decided to keep it.

"Here's something important I want you to remember, Elizabeth," Indira said at our next Clear Light session. "Most people don't realize it, but thoughts are things."

Feeling puzzled, I looked at her. She must have been used to that kind of response because she barely paused before she went on. "Say it after me. 'Thoughts are things.'"

"Thoughts are things."

"Does that make sense to you?"

"Not exactly, no," I said. "You can't see a thought, or feel it, or taste it. It doesn't exist in any of the three dimensions. It seems to me that thoughts are less tangible than puffs of wind. They aren't solid like trees or rocks. They aren't even as substantial as clouds."

"Are you sure?" Indira said. "Everything that exists in the three-dimensional world, from the ring on your finger to a New York sky-scraper to the Universe itself originated as a thought. Look around you. Each object you see existed first as a thought, either in a person's mind or in the mind of God. So thoughts are, indeed, things, and profoundly powerful things too.

"We all manifest what we think about. When we think something, we are putting it out into the world, and it will come back to us again in a physical form. We've both known people who believe nothing good will ever come their way. That's the thinking they release into the world, and that's exactly what comes back to them. Their lives are a series of broken bones, unfaithful lovers, deceitful friends, horrible jobs, and bad weather. On the other hand, there are people who believe they can overcome obstacles to live joyously. These are the people who tell you how lucky they are, how things seem to work harmoniously together for their good.

Of course, the way thoughts manifest themselves in the everyday world is a subtle and complicated process. A child who plants a penny because she believes it will grow into a penny tree is going to be disappointed, no matter how hard she thinks of branches covered with coins. Still, there is no denying that for anything to become real in the physical world, it must first begin as an idea."

I began to look at my own life, what I routinely thought, what I said, what I did, and what happened to me each day. I started to see that all these things were closely tied together. "It seems so clear to me now," I thought. "Why didn't I realize it before?"

Indira returned to New Mexico a few weeks later. I promised myself that I'd save enough money, to visit her when she returned to Vermont the next summer and take the Clear Light Therapy course. In the meantime, I kept going to the meditation group every Friday night. I wanted to know everything about the invisible forces that influence our lives, the things Indira called the Higher Energies.

Indira teaches; "The life force is eternal and universal, and because of its limitless capacity, it is a part of all things. It is everywhere! Moreover, it is a major part of each one of us. Consequently, we all have within us an unlimited power and unlimited potential. As you walk the path of the Initiate, your perceptions expand gradually to accept the higher vibrations of Self. You begin to understand that we experience life through the five senses, or the windows to the soul. We are taught at an early age about these five senses, seeing, hearing, touching, feeling, tasting; but we are not taught about their deeper dimensions that are more sensitive than normally perceived. Those dimensions will open for you as you move toward them. This is called Spiritual Evolvement of the Soul.

Meditation guides you along that path everyday, as you practice your saddanas or daily devotions. The reflection of this Shakti energy comes in the form of life events that you experience everyday.

As you work with God's etheric power, He will have a way of showing you the next move at every turn. Believe in it. Know that this force within you is so powerful that it will pull you into excitement and adventure beyond your wildest dreams. Keep it pure, remain silent, and always remember to bless the process between yourself and the Divine. The more you work with communicating with God through prayer, the more in touch you will be with all of life that surrounds you.

Everything is one with everything. All of this knowledge will become a symbol of strength to you. The world is here to help and support you and the fuller you become in the richness of these energies, the more dimensions you will be able to pull from."

Luckily for me, several women in the meditation group had already learned Clear Light from Indira, and I could continue my therapy sessions with them. Each session was an hour and a half long and extremely intense.

As the work progressed, problem after problem after problem, called blockages, came up to be healed. With the healing and release of each one, I felt like I was going deeper into the true center of my being. I was learning more and more about myself. It astonished me that so many things were hiding inside me. Things my conscious mind had known nothing about. I began to see myself as something like a set of Russian nesting dolls. When I opened up and dealt with one problem, there was always another one waiting inside.

Gradually, like a gaunt, massive tree becoming visible through a mist, the most important issue in my life at the time revealed itself. To my surprise, it was my stormy relationship with my twin sister Priscilla. Much of the pain that came up to be healed during my Clear Light Therapy sessions involved her. I had visions of several past lives we had spent together. Lives when we had also been twins. In one we were members of a tribe on the Amazon River. In another, we were country people in the North of England. Now, in this life, it was time for me to finally separate from her, and de-twin. For my own good, and probably for hers, I needed to settle any leftover business I had with her and become one complete individual. I had to stop being the weak, dominated half of a set of twins. All my life I had wanted the two of us to have a close and loving relationship with each other, but I began to accept that it would never happen. It was not supposed to happen. It was contrary to the lesson I was here to learn for my soul's growth. There was no guilt attached to that realization. Instead, there was a deep freedom I gained in letting go.

After five or six weeks of Clear Light sessions and group meditation, I felt as if I were waking up after a long, dark sleep. All my senses were getting sharper. Each day was like a glorious kaleidoscope of colors, sounds, shapes, smells, feelings, tastes. I could perceive the sacredness in every face I saw. I could read pain, joy, confusion, contentment; whatever anyone near me was feeling. Often I could not only see but also feel what those nearby were feeling. Several times I was overcome by emotions that were coming from the people around me. When I walked in the sunshine, I wanted to sing. When I walked in the rain, I wanted to dance. I found my bliss.

The smallest things delighted me. It was like being on cosmic laughing gas. Buying an ice cream cone for myself was an occasion for hilarious joy. What flavor did I want? It didn't make any difference. They all were fabulously delicious. Their colors were all beautiful. The girl scooping up the ice cream was amazingly lovely. The scoop was a lovely scoop. The cone was a lovely cone. The other people in the ice cream store were radiant with beauty. I found myself laughing the way a baby or a small child does, just from delight in being alive. There were little spiritual lessons in every action, every decision. Everything I saw, everything I did had a deeper dimension. I discovered that spirituality wasn't just going to church or praying or reading the Bible. Washing the dishes could be a spiritual act; so could sweeping the floor, or driving to work, or waving to a friend across the street. It was in being present in the deep dwelling of awareness that resided inside of me.

I felt as though new sensitivities were opening up within me. The perceptions I was now having couldn't be described in terms of the five senses we ordinarily have here on Earth. These were deeper, more profound. I wondered whether my ability to sense a deeper meaning in ordinary things was a sign that my eyes were opening to a previously hidden spiritual world I was beginning to perceive the unlimited realities all around me.

I looked forward to every Friday, when I met with the meditation group at The Klara Simpla. Chanting and singing were as necessary to me as air and light. Of all the different ways of praying, I believe that chanting the name of God is best. God has many names, and he answers to all of them. At home, when one mantra didn't seem to be working for me, I would sing another. I didn't want my meditation to become a mechanical thing. I wanted to use the phrases that moved me most deeply, that would quickly bring me to the place of bliss. I wound up with two favorites. The first was, "Lord Jesus Christ, I lay my life at Thy feet." The second was "Om krya Babaji, na ma om." (Come to me, Babaji, I give my life to you.) I didn't know who this Babaji was, but the mantra struck a powerful chord in me.

"What's the story on Babaji?" I asked my friend Maria one evening. "Who or what is he?"

"Hmm," she said, "that's not the easiest thing to explain. As a matter of fact, a being such as Babaji is basically a mystery. Ordinary human minds can't grasp what he is. Babaji is sometimes called the Yogi-Christ of Modern India. Those who follow him, and there are many, believe that he is an avatar, a divinely-appointed source of blessings from God to humankind. He has full power over death. He has lived, in a perfected youthful form, for hundreds and hundreds of years, even though he looks like a man in his mid-twenties. He appears to only a few people in each generation. He's a tremendously powerful force for good, training and advising men and women who want to bring peace and love into the world. Sometimes these people recognize who he is; often they don't."

"Wow!" I exclaimed.

"I think the best way for you to learn about him is to read a book called *Autobiography of a Yogi,* by Paramahansa Yogananda." She said, and wrote the title and author on a piece of paper for me.

I found a copy of the small, orange-covered book in the book section right downstairs at The Klara Simpla. I picked it up and couldn't put it down. Paramahansa Yogananda was the first of India's great spiritual masters to live and teach extensively in the West. Before he left India in 1920, almost no one outside that part of the world knew anything about Yoga or Indian spiritual practices and beliefs. Yogananda taught many thousands of people about yoga and meditation during his travels through Europe and America. A chapter in his autobiography is devoted to Babaji.

I also picked up two other books that day. *You Can Heal Your Life* by Louise Hay and *Creative Visualization*, by Shakti Gawain. These two books explain how to use mental imagery and affirmations to produce positive changes in one's life. Louise had finally had her "little blue book" published, but had added more information. I knew I wanted to reconnect with her again.

"Elizabeth, you've got to be careful," Maria said after one of our Clear Light sessions. "You are tapping into serious, strong stuff. This process affects your inner self on extremely deep levels. It takes guts to go through it so quickly. It's exhausting, both for your body and your soul. You must care for your physical body especially well now. Look after yourself. Eat properly. Get enough sleep. Don't take too many things on at one time.

"There's something extraordinary about how quickly you're learning. It's taken you only a few months to absorb what it takes others twenty or thirty years, maybe even several lifetimes, to understand. You are being taught at lightning speed. I've never seen anything like it. I believe the Higher Forces are preparing you for a special purpose. Your life purpose."

A picture came before my eyes of two figures, each surrounded by light. It was, of course, the memory of my near-death experience when my late husband and stepson appeared to me and told me it wasn't time for me to join them, that I should go back, that my life's mission hadn't yet been fulfilled.

Despite all the wonderful things that were happening to me, I still disliked and resented Richard. I was furious with my soon to be ex-husband for uprooting my life and abusing me. He had acted like some kind of demented French apache dancer, pushing me around, cursing and threatening me. I didn't acknowledge my part in the drama at all, refusing to see that I had willingly chosen him as my dancing partner.

I passed Richard's house every day as I drove to and from work. His car was always parked outside. "Richard, you insect, I wish your car would blow up," I muttered under my breath one day. After that, whenever I drove by his car, I would picture an explosion. Ka-pow! I'd visualize a bright flash of light, and then pieces of the brown Oldsmobile flying everywhere. I never actually imagined Richard inside the car, but I just couldn't stop myself from mentally exploding the vehicle into smithereens, over and over again.

Indira told me that psychic powers have their foundation in the astral level of the human psyche. (The astral level is an area of existence that can't be comprehended by the ordinary five senses.) "In modern times, most people have ignored these potential powers," she said, "and so the ability to use them has more or less been left to languish away. But the powers are still there. They're intrinsic to human nature. They can be awakened. Like fire or electricity, they're nothing to fool around with. Through meditation, we must draw on our Higher Selves for the knowledge and insight to keep from misusing these powers."

Years before, Meg had told me that it was actually true that practitioners of black magic could cast spells by using candles, chants, and sometimes just a downright nasty and powerful will to do harm. I didn't realize that I also had this capacity. In the Great School of the Universe, I was still in the kindergarten class. But, alas, even kindergartners can sometimes get hold of dynamite.

The ability to clearly project a mental image is a valuable one. Like dancing, almost everyone can do it if they practice, but it's easier for some than for others. Although I wasn't trained at the time to perfect or refine this talent, I had a fair amount of it in its raw form.

Visualizing is how we bring what's in our minds and hearts into the outside world. It's related to what Indira, Shakti, and Louise Hay were talking about when they said that thoughts are things. For example, I can always get a parking place in New York City or any other crowded place. As I approach my destination, I picture myself parking the car exactly where it needs to be. My mantra is, "The people whose car is occupying the parking space is done with needing the space, and they are now releasing it for my use." Then I mentally say "Thank you." It works every time, unless I'm under a lot of stress and can't concentrate properly.

When I was living in Vermont though, I didn't know much about the *power* of visualization. In my anger and ignorance, I played my "Blow Up the Mean Man's Car" game more and more often. Even when I wasn't near it, I'd indulge in quick mental pictures of Richard's car flying to pieces. "After all," I told myself, "it's just pretend. Besides, it's probably therapeutic because it makes me feel better."

Then, one sunny afternoon, Richard's car blew up for real. No one ever could figure out why. Richard was sitting in his office when suddenly his beloved Oldsmobile exploded right outside his window. No one was in or near the car, and the engine was off. Police never found any explosives. An auto mechanic I knew told me that he had never seen a car blow up like that.

I was speechless when I heard about it. I immediately knew what I had done. An energy from the lower astral levels of my body had gone to work on the molecules of that car until it finally blew up. The Higher Powers had chosen not to stop the action; I'm not sure why. Perhaps it was a lesson for me as well as a payback for some of the karmic debt Richard owed.

One thing I do know is that I learned an unforgettable lesson. From that moment on, I stopped using visualization to vent my own petty and vengeful feelings. I stopped wishing that people I didn't like would fall on their noses or off bridges. Before the exploding car incident, whenever I was driving and someone would cut me off or do something else rude or dangerous on the road, I'd mentally flip their car over. I changed those thoughts! I began to visualize that a cop would appear, pull them over, and give them a ticket. It's surprising how often a policeman actually shows up.

My Aunt Claramay called me from Concord, New Hampshire late one Friday afternoon. "Your mother's been taken to Concord Hospital. She fainted in the kitchen today, and the doctors aren't sure what's wrong."

"I'll come right over after work," I said. "I should be there around six-thirty or seven." While I was living in Vermont, I could visit my mother often because she was then living in Grammie's house in Warner, New Hampshire. Usually I loved going there on the weekends, to be with her. The drive was about seventy-five miles through beautiful, rolling New England hills.

The sun was beginning to set as I left Mr. McCarty's law office. I wanted to get through Hillsboro before full dark, because it was the most difficult part of the drive. The road wound through deep woods, and there weren't any highway lights. As I reached Route 114 in Henniker, I began to feel a strange, tingling sensation in my right foot. Then I discovered that I couldn't move my foot at all, and it was pressing hard on the gas pedal. I felt the hairs on the back of my neck stand up.

Something was outside my car, moving alongside but at a distance as I drove. I couldn't see anything, but I could sense a kind of pressing in around me. At first I tried to pretend nothing was happening, but soon I began to see a dim, amorphous shape hovering outside. The dreaded word "entity" came to my mind. Indira had taught me that word. She taught the class, "As your paranormal sensitivities increase, you might well encounter things called entities. Entities are disincarnate beings that exist in another dimension, but they can come into our physical world. They can be evil and spiteful or just mischievous, and they're fully capable of causing great harm."

At the time, I didn't believe her. "I think she's going a little bit overboard now," I thought. "She ought to save this one for Halloween."

One good look through my open car window changed my mind. Now there were two more of the dark shapes moving through the night, swimming beside my car as I sped along. They looked like a flying, black ghost, with shining, evil eyes and garments flapping. One drifted in close, and I suddenly felt a frigid cold with an equally sudden magnetic yank toward it. I heard something. Whether it was a voice or not I don't know, but it sounded like lips smacking with viscous, slobbering lust. A bright, orange-red light darted in through my window. Immediately, it was cast back outside again, leaving behind a venomous stink.

What had thrown the hideous thing out? Then I saw that the car was surrounded by some kind of protective circle containing Beings of Light, and they were working to repel the dark shapes that were coming from every direction. The entities weren't about to go away, though. My foot was still frozen to the gas pedal, and the car was flying even faster. The entities outside looked like they were jockeying for position, each wanting to be the next one to try to get at me.

I struggled to stay on the twisting road. Something was trying to turn the steering wheel so that the car would run off the blacktop. A huge tree swung into view through the front windshield. I jerked the car back onto the road as my right wheels rumbled and bumped along the shoulder of the road. Overhanging branches scraped the passenger's window as my car narrowly missed the tree. My spinning mind tried to make sense of what was happening. It was as if good and evil had become physical realities. I could feel the conflict just as distinctly as I could feel a physical object. I could taste, hear, and smell disaster.

I tried to remember what Indira had told me about entities. What had Indira said a person should do if an entity appeared? There was a mantra. "In the name of God, Christ, and the Masters, I order you to leave. Now! In the name of God, Christ, and the Masters, I order you to leave. Now!" With the earnestness of desperation and shaking my fist as hard as I could. I repeated the words over and over. "In the name of God, Christ, and the Masters, I order you to leave. Now ... Now ... Now!"

By reciting the mantra, everything was changing into slow motion. I felt like I had already repeated the mantra thousands and thousands of times. A heavy wave of inadequacy crashed over me. Was there any way out of this nightmare? Outside, in the normal, three-dimensional world, I could see that a police car was chasing me. The red light was flashing through my rear window, but I didn't care. It was nothing compared to my fear of the entities. A scream choked me; it welled up in my throat but was too deep and painful to utter. Three shadowy creatures peering in my window were carefully watching me and enjoying what they saw. They moved in closer. I could hear their rasping, evil voices.

The road swiftly expanded outward as the car picked up even more speed. A multitude of sensations overwhelmed me. The wind from the car's velocity was causing the skin on my face to stretch backward. My eyes were like slits. My teeth shut. The shadows-darker-than- shadows were even more excited when they saw my contorted face. The Beings of Light tightened up around the car, and their brilliance became a shield.

I couldn't decipher what the vile entities were saying. Then like a radio station tuning in, their guttural words became audible. The glorious ones around me ignored them. There was an imperceptible tightening of their shields. The entities grew more animated as if to say, "Step aside; we've got her. She's ours."

The brilliant celestial powers stayed where they were. One spoke for all, and its voice was like a cosmic trumpet, deep and rich. "You will not touch her. He, the source of all joy and sweetness, virtue and justice, it is He and He alone who decides." After that, there was an uneasy quiet, but I saw that the glee never left the eyes of my attackers.

The scream that was stuck in my throat finally escaped. "Stop, stop, let me stop my car. Please, please, I command you to leave."

Words came from the grunting, belching forms in the darkness. "Get away. She is ours. She is ours."

A bright light appeared far down the road. It didn't look like head-lights. It was a much bigger — more penetrating light. Shielding my eyes from the brilliance, I could make out that it was burning right through the entities. They began to crouch down and double up in great pain. The brilliance was so intense that the creatures became translucent. I saw ugly things like cancerous growths inside them. These growths seared and burned in the light. It came to me later that these hideous, raw spots were the evil in these creatures, the moral flaws they cherished and protected inside themselves, the things they refused to release and give up to God's forgiveness and healing.

At the same time, the figures who protected me were basking in the brilliance, as though it fed their beings and infused them with strength. The angels, and I'm sure they were angels, looked as if the radiance gave them indescribable joy. There were no dark spots inside them. The Beings of Light had been washed clean by their Master's love.

How can I describe what happened in the next moments? In the next few moments, I was overwhelmed by what I witnessed. There was a form inside the radiant light. Afraid, I recoiled from the vision. It was a Lamb, humble and beautiful at the same time, and bearing the wounds of battle. All good things radiated from the Lamb: kindness, compassion, love, justice, mercy, and awesome power. There were tears in His eyes because I had pulled away from Him. He stood at the right hand of the Divine Light source, the great Creator. The Light from the Creator and the grace from the Lamb filled the angels with renewed strength and resolve.

The fiends tried to seize me again, but the angels, with a flourish of wings, catapulted them away from me for the final time. The wicked spirits rose into the air, screaming ineffectually. I thought I heard, "You're really in trouble now." Then they dove steeply, down past the car, away from the intense light, disappearing into billowing smoke.

The light faded. I was alone in the car again. I could move my right foot at last, so I yanked it off the gas pedal and put on the brake. The police siren rang in my ears as I pulled over to the side of the road, tears streaming down my face, I was shaking so hard that I could barely turn off the key as the officer approached.

He spoke into the open window, "Did you know you were going over 120 miles and hour back there?"

My throat was as dry as paper, and it was hard to summon up enough voice to answer him. Besides, what was I going to say? I was afraid he'd arrest me for drunk driving or else for sheer insanity. "My ... my mother's in the hospital, and I'm terribly worried. I had no idea how fast I was driving."

The officer seemed sympathetic as if he sensed my dilemma. He was very kind. "I have to give you a ticket," he said, "but I'll put down that you were just doing eighty, so you won't lose your license. Be careful from now on. You could have gotten into some real trouble back there. By the way, did you see that bright light on the road in front of you? Seems to be gone now." I nodded yes.

Still trembling, I drove straight to the hospital in Concord. When I arrived, I learned my mother was going to be fine, but the doctors were keeping her overnight for observation. Exhausted, I spent the night in Grammie's house and brought Mother home the next morning.

Often over the years since that night I've pondered that trip from Brattleboro to Concord by way of Heaven and Hell. The memory of the extreme contrast between the light and the darkness has never left me. Sometimes the words of an old hymn come into my mind:

> *Trust in the Lord*
> *With all your heart*
> *Lean not on your own understanding*
> *In all thy ways acknowledge Him*
> *And He shall direct thy path.*

> —PROVERBS *3: 5-6*

As the months went by, I missed Indira's classes and meditations. Sadly, I began longing to return to New Jersey. I missed my family. I wanted to return to them and provide a good home for my sons. Vermont was too far away. Nine months was long enough to be away from my family and friends. I knew I would go back to Vermont for the Clear Light Therapy class next summer. I was still traumatized by my poor decisions of 1985, and needed to be with my children and family.

I also wanted to take classes and train with Louise Hay, who held weekly healing workshops in West Hollywood, California.

Every day I prayed, "Please Lord, let me know whether I should return home. If it's right for me and everyone else concerned, please send me a sign."

CHAPTER 9

Back to New Jersey

ONE DAY AS I WAS walking back to work after lunch, I saw a playing card lying face up on the sidewalk; the nine of spades, which is the card of reversals, of going back to where you came from. Then *I knew!* My heart leapt and I went into instant bliss. Within days, I got a call from my friend Karl, chief pilot for a company based at the Westchester County Airport. He told me that Xerox needed a flight attendant for its private hangar there. Was I interested in interviewing for the job? The airport was in White Plains, New York, just a twenty-minute drive from my family home in New Jersey. I couldn't get my bags packed fast enough.

Within twenty-four hours after this event, I received a call from White Planes Airport asking me to come back home and do some flying for Xerox Corporation. I had spent seven years working in aviation, and missed the work. This new opportunity thrilled me.

"Elizabeth, I think you're making a tremendous mistake," my friend Maria announced. "I can understand why you want to get out of Vermont and go back to New Jersey, but why in the world are you going to move into your ex-husband's house? You've told me plenty of times that it's all over between you two, and that you will never, never get back together again. I think you'll just be making trouble for yourself if you go."

Oh, I have my reasons," I said. "I've prayed and meditated about it, and I've gotten a strong impression that's what I should do. My first husband, Dick and I are still friends, and, anyway, Dick's not going to charge me to stay in the guest bedroom if I help him straighten up his house. I really have no other choice at this time. Plus, the house is near Westchester Airport so I'll have an easy commute to work."

Vance, my oldest son, was living in Dick's house too, and I hadn't seen him for a long time. The house was roomy and pleasant, like the other houses in a quiet, green Bergen County suburb. Staying there wouldn't be too bad. Besides, it was only going to be temporary.

There was a little diorama in the back of my mind, a picture I barely acknowledged but, being hidden the deepest, was probably the strongest reason I was going back to my ex-husband's house. I saw Dick, Vance, Jeffrey and me all peaceful and happy, living the lives God intended us to live. I didn't picture Dick and me married again, but I did see both our sons loving us and us delighting in them. I saw Vance, bright and musical, beginning to find his way in the world; along with Jeffrey, the intelligent, serious college student, working towards becoming a doctor; and Dick, the loving father, grown wiser and more patient and justly proud of our sons. Finally there was me, at last justified and appreciated for my years of work and caring.

"Don't worry about me, Maria," I said. "I'm going to be just fine." How was I to know that all of that was a pipedream of illusion?

The day before Thanksgiving in 1985, I returned to Waldwick, New Jersey, leaving all of my possessions in the small apartment in Vermont. An uneasy feeling came over me as I walked up the pathway to Dick's house. I noticed some trash in the brown, weedy grass; and the glass on the front door was cracked diagonally from side to side. "Oh, Well," I said to myself, "I knew things around here would need a little sprucing up. Men aren't usually very good housekeepers." I opened the door and stepped inside.

It hit me like a slap – a practically visible wall of stale beer stink. I gasped and looked around. This place is a stable, I thought, but then I changed my mind. Stables get cleaned out sometimes. The dirt on the floors in the living room and kitchen was so thick that it had made its own carpet. Open bottles of alcohol were everywhere. The sinks, bathtub and toilet looked like they hadn't been cleaned since the Nixon Administration. All the ashtrays were filled to overflowing except for one that had fallen off its table and spilled its contents onto the already dirty rug.

Dick tried to make me feel at home. "It's good to have you here," he said. "The three of us under one roof again. Now all we need is Jeffrey to make it a foursome."

I shuddered. The idea of Jeffrey being in this wretched place appalled me. I said a silent prayer of thanks that he was away at college.

My son Vance looked too thin. His skin was so pasty that he looked like he might be coming down with some sort of wasting disease. "Something's wrong, Vance," I said.

"No, Mom." he said. "Everything's cool, really. Just great." His pupils were pinpoints, and he seemed to have trouble keeping me in focus. "Just great," he said again, and then he sniffed and blew his nose.

Vance had pneumonia at three, and almost died. While he was sick, he was running in the house, and ran smack into the couch, knocking his front teeth back into his jaw. The baby teeth grew out, but his permanent teeth came in as buckteeth. They could not be fixed until he got braces at the age of ten. Vance was harassed and bullied throughout his grade school and middle school years. He was sad a lot, and although I tried to work with him, upsets kept happening. In high school, he got involved in drugs, and became difficult to handle. I finally sent him to live with his father just after his eighteenth birthday and before he graduated from high school.

While Vance was too skinny, Dick, as he sat in his grubby recliner, looked unhealthily swollen and out of shape. Clearly, drinking with the "guys" on Friday nights was probably the only social thing in his life.

"Let me tell you a little secret," Dick said, leaning forward. "I don't know what I'd do without good ole' Vance living here with me. I hate being alone, just can't stand living by myself. So maybe our son doesn't eat all his green vegetables, and maybe he likes to have his friends over sometimes and they like to have a little fun. Well I say, 'So what?' He's doing okay, and so am I."

"Things aren't right around here, Dick," I said, "and you know it."

"Everything's fine," he said. "All we need is a little tidying up."

In a few minutes Vance retreated to his room up in the attic, and Dick fell asleep in his chair, his mouth open and a beer can in his hand.

My skin was tingling. I could sense apathy, fear, anger, and great negativity in every room. I started to feel dizzy. The walls were pressing in. There wasn't enough air to breathe. I closed my eyes. Bad things had happened in this house – things a lot worse than mess and dirt. All I wanted was to turn around and run away.

Then I remembered something I had learned from reading Louise Hay's book, *You Can Heal Your Life*. "*Everything that happens to you,*" she had said, "*all the events in your life are a series of tests, a set of sacred assignments. Each change that comes, even if it seems terrible or painful at the time, can bring you closer to the enlightenment and upliftment of your soul. Progress comes from understanding why you were put into a particular situation, overcoming your fear and resistance and, finally, comprehending the lesson that is there for you to learn. Always remember that you are safe, and it's only change. Embracing change helps you to drop your fear, and not set up thoughts of failure or helplessness.*"

What was the lesson I was supposed to learn from this mess? I didn't have an answer. By the end of the evening, in my "guest room in the attic," staring at the dusty mattress on the floor, I wanted to throw myself down and cry, just as I had when I was a little girl. Instead, I crawled between the dingy sheets and tried to get some sleep. "I should be grateful for all things, even this," I said to myself over and over again, but I didn't feel grateful. I just felt wretched. How was I supposed to thank God for letting me be broke and living in a dump? Should I say, "*Thank You, Lord, for my failed marriage, and thank you that my son is using drugs?*" The whole thing seemed preposterous.

After a restless, dream-filled sleep, I awoke and felt a quiet peace. My faith was strengthened and I knew all would work out for me. There must have been angels helping me all night long. One of Louise Hay's songs echoed through me:

Doors opening,
Doors Closing,
Doors opening, I'm opening
I am safe, it's only change.
I am safe, it' only change.

The first two things I cleaned were the refrigerator and the stove. Although it was November and cold, I had to go outside every few minutes and get some uncontaminated air. I removed many, many hard, crusty things, softly decaying blobs, and luxuriant gardens of variously colored mold. A jackhammer and a fire hose would have come in handy. By the time I finished cleaning I was exhausted and nauseated, but I had the satisfaction of knowing that no one would die of ptomaine poisoning from eating food from that kitchen.

It wasn't easy living at Dick's house. It was obvious that Dick and Vance were stuck in a kind of emotional quicksand and didn't know how to get out. Vance's friends came over every Friday night. Sullen and grubby, their usual amusements were pornographic videos, alcohol, marihuana, cocaine, and whatever other drugs they were clever enough to poison themselves with. Dick, I discovered, knew all about these wholesome little get-togethers. Sometimes he joined in.

Several years earlier, when Vance was eighteen, I had sent him to live with his father. Vance had started taking drugs, and I didn't want him around Jeffrey, then thirteen, and Nilas and Caroline, two foster teenagers who were also living with me. Dick promised me then that he would keep a sharp eye on our son and make sure he stopped messing around with drugs. I believed him. I didn't realize that what I did was like taking matches away from Vance and then handing him a blowtorch instead.

It was the memory of the failed marriage that tempered things now. Perhaps this situation was a chance to make up for the past and help them change. This deep desire bolstered my spineless backbone with courage. It completely subdued my "yellow streak" and allowed me to literally whistle in the dark, although I endured a constant trembling uncertainty.

My natural instinct was to flee this. Normally I would have run away, but my being there was not just ordinary. It was not a coincidence. I learned a lot in my nine months away, and this experience would turn out to be one of the most extraordinary events in my life.

During my four-month stay in Waldwick, I was able to get in to New York City and participate in the "Hayrides." These meetings, led by Louise Hay, were not called healing meetings; however, they turned out to be extremely healing for the thousands of people who participated in them. The Hayrides were a support group for people with AIDS or any other physical disturbance. We got together, supported each other, and networked. We'd sing, we'd meditate, and listen to Louise's talk.

There were body tables set up in the back of the room where body workers, myself included, would work with anyone who chose to come and lie down. We'd all share our successes and fears, do visualizations, and work on loving ourselves as well as creating loving responses to each other.

I participated in the Hayrides for two years, and witnessed a lot of healing of the consciousness. Many who came on a regular basis grew so much that their hearts truly opened. There were lawyers, film people, actors, restaurant owners, bankers, wall-street brokers, and hundreds of others from all walks of life. People would arrive broken, desperate, frightened and, through Louise's guidance, would find their smile again. Louise's focus, dedication and devotion drove the work forward. There was never any financial exchange.

It certainly helped me through my "adjustment of change" era. I wouldn't trade the experience for anything. The gratitude and love it brought into my life stayed with me. I will always be humbled for the opportunity. This truly is the way we should be living our lives. The Hayrides gave me strength to continue on in my circumstances, knowing, somehow, all would eventually work out.

I miss the Hayride's. Many of the things we did were extremely personal and intangible. The relationships we formed were profound because they came from deep, universal love.

I accepted I had no choice in the situation with Dick, and worked to feel gratitude for Dick's repulsive, dubious shelter. By being *grateful* I don't mean resigning myself to self-pity and martyrdom. No! I had to see it as a learning moment. I struggled to find real gratitude. This desire for gratitude was a desperate feeling. I didn't have any strength or vitality. It felt like a dead body without a soul. I struggled hard to let in some light. But instead, I had an overwhelming desire to throw myself on the bed and sob with the hysterical abandon of a small child. The struggle was so powerful I felt dizzy, as if the walls were caving in on me.

"You've got to get out of here," I said over and over again to Dick, "and you know it. Both of you are in terrible shape."

"I suppose you're right," Dick would say, "but I can't seem to find the energy. Time goes by, and things stay just the way they are."

One evening I was especially upset and said exactly what was on my mind. "You've got to separate yourself from Vance. It's obvious you're scared of being alone so you let Vance do whatever he wants. Unfortunately, he only wants two things – one is to get high, and the other is to get even higher.

"I've told you many times that I can fix this place up for you. You should sell it and go somewhere else, somewhere smaller and easier for you to take care of. Nobody in their right mind would buy this house the way it is now, but I'm sure I can get it looking nice again.

"Vance needs to get away too. He should be out on his own, taking responsibility for himself. He's a man now. He should start acting like one." I said.

Circumstances were not pleasant in the Waldwick house. I had little money, and was not working on a regular basis. Things appeared to be hopeless and I was fighting desperation and despair. I cried out in my dreams. The holidays came and went. Nothing changed. Every night I prayed, *"Mother Mary, please, please help me find a place of my own. Help me to understand what it happening to me. Help me to know what to do."*

In mid-February, I got my answer in a dream. I felt the Holy Mother's energies, and a voice spoke to me saying, *"Don't worry, dear one. You will find a place to live. It will be a place you will love. I will give it to you for two years. On March seventh I will send you a man who will help and guide you."*

I could hardly wait until March seventh. But when the day came, I didn't get the house Mother Mary promised me. All that happened was that I met a realtor named Bill who took me to see some places that were impossibly expensive. At the end of the day I was tired, disgusted and disappointed; furious with Spirit and even more furious with dumb old Bill, the realtor.

After several weeks of searching, at the Spring Equinox on March 21st, Bill called and said he wanted to show me a townhouse in Mahwah, New Jersey. "I think you'll really like it," he said. "I have a feeling that you just belong there. It's a real beauty."

"Okay," I said, not daring to ask how much the rent was.

As soon as I saw the townhouse, I had to agree with Bill that it was a real beauty. I had been to this condo complex before. "I love it here," I said. "I feel at home already. Just give me a few minutes to do something, okay?"

With that, I sat down on the floor in the bare living room and began to meditate. Bill sat in the window seat and waited patiently. He didn't say a word, bless him, and he acted as unsurprised as if all his clients plopped down on the floor and meditated when they found a place they wanted.

"Bill," I said, after a few minutes, "how much is the rent?"

"Sixteen hundred a month," he said. I gulped. Sixteen hundred dollars was impossible for me, of course. It might as well have been sixteen billion.

I closed my eyes again. Almost instantly I sensed the ghost of an old man standing in the kitchen. He spoke to me telepathically. "Elizabeth, you don't know me, but I used to live here with my dear wife. On January twelfth I had a heart attack and collapsed and died in the driveway right outside. Then my wife moved into a smaller apartment. That's why this townhouse is up for rent."

Bill looked shocked when I told him about the ghost of the old man. "You're right, Elizabeth. An older couple did live here, and the husband died of a heart attack in the driveway, just the way you said. I'm flabbergasted."

"He told me some other things too," I said. "He said he'd been holding this place for me since his death two months ago. He said I should ask for a two-year lease and offer eight hundred dollars a month for the first year and a thousand a month for the second."

"The owner will never accept that," Bill said.

"Make the offer anyway," I said.

Bill went back to his office to make the call while I stayed in the living room to meditate some more. I thanked Spirit for giving me this opportunity. Through Her grace, the Holy Mother had given me this wonderful, beautiful place to live. I knew for sure that I would be there for the next two years, as promised. My dream had been fulfilled before I even saw the townhouse.

Bill was smiling and shaking his head in wonder when he came back. He handed me the lease to sign. "How did you know the landlord would accept your offer?" he said. "Mr. Grogan, the owner, had three offers on this condo today. One was from a woman who has two small children and a dog. She offered eleven hundred a month. The second bid was from three college boys, and they were willing to pay twelve hundred a month. But the landlord chose you, even though you put in the lowest offer. Maybe it's because you don't have any little kids, you're not a college boy, and you want a two-year lease."

"I couldn't be happier," I said. "There's only one problem left. I don't have any money."

Bill scratched his head, looked down at the lease, and then did something absolutely amazing. He took out his checkbook and wrote me a check for three thousand six hundred dollars. "This should be enough to make the deposit, pay the first two months' rent, and move in your furniture and things. I don't know why I'm doing this, " he said, "but it feels right. I know that somehow it'll all come back to me. If that spirit in the kitchen was saving this place for you, I guess you'd better have it."

"I'd never take this money if I wasn't desperate. You'll get every cent back at some point."

"I am sure of that," Bill answered, blinking as if he could not believe what just happened.

David and Chris, my twin sister and her boyfriend, came up to Vermont to help me, and I moved back to New Jersey in less than a week. The Holy Mother wasn't done pouring out her gifts to me. When I arrived in Brattleboro to move, a letter was waiting for me. It was from Evelyn, my angel friend at the airport. She was asking if I planned to return to New Jersey and if we could be roommates. Her mother was moving and she needed a place to live. She could not remain in New York City.

As extra icing on the cake, Evelyn moved in to share the town house with me. We each were paying just four hundred dollars a month to live in this beautiful place with its trees and green lawns, not to mention its fine clubhouse, tennis courts, and pool. It was delightful.

The Holy Mother provided me with the opportunity to renew myself with her energies. I marveled at what had opened up for me. I was ready to benefit from all the gifts the Holy Spirit might give me and remained devoted with my faith and prayers. I watched for every sign, every change around me and accepted each with open arms when it arrived. I had my moments of doubt, of course, but they were only that – moments. I didn't allow them to get a grip on me. I knew Spirit was communicating with me and guiding me. The more I trusted Her, the more She was able to reveal Herself. My energy and meditations quickened my spiritual opportunities, and they exploded open like popcorn in a popper. I knew the power was within me. My heart was filled with gratitude.

Within a month of my move, Dick told me he couldn't stand his living situation any more. He was finally, willing to do something about it.

"If you promise to sell the house and relocate," I said, "I'll give the place another cleaning, top to bottom. I'll even paint whatever needs painting and hang new curtains. Also, I want you to engage Bill as your realtor. He's been wonderful to me, and I know he'll do the best job selling your house."

Dick was skeptical, but he finally agreed. Not only did Bill sell the house quickly and at a great price, but he also helped me paint, hang curtains and clean the floors to get it ready to put it on the market.

In the meantime, Dick put in for a transfer to a different drug store as a pharmacist. He found a condominium near his new job. "It's great living in my new condo," he told me a few weeks after his move. "I enjoy working here. I feel like I've left a lot of old, ugly baggage behind me. I'm making a new beginning. Thanks for everything, Beth."

Vance was the only one who wasn't happy. He still wanted to cling to his careless, drug-filled way of living. His transformation was to come later.

Just to keep the Universe in balance, I was able to repay Bill for his many kindnesses.

One year after he found me the condo, Bill contacted me and told me he was very upset about his daughter, Carol. She had changed from a sunny, friendly girl into someone sullen and resentful. She had been in two car crashes in one month. Her grades were falling. She had started smoking and was hanging around with the wrong crowd in high school. "I don't know what to do," he said. "I'm worried. It's wrecking our family. Do you think you could counsel her, along with me and my wife?"

Of course I told him I would. Each visit, I deducted my regular fee from the $3,600 that Bill had given me for the deposit and first two months rent on my town house. The counseling lasted almost exactly as long as it took me to pay Bill back for his check. By the end of the sessions Carol had stopped smoking, graduated from high school with honors, and was going to Syracuse University. She's now associated with one of the top advertising companies in New York City. It was a joy to help her and her parents. It still brings me happiness to think about it.

In late July of 1987, my roommate Evelyn and I flew out to Santa Fe, New Mexico for the Harmonic Convergence. We stayed and fasted for three weeks with the Clear Light Group. The *Harmonic Convergence* is the name given to one of the world's first globally synchronized meditation events, which occurred on August 16-17, 1987.

The convergence corresponds with a great shift in the earth's energy from warlike to peaceful. According to Jose' Argüelles, the principal organizer, the event came at the end of these nine "hell" cycles marking the beginning of a new age of universal peace. Adherents believed that signs indicated a "major energy shift" was about to occur, a turning point in Earth's collective karma and dharma. This powerful energy was enough to change the global perspective of man from one of conflict to one of co-operation. Actress and author Shirley MacLaine called it a *"window of light,"* that allowed access to higher realms of awareness. Little did I know how spot on she was.

According to Argüelles, the Harmonic Convergence also began the final twenty-five year countdown to the end of the Mayan Long Count in 2012. It marked the end of history and the beginning of a new 5,125-year cycle on earth. Evils of the modern world, war, materialism, violence, abuses, injustice, and oppression, would end with the birth of the Sixth Sun and Fifth Dimensional energies would rain down on the Earth beginning on December 21, 2012.

We fasted on juice, fruit and water for twenty-one days, did several sweat lodges, and by the date of the convergence were clear, sensitive, and ready to receive the energies pouring down from the center of the galaxy

On the day of the convergence, we all called for a day of silence. I remember clearly going outside in the canyons of Santa Fe, New Mexico, laying down on a blanket and actually vibrating to the new energies, as I basked in the sun and the astrological line up of planetary vibrations.

CHAPTER 10

Hawaii
Land of Enchantment

AFTER ABOUT EIGHTEEN MONTHS OF traveling back to Vermont every week-end for my Saturday morning weekly meditations, a 185 mile drive each way, everything in my life was about to undergo a seismic shift.

I was in my new condo, teaching, doing healing work, and had built up a nice meditation group in Mahwah, New Jersey. The Clear Light Group, Indira, Rob, William, Baba and Dennis had moved to Maui, Hawaii. A place I had longed to visit.

Floating in the middle of the Pacific Ocean, this multicultural, heavenly natural group of islands, lay in the middle of a cobalt blue ocean. I had always heard that these Polynesian islands have sunrises and sunsets so spectacular that they can induce powerful, mesmerizing meditations.

Hawaii is the land of enchantment. I was searching for spiritual enlightenment. Never in my life could I have dreamed what would happen to me in Kipahulu, a forty-five minute drive down a dirt road, beyond Hana, on the other side of Haleakala.

I made three trips to Maui. During each trip I experienced several deeply penetrating spiritual experiences. The first one, in November, 1986, was profound. I flew directly into Hana with Nancy, another Clear Light student, for a two-week retreat. Dennis met the group and drove us to their new home. The property contained a small group of cabins on a large hill. If you looked upwards high enough, you could see to top of Haleakala.

The new Clear Light Camp was located just past the seven sacred pools, and not far from Hanavie, a waterfall in the dense tropical forest. Kipahulu, means "fetch from exhausted gardens." It is a remote farming community in East Maui, about ten miles south of Hana. The town didn't have public electric or water utilities. Residents sourced water from streams and rain showers, much like they do in Bermuda. We showered at the waterfall, which had rainbow rings of water dancing around it.

Kipahulu is a paradise of rainforests, waterfalls, pools, mountain valleys, and sweeping ocean views. Upper Kipahulu, was part of the National Park registry to preserve the natural and cultural heritage of the valley.

In September, 1986, before I arrived on the island, one night while sleeping, I awoke at 3:00 a.m. in what felt like another time and space. I was having a nightmare:

In the dream, my twin sister, Chris and I were in a car, she was driving. We were on our way to Grammies house in Warner, New Hampshire. We went around a curve, across a covered bridge and began to go over an embankment, straight toward the Warner River. I jumped out of the passenger side of the car, fell onto the ground, and then held the car with my hands to stop it from going over the cliff. I began to pray, and called on the Masters to help me get the car back up onto safe ground. I was afraid my back would give out. Some of my inner thoughts were negative, as I began to remember the emotions, anger and pettiness sisters have between them. Each time I felt and remembered a negative thought or action between my twin and myself, I kept saying, *"It doesn't matter. This won't happen. This won't happen,"* I was determined that the car would get safely back on the road. It was taking all of my inner strength to hold on.

Finally, the car was safely level on top of the cliff. Then suddenly I felt a soft rain. I was aware of how I was dressed and of a house in the trees. I had never seen it before. As I began to walk toward the house, I knew help would be inside.

I woke up startled. The bed sheets were drenched. I was physically exhausted. Every ounce of energy was drained from my body. I realized that this was astral energy, which is used to turn possible unpleasant or dangerous events around, through love and the Law of Karma. I felt I had somehow just saved my sister's life.

In November of 1986, I went to Hawaii, on a spiritual retreat. The dream continued to weigh down on me in Hawaii. I could not let go of an uneasy feeling. The afternoon of November 11th, at approximately 2:00 p.m.. I was in deep meditation. I heard a voice say to me. "Your sister died." I "felt", deep inside myself, something had happened. For the rest of the day I struggled with coldness and negative energies. The group became aware of what I was struggling with and worked on me energetically for several hours. This continued through the evening. I went to bed exhausted with a heavy heart.

By morning I was aware on the inner levels that all was well. During the morning meditation, I sensed that I needed to call my mother who now lived in Grammie's house in Warner, New Hampshire. My mother answered the phone.

"What happened to Chris," I asked her immediately.

"How did you know? Who called you?" My mother asked anxiously.

She was surprised that I knew about the accident.

My sister was driving back to New York City from Warner on the evening of November 11th at 7:00 p.m. (2:00 p.m. Maui time) when the car slipped on ice, flew into the air, and landed at the bottom of a thirty-five foot ravine. The car turned over several times. Everything in the car was crushed except where my sister sat. The area around her was intact and she walked away from the accident without a scratch.

I was astonished at my mother's words, and the dream two months before came into full focus. Was it a dream, or a precognitive experience? The feelings within my being were indescribable.

It was then that I noticed the soft rain, so familiar in Hawaii at that time of year, and the clothes I was wearing. They were the same as in the dream, and I was within the house I had seen beyond the trees

I returned to Hawaii for another spiritual retreat with the Clear Light Group in April 1987, and had a completely different, but beautifully blessed experience. This time I was escorted by two of my clients, Bruce and Mark. Since I had worked in corporate aviation, I was able to arrange some special advantages on this trip. We were "given" a hut with the bedrooms actually on the beach, in Lahania for a few days. Since it was Bruce and Mark's first time to the islands, we decided to take the fifty-four mile drive around the base of Haleakala to Hana, as well as drive to the top of the world's largest dormant volcano to watch the sunrise.

We awoke at 3:30 am for the drive up the side of Haleakala to experience one of the world's most beautiful and unique sunrise at the 10,000-foot summit of the volcanic mountain. Because I was from New England and had been to Mt. Washington in New Hampshire, I knew we had to have some warm clothing and water. We packed snacks and drinks in the car and began the drive.

Arriving at the top of the famous Haleakala Crater, the highest peak on the island of Maui, we witnessed, through the dark and foggy clouds, an explosion of color, as the sun rose above the clouds.

Then, out of the center of the crater, in a foggy mist, rose a figure within a brilliant golden amber light. I recognized the figure as that of the great Yogi, Paramahansa Yogananda, and tears began to flow from the eyes of everyone. Telepathically he gave this thought to this small, searching group; *"Giving love to all, feeling the love of God, seeing His presence in everyone, and having but one desire — for His constant presence in the temple of your consciousness — that is the way to live in this world. Begin with yourself. There is no time to waste. It is your duty to do your part to bring God's kingdom on earth. As we realize the presence and the love of God within, we develop our ability to radiate it without. This is the practical answer to the troubles of humankind, for there is a dynamic relationship between our consciousness and world conditions."*

Then he was gone. Speechless and overwhelmed, we walked back to the rental car and began the 28-mile, downhill ride back to sea level, stopping along the way to enjoy the view. Our hearts were filled with joy, there simply was nothing to say. We shared the powerful energy of Light.

A few days later, while meditating, another spiritual experience came upon me. I closed my eyes and began to sing the mantra of the day, along with the rest of the group. There were about twenty students, plus the five Clear Light teachers. As I fell backward into a deep meditation, quite suddenly, the room and the people were gone. Again, as years before, I experienced a dark tunnel with Light at the other side beckoning me forward. Then, as quickly as it had come, it was gone. I opened my eyes with relief, and found that I was no longer in the tunnel. I spun around to look behind me for the tunnel but it was not there.

Suddenly my worldly feelings faded away; everything was gone. I began floating upwards, higher and higher. Up I went. Out of the top of my head. I realized I was reaching out, reaching, reaching. What was I reaching for? I felt myself floating towards another tunnel, while being drawn toward a bright Light. With an awareness of great relief, I sensed the lifting of a heavy burden of pain and fear. As I traveled, I noticed that whatever I was stretching my arm out to was just beyond my reach.

My internal thoughts were still clearing as the bright Light swirled toward the perimeters of my subconscious. I was aware of traveling through the Universe, then suddenly, through a second Universe, but the planets and stars were shaped differently. I was brought up again into a third Universe. It felt like waves of mercurial light, not necessarily planets or stars, but just a sense of being, while floating within the vibration of such an incredible sense of Love. I felt as if I were in rings like the kind babies play with and stack on a stick. They were vibrant colors of red, orange, green, yellow, blue, indigo, and violet. Once I came to the top of the violet ring, everything flattened out.

Why was it so quiet? Where was the music of the mantra that had ripped through my senses a moment ago? Or was it really only a moment ago?

Time seemed to have disappeared. I struggled to shake myself back into awareness. Fear gripped my heart as I struggled to shake myself back into physical consciousness. Something was happening to me beyond my control. Something was very different. My body was enormously different. I realized that the body I was in felt transparent and weightless. A deeper fear gripped my returning awareness. Had I been harmed? Was I dead? I had often wondered what it would be like to die, and pass beyond the boundaries of space and time.

Gravitational forces were suspended. Space and time seemed blotted out. Again I was aware of the sensation of weightless movement. I was rising. I was escaping. It was like the first plunge on a roller coaster, but a roller coaster turned upside down; it was like falling upward.

Doubts and fears hit me like lightening bolts. Was there an afterlife? A Heaven? My beloved Grammie had promised me that a loving, all-powerful God existed, and that all souls joined Him after life. There simply was no doubt about it. It's easy to believe when you're little, walking hand-in-hand with your grandmother through the woods, or sitting close to her by the fire. But was there really such a thing as life after death? I wondered, while helplessly flying through the seven rings of Light towards a greater, more brilliant Light. My eyes widened. Did I still have eyes, or was this just an illusion? What if death really was a dark, heavy door banging shut, and after that final slam there was nothing at all? At that moment I felt more like a piece of nothingness than I ever had before. But I was still not completely nothing. I was aware of myself. I was still thinking. That was something. I started the mantra, *"I think, therefore I am, I think, therefore I am."* I couldn't imagine nothingness. There was no category in my mind or experience for such a notion. Nothingness conflicted with all my training and instincts. Nothingness as the final stage of life would make a mockery of humanity, I thought. Either human beings have Souls, or they dream them up to avoid the dread of an endless void. One cannot live without hope, even if it is a false hope. Still, I realized with a shock of joy and relief, I was continuing to think and feel. *I existed!*

Slivers of recollection zoomed past me. I numbly grappled with them before they slipped away. I had heard someone saying something of great significance. What was it? Try, try, try to call it back. The words came again, like dancing, prismatic lights. With great effort my mind reached out and grasped them. It had been a man speaking. "Elizabeth is having a healing. We must cover and protect her!" Then a female voice shouted, "She's in a deep trance. We must keep a close eye on her!" Then there were other voices too, but a mist rolled over them and they disappeared. Half-formed shapes faded in and out of view. I struggled to focus.

Shapes of beings slowly crept into view beyond the bounds of my awareness again. I struggled to focus, to comprehend. They were surrounded with Light. Inside I knew this was not the same as my last cosmic trip.

I thought, now I am in the middle of the great mystery. I had waited all my life to know the truth about God. I tried to look ahead, to see, but everything became blurred with a strong, bright amber light. Should I be afraid? I was afraid, that was certain, but should I be? At least I was feeling something. I felt as it I was being purposely led somewhere. In a state of wonder, I wanted to jump up and down with joy. My curiosity was focused and strong. Suddenly I felt no fear. There were Light beings and spirals of Light swirling around me. They gave me hope as I continued my ascension. I had the distinct impression that time no longer existed; neither did space. Yet, paradoxically, my thoughts still flowed in something like a time sequence. I felt as if I was moving somewhere.

Yes, I still existed, and that was good. Or was it? It all depended on the nature of this new sense of being. What if this upward climb went on and on forever? Would I be pulled into the bright light forever with this upward rush? My heart pounded in my chest. Did I still have a heart, a chest? I remembered stories my mother and grandmother had told me, accounts of Heaven, Hell and the afterlife. Why was I taking this trip and what was its purpose?

The day before this, I thought it was life-shatteringly important to simply take a shower and get dressed. I remembered the urgency I had felt to get to the Food Mart with William so we could find just the right items to fix for dinner—now it all seemed a million miles away. A few nights earlier, I had looked into the center of a crater and had seen a great master teacher. For a moment I marveled at the size of the Universe. There seemed to be more than one. I pondered the meaning of existence. I remembered how small I had felt smaller than a dot on the eye of the smallest ant.

Maybe I should have meditated more, studied more and opened my eyes to the real essentials of life. But there had always been more immediate distractions. Daily life questions and concerns occupied my attention. What should I wear? Whether I should fix roast beef or fish for dinner? What was a good book to read? How to make enough money to keep going?

Panic seized me again. What if this seemingly upward fall really did go on forever? What would I do then? I tried to force myself to move farther along, hoping to get closer to the bright Light beaming from far away. My mind kept up its zigzag dance from the molecules to circles of light to the awareness of three Universes, and anything in between. Was this what "rising up" was?

Indira and the Clear Light Group had taken their beliefs from Eastern religions, I thought. For them, all things were part of the *Cosmic Unconscious*. Everything was God and God was everything. God was impersonal, a life force, the unknowable principle behind the curtain. They believed that life is fulfilled only as each one of us loses his or her individual identity and sinks back, disappearing into the "nothingness of what is." I hadn't been impressed either with an Americanized, homogenized version of paganism, Hinduism and Buddhism.

Everyone was desperate to find the meaning behind their hurried pace of life. In desperation they created many varieties of gods *in their own image*. The ego ruled in many cases. I decided to set aside the other jumbling thoughts crowding for attention. I had to make sense out of all this craziness. I needed to find a definite reason for what was happening while I still had time.

I believed strongly in the Lord Jesus Christ and the God, Jehovah of the Bible. I was told the Bible stories by my mother, grandmother, and my cousins. I was brought up with a strong New England Baptist background. I knew I had received The Lord's blessings many times. After all, hadn't He brought me to everyone I ever loved?

The sensation of acceleration snapped me out of my thoughts. I was rapidly speeding toward the bright Light. On my left and right I started to notice flashes of light and patches of various, brilliant colors; amber, aqua, magenta. It was all rushing around with a speed that made me dizzy and nausea. My mind reeled back to the question of religion. Not only had I known atheists and so-called New Age people, but I had also come across those who spoke about God as though they knew everything about Him, right down to the color of His beard. Of course, there was no question that He had a beard. the Almighty was without doubt a Him. These people knew for sure that there was life after death. The Bible said so. They were stuffy, hypocritical, and always attacking anyone who questioned their beliefs. They believed they had the only valid tickets to Heaven. Everyone else was headed for a place where there was a lot of suffering and emotional turmoil. How could such bigoted people have the real information about the afterlife? Each place of worship had its own particular set of rules. It's tidy collection of dos and don'ts. There must be a hundred explanations of what God is, what He does, and why He does it. What was the truth?

The surrounding light intensity was changing into a rosy-colored hue as I continued to search for answers. How many possible ways were there to explain existence? Our earth reality demands an explanation.

Where was I being led, or rather, what was I being sucked into like a whirlpool? I longed for the Universe to explain itself. Had it existed forever, or did it have a beginning sometime in the past? Every machine or work of art has a creator, someone who thought of it, and then made it. The process is thinking, talking, and action. After all, grandfather clocks, Mona Lisa's, and houses, even very little houses, don't suddenly appear out of nowhere. So how could something as enormous and complex, as beautifully ordered as the Universe just appear out of nothing? Who made it? How did it get here? And, for that matter, what would explain the unique qualities of human beings, their personalities, their creativity, their ability to think abstractly, and, especially, their capacity for unselfishness and love?

Again the lightness deepened. I was certain now that I had burst through the barrier of time and had entered a strange sort of new existence. My body felt very different. It became light and transparent. Then terror again seized my thoughts. What would I do if this actually did go on forever? Oh my, what then? I tried to force myself deeper into an area, where a bright Light was beaming from the center. I made out a distinct form of light a little way ahead of me—a dim amber light.

The brilliant radiance obscured the colorful shapes suddenly appearing. First I thought they might be angels. Did human-like creatures with wings exist anywhere outside fantasy and imagination? Perhaps the idea of angels was silly, outrageous, and foolish. But until this meditation and out-of-body travel, I would have thought everything I was experiencing right now was unfathomable.

Things seemed clearer in this new environment. My mind felt more lucid and agile than it had before this experience. I was thinking faster, much faster. I was analyzing multiple reasons for human existence so quickly that it seemed I was thinking three or four thoughts all at the same time. Suddenly everything came into focus. I realized it was simple. The possible reasons for how and why we came to exist were not endless. There were only three. All the religious, philosophical, and scientific theories I could think of boiled down to three basic solutions.

Suddenly I was turning upward and outward, struggling to keep my center and not be pulled out of myself. This experience was very different than the one I had during the car accident nine years ago. I could see a bright Light that wanted to envelop me. The Light drew me forward. I think I wanted to go with it, but would the Light devour me? Did it want to eradicate me in its bright flames? With that thought, a calmness washed over and through me. I must get my thoughts in order. It's the only way I can stop spinning out of control. Yet I knew I was in no danger. It was as if I was being summoned to a special place in the Universe.

Where was I? What had I been thinking? About the origin of the Universe and the idea that there were only three possible solutions to the riddle life and of how we got here. The first explanation was that the whole Universe just appeared, alakazam and presto-change-o, out of nothing. I rejected that idea instantly. It didn't make sense; it went in one brain cell and out another. Everything we experience has a purpose. There were two possibilities left. Either a personal beginning or an impersonal beginning. The Universe was ultimately the result of either impersonal "matter" configured by time plus chance, or it could be that the Universe was created by a purposeful, thinking entity. It was either a random process or a living creator — "A" or "B."

On an earthly scale, every action has a reaction; every choice has a consequence. What if, oh God, what if our choices and actions on the earth somehow impact this strange afterlife, or our next life, if any? That's what Grammie Hemphill always taught me. We are creating our next lifetime with the actions and decisions we make in this lifetime. I wish I'd thought more about consequences. Then it occurred to me that maybe earthly life, which I suddenly realized was very short, actually could be a kind of preparation for an ultimate union with the creator. How fabulous that would be.

The golden amber figure of light ahead of me was glowing brighter now. I tried to dismiss the suspicion that it was an angel. Probably the vibrating Light was just some kind of cosmic glare, or maybe my eyes were just dazzled. No, the entity was still there, its amber Light getting brighter all the time. It kept traveling along, just ahead of me. Oh, Lord, what if this was an escort? Where was it taking me to? Did I really want to go wherever that was? Did I have a choice?

The glowing Light was now joined by others. Some were made of various colored lights. But there were others too, and they had no

Light at all. They were the shadows of shadows, or darkness intensified, the opposite of matter, black holes. They seemed ominous and full of treachery. Then I realized they were all clothed in white, and the darkness was a reflection of the background behind them. As I looked closer, the brighter objects began to far outnumber the darker ones.

The darkness continued to brighten and the mist gradually dispersed. I had the distinct impression I was drawing near something important, but what it was I didn't know.

CHAPTER 11

The Journey of the Soul
Mentor — My New Guide

MY HEART WAS BEATING FAST. I had to prepare. Prepare for what? Oh, I wish I had paid more attention when I had time! Where was I? The world came into being in one of two possible ways, there's just no way around it: a) personal and b) impersonal. Since reality cannot have emerged out of absolute nothingness, something has to be eternal, either matter or a personal being. What are the implications of each? One would tend to have moral, ethical, and relational overtones, whereas the other would not. Was God truly a personal God? I was terrified. I was running out of time.

The Light was bright, and its attraction was irresistible. My falling upwards came to a full stop. Suddenly, I heard beautiful, tone perfect, chanting. There was a group of people, dressed in orange robes, sitting in a circle chanting. Love and devotion rippled through my mind and spirit with the rhythm of the music. Peace fell upon me like a soft, warm blanket.

Then the music stopped, and all of the figures bowed in devotion. What? Why, I thought. I slowly turned around and with a sharp, deep gasp, fell to my knees. In an oblong circle of White Light stood a female figure holding a ring of flowers. She was dress in blue and her head was covered with a white shawl.

"Close is the beat of my heart, when I fall at the feet of the Divine Mother," William's song flowed through my mind.

"Behold, Elizabeth, it is I."

Tears flowing down, I whispered, "I'm dead. I'm dead. How wonderful. How wonderful."

"No dear one, you're not dead. You are very much alive. I have brought you here to ask you to work with me on the earth plane."

I instantly fell at Her feet. "Divine Mother, I surrender to you. Thy will be done."

"You will become my spokesperson on the earth plane. You are here to attend some other world classes and to meet your new guide, Mentor, who will work with you upon your return." Mary said, smiling.

Her smile, brighter that the brightest white, enveloped me. Humbled, my own feelings of unworthiness filled me. "How could I ever possibly do this?" my quivering body asked.

The Divine Mother walked over to me and explained, "You are on a timeline that created the perfect opening for this work to be done. Your ancestors and relatives on both sides have accomplished great things on earth; from Alfred Kinsey to Grammie Hemphill. Out of the four girls, you are the one who chose to advance and raise your vibration. Your prayers and desires have been answered. However, it won't be at all easy for you, Elizabeth. You must finish up your old karma, and begin the new training simultaneously.

"You will learn more about pain, release, surrender, and letting go." She continued. "You will be taken to the unexplored regions of the unconscious and its mysteries will be revealed. You will bring a new healing service and chakra system to the planet, so the souls housed there can advance and raise their vibration, voluntarily."

The Light vibration was so intense, I felt as if I was disappearing into the Bliss. "How can I ever achieve the necessary physical and mental state to carry out this precious mission?"

"It's your karma, Elizabeth. You can and will achieve this." Mary replied. "You will be given the energy and ability to do so. You will write many teaching books, but the ninth book the world will embrace with its lessons of Truth."

Not quite comprehending what I was in for, I replied, "Your will is my will."

Then an amazing thing happened. Mary took the wreath of flowers she held and placed them on my head. Taking a moment to lift up my chin and look deep into my eyes, She whispered, "Thank you for being with me at the cross," as she leaned over to kiss my cheek.

Instantly, I collapsed at the impact of Her kiss, and fell into a divine swoon.

Suddenly I was in a great hall. It was filled with Light—exquisite, living Light, brilliant, quiet, with *an out-of-this-world* peace about it. Whatever had happened I could not fathom.

A moment before I had been kneeling at the feet of the Divine Mother. Now I was in a place I had never been in before. I glanced ahead and saw someone coming towards me—someone—and then a cry of joy escaped my lips. "Oh, Joe, Joe."

He smiled in such a tender and amused way, with such a gentle love, I had to shake the tears out of my eyes.

"Tell me about what's happening here," I cried. "Oh Joe, tell me all about it."

"You never doubted, as you passed through your journey of tests, Beth. How wonderful of you. Your not doubting is what allowed you become a part of this new energy vibration. Later you will meet your new guide and he will assist you in writing the things that are yours to tell."

"How marvelous," I exclaimed, "How very marvelous."

My Beth, how very proud of you I am."

"You're proud of me?" I gasped in surprise.

"Of course, my dear. You've overcome the darkness. When you reached for me that night of the car accident, the entire Universe was aware and listened. Your words will live forever, my precious one.

"Then I can stay? We can go on together?" I cried eagerly. From the beginning of this experience I had the inner feeling that I would have to return to earth, and my daily routine of normal, mortal living.

"Not yet, Beth. Not yet. You and I are true soul mates and we belong together, but for a little while our assignments are on different planes. You still have your body."

"I do?" I asked surprised. "Then what am I doing here, now? How on earth did I get here?"

"You rent the fabric of the veil of unbelief. But come along, Beth. They're waiting for you."

"Who?"

"*The Great White Brotherhood of Light*—the assembly and noble great ones whom God has reserved for Himself, which the earth plane knows not of. You are now in your new Soul Pod, which you attained by raising your vibrational frequency in earth. You have new guides as well as a new Soul teacher, *Mentor*. He is assigned to this pod by Saint Michael, who heads up all of the Angels who dwell in the Seventh Dimension. You have just completed one of the journeys of the Soul."

Joe took me to a large beautifully wood carved door that opened at our approach.

"Enter, my darling Elizabeth and always remember that I shall see you again in time."

I quickly reached out my hand to stop him, but he was already moving away. Immediately I was ushered into this great assembly.

The place, room, temple, assembly room, whatever you want to call it was like nothing I had ever before beheld. It was immense in its unbelievable expanse and majesty. There are no words in any language to describe the awe and magnificence of it.

There was music—*Ardas*—prayer beyond prayer—chanting through my soul, only more glorious, more triumphant, more divine. My inner melody was but a faint echo of this heavenly song of Universal triumph. There were no words. It was more than sound. It became a vibration *of power*, so alive that it could be felt and seen. It was Light— the great Light of Almighty God as it flowed out from the bosom of eternity, to create, to manifest, and to redeem; to make alive, to exist, to uplift, to exalt and to glorify. It was the great divine Light of Christ consciousness, the very power of existence and creation of life.

I called this ancient mantra, *Ardas*, my song of gratitude. It was that. It became my "Thank You" prayer of loving devotion. With deep gratitude, every blessing multiplied a hundred-fold, almost automatically. As my gratitude increased, my blessings increased. It was the complete fulfillment of multiplying and replenishing the blessings on earth. Through gratitude I could transmute tragedy into joy, failure into success, loss into blessings, sickness into health—darkness into Light. The Law of Thanks-giving and gratitude is the Divine Law of multiplication. It is the Law that brings forth the creation and manifestation of increase.

As gratitude poured into my being in its complete fullness, I realized the purpose and the power of such infinite harmony. It is the song of love, devotion and gratitude that can clothe one in complete glory. It is the celestial symphony of the Universe. It is the *"new song"* that is not understood through words but felt and released from the center of the Soul. It is divine, perfect Love. It is developed and strengthened from within by being grateful for every little blessing received—and those little blessings will begin to multiply.

The utterly magnificent room was circular in its immense dimensions of breathtaking grandeur. There were rows upon rows of people seated within the ever-expanding circle. I recognized these people as some of the shadows I had seen during my upward fall. They were all dressed in white, and many had just arrived. They were the Souls who had recently passed over.

The floor seemed to be made of glass, or clear quartz crystal, or perhaps one large perfect diamond. It reflected light and the rainbow spectrum of colors with sparkling brilliance. Only the center, about a twenty-foot space, was open and occupied by just one person.

The individual standing in the center welcomed me forward. I walked down one of the many aisles that led from the great doors to the outer walls of the great assembly room, into that inner open space. It is most difficult to describe the celestial magnitude of the experience.

The individual presiding over this particular assembly was glory personified. A great love and light flowed from his being, his robes, his eyes, his very fingertips. I could not stand in this place, before such hallowed ones. I sat down upon my knees and bowed my head in a profound reverence to be in the presence of Mentor. My flowing tears washed my face.

With an indescribable smile, Mentor greeted me, "Arise, Elizabeth, and welcome to your new soul school. We have been waiting for you."

Then I heard, or rather felt, every voice in that vast assembly hall whisper softly, "Welcome, Elizabeth." I had the sudden feeling that I knew each and every individual in that divine assembly, as though I were clasping and shaking their hand, and they mine. Every trace of self-consciousness vanished, and I stood up straight, while a great white light seemed to pour over me and through me.

Mentor spoke to me telepathically, "The whole heavens are rejoicing over you, Elizabeth, for you have been able to pass through the veil of blindness and unbelief.

"The veil of blindness and unbelief?" I repeated, for I had recalled Joe saying the same thing, and I desired to know the meaning of those words.

"Yes, you have pulled back the fabric of the veil of unbelief. It is only this veil that shuts mankind out and away from us.

"Recently, that veil has grown more solid than steel, or concrete, or marble, or any known physical substance in existence. Its density has increased through the ages. It is built from the very hardness of men's hearts, which have now become harder than any other substance in the universe. It is re-enforced through the blindness of their minds and woven of gross wickedness. A completely hardened heart is one of the most wicked conditions possible to attain. It is often caused by minds that *will not see*. This condition does not belong just to the criminals. Often their hearts are softer than one who calls himself a saint. When you choose to believe all things, you make all things possible.

"Raising your vibration and creating the ability to change soul schools in one lifetime has been next to impossible before the 1960's.

However, a soul enters the body on earth for a specific purpose and mission. The purpose is to grow in love, to shed any previous lifetime attachments, prejudices, and judgments and to embrace the steadfast, ever-loving universe. Each lifetime brings the soul closer to the heartbeat of God. The 1960's was a game changer because children were born with stronger DNA, more strands of DNA, along with extra spiritual powers and insights. These are your indigo, rainbow, and crystal children, and some autistic children as well. In the millennium teens, we will have the new souls of the *far-seeing children* being born, who will eventually help to bring about peace on earth,

"The overcoming of unbelief is accomplished mostly by those who offer up their broken hearts upon the altar of God, without rebellion, bitterness or self-pity. It must be offered with a love and devotion from a place of truly desiring God's will to be accomplished, rather than the influence of the ego. Therefore it becomes a dedication of thanks, or praise, or divine love that can melt the heart completely. Thus the veil can be lifted by anyone on earth who desires the perfect gift of grace and divine love. It is the offering of a broken heart, mingled with melting, inner tenderness that overcomes the unbelief. It can pull back the veil to see through its screen.

"Millions of people on earth are suffering from heartbreak." I offered.

"Yes, Elizabeth, but they are misusing their greatest instrument of divine glory. Instead of offering their heartbreak to God in praise and thanksgiving for the power it contains, and truly desiring the cleansing heartbreak to continue, if it be His will, they harden their hearts even more. This increases the tears in their eyes, and the darkness in their souls. Over time, the great veil becomes more impenetrable.

"Glory and grace to all who can pierce this veil." I felt those words echo and vibrate through the hall, while breathed in and out simultaneously by the multitude gathered.

"We cannot rend the veil for anyone on earth because it is made of mortal vibrations, and only man can rend it. Each individual must do this for himself, and each one who accomplishes this makes it easier for those who follow, especially if they are on the ancestral time line. This is why the heavens have rejoiced over your accomplishment, Elizabeth. You finally took your heartbreak and offered it to God, with no restrictions, along with the very power and weight of your burdens. When that energy was transmuted, it could rend the veil for you. You allowed your heart to become softened, instead of hardened, by the experience of losing your husband so suddenly and quickly, as well as other sorrows. You could learn to believe and trust without question, without doubt.

"It is heartbreak that causes the hard heart to crack, or open—and that opening can be used for advancement. This experience is overwhelming in its full manifestation. Sadly, some people reinforce their internal heartache, sealing it in the sorrow and shriveling up to the very fibers of the soul. Each individual gets to choose how he reacts to his feelings of sorrow and loss. The grace of God's power of Light can descend upon him, or the blindness and bitterness of hell can enfold him in darkness forever."

"How divine. How beautiful it is to know these things," I cried. I was filled with the marvel and wonder of the simplicity of it all.

"Yes, it is beautiful. As for you, Elizabeth, the veil is gone forever. You can pass through it, to and fro, as the occasion requires.

"You must return back to earth, because there is still a great amount of work for you to do on the earth plane. You are needed there in your tangible, mortal form. Your work will be varied, according to the needs of those you meet. Many will resist your message, but the ones who are open and listen will find their lives changed and their vibrations lifted up forever.

"You must allow yourself to love again, Elizabeth. This is very important because you will write about it, uplifting hearts and bringing hope to the disillusioned. Life continues after loss, and the soul has the ability to be raised up to higher levels because of loss. To dwell on it and allow the loss to envelope your consciousness seals you off from potential soul growth.

All who walk the planet need to experience this lesson. This knowledge will lift much pain and suffering as well as the base tendency of reciprocity. A human being can never right a wrong without the divine power of Grace, which only God can give. This is natural law.

"You will also be privileged to write an account of your near death experience, or out-of-body experience, however you want to say it. If you need help, your invisible guides will help you."

Mentor ceased speaking and I glanced at the multitudes surrounding me. I felt their loving energy pouring out to me. I felt I knew each and every one of them—that our hearts blended as one, in complete, everlasting unity. I was sure they each knew me, perhaps better that I knew myself, or them. They had witnessed my progress throughout many lifetimes, had given me their strength and support, and had directed Light my way as I accepted their offer of help.

How one mortal body could endure the grace and greatness of this experience was mine to keep within my heart. I do not know how all this happened except that, perhaps, my body quickened with a higher vibration, directed by the spirit of God.

These great beings were clothed, but not in any kind of cloth material, but pure, spun Light. It was glorified light, blazing in splendor—a living, vibrating, eternal Light.

There were both men and women in this meeting hall. All were as one in the great love they sent out to enfold all, the earth, mankind, and the universe.

The vibrations of that song, *Ardas,* that had been developing in my heart was their song. It was the very song that only God and the righteous can learn, *prayer beyond prayer.* It had only been a faint echo in my soul, yet that faint echo had become a part of my living power of fulfillment. Then I realized why it's one of the oldest mantras known. It is the pure vibration of gratitude and love along with praise and pure devotion. When any heart opens, even a tiny crack, to permit the rhythm and tune to enter within, it heals and helps to open the soul, raising the vibration to manifest even greater things.

When this precious melody of love becomes the living essence of one's being, its power begins to manifest. It is the vibration of spontaneous, glorified life itself. It is for all mankind to express and those who only will develop the "ears to hear," which means the power to *feel*. The song will become a power of ever increasing strength. Each individual who develops the power to hear it has the ability to multiply its volume and send it out to touch the burdened hearts of a weary world. That mantra song is a prayer, a spontaneous prayer, pure and undefiled. It is not a "God give me" prayer. He who sings this song in his soul shall receive grace and peace. Born of love, it is a song of great gratitude. The things of this earth shall be added to him one-hundred fold.

Ardas was the song, an inner song of praise, that lifted me from a lifetime of grief and loss to a rebirth, a life a hundred fold better. Yet this power of improving and increasing is not the song's full purpose. The power to multiply blessings is the foundation upon which it operates.

Ardas' purpose is to open and melt the heart so the veil of unbelief can be conquered. It produces and develops a love so great that all things melt before it. It contains a love that forgets itself completely. With such infinite tenderness, the heart desires only His will be done. It completes this letting-go process of all personal disappointments and desires—and then and only then can a person find grace and peace, for that alone is His will.

It was then that I understood pain, suffering, and heartbreak in their true Light—and not as a punishment sent by God. They are a blessing that contains the keys for soul progress. Light, power, and complete dominion over body and mind. In themselves they were just what they appeared to be, unbearable burdens, but when accepted and enfolded in the faith and love of man they can be transmuted into utter glory. Man has true dominion over them, if he can but just learn to use this gift. Loss and sorrow contain the power of turning darkness into light, poverty into plenty, heartbreak into ecstasy, pain into joy. Within man are the keys. The power and dominion to rule over the inner turmoil of the mind, to subdue them, be thankful for the lessons they bring, and release them. Otherwise, man can be destroyed by them.

How simple it was when you understand. Truly the "Mysteries of Godliness" are but the mysteries of the great but simple truths of Natural Law. The understanding of these laws is eternal truth—the truth, which if used, will make one forever free.

Mentor's first lesson

Suddenly there was a shift in the great hall, and all eyes were focused on me. Then the great teacher, Mentor, began to speak.

"Look closely, Elizabeth, and get a clear view of the world," spoke the soft, vibrating, penetrating voice of the Master One leading the assembly. "The greatest drama of the universe is being enacted upon the earth at the present time. Your planet is at a stage the entire universe has been anticipating. This drama is almost over. The climax is drawing near.

"Mankind is in an extremely difficult situation; a severe test or trial occurring in the second decade of the new millennium is coming. During this era, different social forces or intellectual influences come together and cause new worldwide developments.

"The powers that be, the forces of Light and darkness, are pouring out their energies, for we are approaching Judgment Day, not as it has been understood, but as it is in the earth's reality. It is not just a day, as man has been thinking, but an era, a period of time, in which each man must judge himself. Is he prepared and ready to ascend into a new world, the *realms of light*, or will he continue in the inferior world, to progress slowly through the coming ages? Each man sets his own pace, continues at his own speed, and makes his own choices. It is almost possible to predict the exact future of each individual. For the seeds they plant within their hearts, and abide by, such they will reap. This is the law of character development.

"No one needs to be told which tree in the orchard will produce the best crop, for it is pre-determined with the planting of the seeds. Those who sow with the wind must reap the whirlwind. For some, the second death is all they have left," added the guide.

"The second death?" I held my hand to my heart and took several deep breaths. "Is there really a second death?"

"Some call it an awakening, or a deeply penetrating spiritual experience, but look and you will understand the great mercy in that action. Look down at the earth, Elizabeth."

I looked down and realized that the crystal glass floor was a telescope, a great lens. From it, not knowing how or why, I was able to view the entire earth, and the inhabitants within. I saw the great forces of Light being poured down upon the earth's surface from this group, and thousands of other groups as well, in an ever increasing of brilliance. From all of the pods in all of the higher vibrations, Light was pouring out with increasing measure upon all life on earth.

This Master teacher, Mentor, took the time to explain to me that I was in a pod with a very high vibration of light. The *Many Mansions* spoken about in holy books were referring to the different dimensions, sections and levels of heaven.

"After death," Mentor explained, "the super conscious mind enters the world of after life and begin their life review. This is a *state of awareness* where we begin to judge ourselves. Hidden memories and actions of our past lives are revealed. We witness our decisions and know if we learned our life lessons. Then we are sent back to the pod the soul originated from and greeted by our loved ones. Understanding, adhering to, and absorbing love and forgiveness is the next stage. We sit with our peers and guides, and process our recent life experiences.

"Then a new pattern is designed, and a new life is planned and created. This is why souls are reborn in certain geographical areas and in certain bodies, with specific habits and mindsets.

"There are different vibrations and levels of the soul school and it is quite difficult to ascend to a higher level. The advancement of the soul can only be done through living another life in a specific location, on a specific planet, aligned with your soul's vibration. The soul levels are beginner, intermediate, advanced, and self-realization. Each level brings you to a different dwelling place automatically. It is in the self-realization level that souls train to become teachers and guides to the lower level souls. This is a great honor and must be developed and learned. One cannot ever interfere with the natural unfolding of another soul.

"Lastly, there are certain souls that must go to a place of separation, because of their cruel and evil deeds while living in the body. Those that torture, maim, and kill others, or who commit heinous crimes against groups and nations must be put in a place of solitude for some time. This is determined at the place of life review. These souls do not travel along the same wavelengths as the other souls.

"Those whose soul's character was too weak to turn away human temptations, who have been impeded by evil, or harmed others, are led into seclusion and isolation and will remain there for quite some time; until the heart begins to have the desire to open up again.

"Unless one learns to fulfill the laws of righteousness, while living on the planet earth in this lifetime, he cannot be exalted into the higher Celestial realms. Death does not create a divine being or a celestial change in anyone. It only reveals to the soul, what he really is, his worthiness or unworthiness, as the case may be. It is the complete unveiling of the *character* of the soul, of himself to himself, and is often quite shocking." Mentor concluded.

As the light poured down from the great divine realms of God, I saw many of the humble, seeking ones meditating, praying, while lifting up their heads to listen. I beheld this Light as it penetrated their hearts, just as it had mine. I saw it warm their souls as its righteousness began to increase on earth. I felt the singing of the mantra *Ardas,* a song of everlasting thanks, touch their hearts with its healing, awakening power. Then I saw their response to its glory. I saw the power of it, and the breathtaking wonder and majesty of it. I felt its magnitude and the everlasting thanksgiving in their hearts.

Mentor added, "The only people who cannot be helped are those who are sealed—either by believing that they already possess all Light and all truth—or those who are completely hardened by crime. No one in a mortal body can possibly possess all the Light—for if he could, he would no longer be mortal. But in only those who realize that they cannot and do not possess all the Light, is it possible to receive and open to receive more, and more."

Then I comprehended the constant, tender care that had been so freely given to me. My heart melted completely into tears of deep, everlasting gratitude. I beheld the literal, breath taking, wondrous feeling of fulfillment of: *"The meek shall inherit the earth,"* as it began to unfold. I saw their meekness develop and become powerful in its strength as the haughty attitude began to be cast from their high and mighty seats.

I had a moment of great difficulty as I realized that some of the proudest were leaders of the churches. As I watched and absorbed this scene, I felt an unspeakable shame come over me for them. Very few who claimed to be ambassadors or representatives of God, in whatever religion, had any God-centered traits. I bowed my head and wished with all of my soul that I could, in some way, make up for the complete mockery of their empty service.

I then focused on the commencement of the meek and the beginning of the re-dedication of the earth to them. I watched them begin to rise from their humble stations, as they were slowly being filled with light, according to their individual capacities. The light they received was the New Light from the double helix, the great amber Light emanating from the Fifth Dimension; The divine Light containing the power of the Almighty.

I was then given the Holy Anointing and the words; Mentor explained, "Elizabeth, you are ordained with a holy calling to help spread the sacred Light.

"Give it to none who are unworthy, lest it injure or consume them, I was instructed. "Allow your peace to return to you whenever you contact those who could not receive it, or who were unworthy. Pray that their soul peace is returned to their hearts.

"Give out the Light, Elizabeth. Let it shine forth, but only to the degree that each individual is prepared to receive it, lest too much at one time destroys the effort.

"Tread carefully along the sacred highway of the divine. Whenever there is a task too difficult, just call out, and someone will come. The strength of all is the power of each one of us, and this is the power of Oneness. The power of unity and of true brotherhood in the Divine," touching my heart, head, and my left hand, Mentor bowed.

The others cried out to me, "God be with you, forever and ever." The song increased in volume and splendor, and glory.

I, too, was covered with the cloth of White Light, while kneeling in the hallway of eternity, as a humble child of earth who had just completed their initiation. Then I heard, "Go back, you must go back. It's not your time to join us,"

Joe called out to me from somewhere far away. It felt like he was placing his thoughts directly into my being. "Go back, go back. There is work left that you still have to do. I release you, Elizabeth. You must learn to love again. Love never dies. It continues on forever. You must write. There are things waiting for you to learn and discover and there are things you must write about."

I didn't know whether the words were separate from me or within me. Wherever they were, I didn't want to hear them. I began to realize that my body was changed. As I reached forward, I saw an amber Light glowing through my hand and arm. I felt weightless. There were no physical limitations. I was made of Light. I could see Light passing through me. My thoughts were clear. I was aware that my new body was the double of my ordinary body, but it wasn't made of any physical material. This body was transparent Light. Any sense of time or distance was obliterated. I knew absolutely that I was one with all things. Rain and sunlight could pass through me, but I wouldn't feel them, and they wouldn't be able to affect me. I felt as if the molecular structure of my body had melted like a patch of snow in the spring sunlight.

Just as movement is unimpeded in this spiritual state, so, I discovered, is thought. I could feel ideas and images flying out of my mind, faster and faster. My thoughts became clear and effortless. They instantaneously shot outward, and the replies from Joe, came back to me just as quickly. "Go back, you must go back. You must write." The telepathic message from Joe was coming directly into my being, similar to my other experience long ago, but with more intensity and clarity.

Within the glow of the soft golden, white Light, Joe was holding his arms out, as if to stop me from turning around or coming any closer. Yet even as Mentor, gestured for me to go back to earth, a brilliant yellow Light behind Joe drew me onward. The force of love from that golden Light was immensely powerful, unlike any I had ever felt before. It was a desire that filled my entire being, and went beyond me; filling the tunnel I was back in, and all space behind and before me. I felt as if I had been returning from a very familiar place, one I recognized, longed for and loved. I hung suspended, lost in timelessness, as the clear, bright Light blinded me for a moment.

Then I surrendered to it. I received my answer in the brightness of that experience. I knew the angels, the Divine Mother, and God were real and ever present. My faith had been renewed and restored. My character, way of life, belief system, teaching, and lifetime training became an active part of my being. At that moment, all I wanted was to be completely immersed in the Light and be filled with the great love that was there. I wanted to realize and receive more and more knowledge.

Somehow I realized there had been some sort of a soul switch. I knew I would never be the same. I felt as if someone or something else was in my physical body and whatever it was, I knew it would be a vast improvement. I was aware that I had given permission for whatever was going on; I realized that I was on a new life path that would need training and refinement,

A part of me floated back into the golden Light beyond. A new awareness and new body emerged, as if I had been reborn. I knew I had had been given the golden key to the Universe. Whatever was I to do with it?

Upon entering back into my earth body, I stretched and moaned, and slowly opened my eyes, enveloped in a migraine headache. William and Dini were nearby, carefully monitoring my sleeping body.

"She's had a healing," Dini exclaimed.

"Go get her some ginger tea," William instructed, "She needs water."

Well trained in First Aid, William checked my vital signs. "Elizabeth," he said gently, "You've been in an unconscious state for three days. I knew you were okay because of your body movements. We all knew you were having a healing because, at one point, you were surrounded by a light blue halo Light that filled the entire room."

"Tell us what happened," Dini said excitedly as she brought back the cup of tea.

My head was pounding and I simply could not speak.

"We need to leave her here in quiet," William explained. "She's not fully back yet. Stay here Elizabeth, and rest. In about an hour I'll come back and take you for a walk. You need grounding."

William returned an hour later and we went out the back to walk slowly up the lower side of Haleakala. It still wasn't easy to speak, or find balance to walk, but William hung on to my arm as we moved along.

I knew I could never explain all that had occurred on my journey. I told him that I had met some great prophets and had been to the Divine Mother's Loca. I had gone through a transformation that I needed to process, accept, and understand.

"Elizabeth, you have had an incredible experience, something that the sages, prophets, and spiritual leaders can only guess about. People have meditated and prayed for lifetimes and have never come close to what you just encountered." William explained in amazement.

"William, the retreat is almost over. We go home the day after tomorrow, and I really don't want to talk much. I just want to take it all inside, meditate, and prepare for my return home." I shared. "I want to go into silence until we leave for Hana tomorrow."

Smiling, William completely understood. He became very protective of me through those hours. When we were driving back to Hana to catch the plane back to Newark Airport in New Jersey, I leaned over to hug and kiss him on the cheek.

"Thank you for everything, William, and especially for protecting me and saving my life." I said, smiling with deep feelings of wonder and gratitude.

I felt like I was done with Hawaii, done with the Clear Light Group, and on a new path. Whatever transformation I had been through was profound, and had changed my life forever.

As I dozed on the flight home, I heard Mentor's words over and over. *"We are all Light beings working through the earth experience. By accepting God's love, we are fueled to expand love to our families, community, loved ones, and to ourselves. Always remember, Elizabeth, to love every breath, every moment, everyone, and everything. This is the path to Ascension."*

CHAPTER 12

The Divine Mother Gave Me a New Home

IN OCTOBER OF 1987, MY second fall in the Mahwah condo at Ramapo Ridge, Bill, the realtor stopped by for a visit. He had some paperwork and a newspaper article with him. "I don't think you should renew your lease here," he began.

"Why?" I interrupted. "I love it here."

"I am sure the landlord will raise the rent beyond your reach. New Jersey has just passed laws to allow Affordable Housing, and Mahwah had been chosen as one of the towns to build them. I brought you the newspaper article about it, and the papers you need to fill out to apply for HUD housing. I am sure you would qualify.

"They are building 3,000 condo units right around the corner on Ridge Road, and it would be better for you to own property." Bill explained. "Also, put Vance on as living with you. That way you can get a larger two-bedroom unit. Even if he doesn't live there, you could use the space. You will need the last three years of tax returns for both you and Vance."

Bill guided me with the paperwork over the next three days. We finally got it into the mail, tax returns and all. "I hope you'll hear before your lease is up in April," Bill said.

Within a week after mailing out the paperwork, Evelyn came and told me she had to move back to New York, and I would no longer have a roommate. "What am I going to do?" I whined. "The rent is up to a thousand dollars and I can't pay it all myself."

"Why don't you go down to Teterboro Airport and try to get one of the pilots to rent a room? After all, you did that after Jeffrey moved out and went to Lehigh." Evelyn suggested. "Maybe you'll get lucky."

That's exactly what I wound up doing. Evelyn moved out around Thanksgiving of 1987, and Bret, an American Airlines pilot, moved in on the first of December.

Nowhere in my consciousness was the memory of the dream I had before I moved into Sunset Court. Mary had said, "I will give you this place for two years, and you will love it."

The day that Bret moved in, I had a strong psychic impression. He was explaining to me that he never knew how long he would stay in one place, because he moved as American Airlines demanded, so he would rent on a month-to-month basis.

"You'll be moving out on March 18th!" I exclaimed.

"Oh great, someone tells me the day I'm moving out on the day I'm moving in," he retorted. We both had a good laugh.

Rooming with Brett was perfect. He was hardly ever there, always paid the rent on time, and was cheerful. I enjoyed that brief time with him.

On March 18th, 1988 two things happened. Around 10:00 am the phone rang for Bret. It was American Airlines, transferring him to Washington D.C. immediately.

About two hours later, the mail came, containing a letter from Hackensack's Bergen County Affordable Housing. Vance and I had been accepted into the HUD Program and could buy housing in either Haveninan or Ridge Gardens.

Like most people who really don't like change, I reacted by digging my heels in the ground. I did not want to move from Sunset Court. In my blindness, I was sure I could get another pilot as a roommate. I did not even consider a possible rent hike.

Suddenly life became a bit complicated. The lease was up on April 1st; the units being offered were not built yet; the pilots I interviewed were angry, contentious, and no one I wanted to share my home with. I really had to take some time to meditate and think.

On the Spring Equinox, I was visiting some friends in Milford, Pennsylvania. One of them, Roy, was a realtor so I shared my dilemma with him. "Go and see the property, Elizabeth," he suggested. "At least get an idea of what is offered. Let me know if I can help you in any way. You've helped so many people in this area, as well as raised a lot of funds for the humane society here. You deserve to own your own home."

Reluctantly, I went to see the Ridge Gardens condos the next day. I liked their design better than the other choices.

"Hi, I'm looking for one of the HUD condo's. Where can I see a model?" I asked the front desk attendant.

"Oh my, I'm not sure there are any left," she anxiously responded. "We only have two buildings set aside, with various style and sizes, and they're going fast. Especially the one and two bedrooms."

"I'd like to at least look at one," I said, with a worried look on my face.

"We don't have any HUD styles to show you, but look and the general one bedroom, and you'll get the idea. The HUD buildings are down in the back, and not complete yet."

"When do you expect we could take occupancy?" I asked back.

"Supposedly by mid-August," she responded. "You go ahead over and walk through the model, and I'll go and check to see what's available for you. A two bedroom. Right?

Smiling and shaking my head, "Yes," I headed toward the building across the street for the walk through. I was lucky I was alone, because the force of light and energy that day was overpowering. As I walked through the front door and headed towards the kitchen, I sensed starlight pouring on me. That's correct, starlight, like Tinkerbell. Closing my eyes for a moment and falling into a light swoon, I saw Mentor once again.

The telepathic message was, *"You must move out of Sunset Court by the first of April, Elizabeth. The lease is up and you must return the property back to the owner, Your invisible angels and guides will be supporting you through this change, which will be better for you as well as benefit both you and Vance. There are many people who will be of help to you. You will spend the summer in Ridgewood at your office complex, and work part time in a law office. When you pack, be sure to include a warm sweater because you'll need one. This condo is your gift from the Universe. Trust where you are being led."*

My head was spinning, and I was gasping for breath. Then suddenly, the vision was gone, and I began to feel strength, security, and a feeling this was right for me. Slowly, I walked back to the Ridge Gardens condo office. The girl had just returned as well.

"There is only one unit left," she told me with a smile.

"Well, I have to be on the first floor," I responded.

"You are. The number is 1502 and it's on Faulkner Court. It will be down in the back of Faulkner, near the woods and a little creek. It's not built yet, but you can drive over and see the property."

Here is a map of where the building will be located. I need a $3,500 deposit and you're good to go."

I took in a deep breath, wondering where that was going to come from, and said to her, "Can I come back tomorrow afternoon with the check? I will fill out the papers then."

"Well, if you fill out the papers now, to show good intent, I will hold it for twenty-four hours for you. We close at four pm everyday, so you will have to be here before then."

Taking the stack of forms from her, I replied, "Don't worry, I'll be here." With a shaking hand, I filled out the papers, simply trusting the universe.

It was late afternoon when I arrived back at Sunset Court. "Oh my, what have I done?" I thought. "How will this ever work out for me?" Then I reminded myself of Louise Hay's affirmation, *"I am safe, its only change."* Slowly I began to relax and accept what was coming my way. Louise taught us to go with the flow of our thoughts. I decided to do just that now.

I knew the owner of Ridgewood Movers from high school. Robert Meyers, I need to call Robert Meyers. Going along with my thoughts, I picked up the phone and called him.

"Hi Robert, how are you doing? I need to move and keep my things in storage for awhile.

"When Elizabeth? We're pretty busy."

"I have to be out of this condo by the end of this month."

"Wow, that's hardly enough time. Can I come by tomorrow to see what this will entail? How about noontime?"

"Okay, that's fine, and thank you," I said, feeling very thankful that this could be managed.

"It will be good to see you again, Elizabeth."

Okay, one down and a few to go. While I was cooking dinner, two more thoughts came to me. One was to call Roy in Milford, PA, and the other was to ask Maureen if I could stay in our office on Wilsey Square for the summer. We had a shower and a galley kitchen. Each massage room had a futon, so I knew I would be just fine. I had absolutely no fear.

It was early evening. I still had time to call Roy. "Hi Roy, how are you doing? I saw the condos today and found out there is only one two-bedroom left. Luckily it's on the first floor. The only thing is they need $3,500 by tomorrow. I filled out the paperwork and they're holding it for me until tomorrow at four."

"That's okay, Elizabeth. I have to go into New York City tomorrow and can drop off a check for the deposit to you on my way in."

I could not believe my ears. Taking in a deep breath, I asked, "What?"

"I've already discussed it with my wife, and we both agreed to give you the down payment, however, we will need it back at some point. We can make payment arrangements. I figure you may need a year to get it back to us."

"Oh, how can I ever thank you?" I gasped.

"You already have," he answered.

I'll meet you in Mahwah around nine in the morning? I'll come to Sunset Court, as it's right off the New York State Thruway. Just have the coffee ready."

Okay, I will and thank you so much."

Next was Maureen, the woman I was renting office space from in Ridgewood. I had just expanded into two more rooms with large closets. I knew I could manage there until the new condo was completed. She agreed but stressed that I could not stay much longer than the end of September. I felt certain that would work out as well.

Well, March 22, 1988 was certainly a day to remember. I felt as if I had moved heaven and earth, but it was only the beginning, After all, when the Holy Mother arranges housing for you, how could you not expect anything less than one miracle after another?

Roy arrived at 9:00 am as planned, and Robert arrived at noontime. "You have a lot of stiff here, Elizabeth." Robert said. "I thought it was a small one-story condo, not two sprawling floors. This is such a nice place. Why are you moving?"

"I'm buying one of the HUD units around the corner at Ridge Gardens, and my lease is up here on April 1st."

"Well, my estimate for moving is $980 and that does not include $120 a month storage."

I gulped. "I can do the monthly storage easily, but the $980 will be difficult."

"Hmmm. Where did you get that unique and beautiful kitchen table, Elizabeth?" Robert asked.

"Oh it's really a dining room table, but I took the leaves out so it would fit in the kitchen. It was imported from Denmark and is solid teak. It cost me over $1.500 and I do love it."

We can barter for your move. I like it a lot and I know my wife will love it. How about you sell it to me for $800 and then pay $180 for me to move all of your items into storage?" He asked with anticipation. It comes with four chairs?"

"Six," I replied, closing my eyes. I took another one of those deep breaths, and knew I had to *let go*. "Okay," I agreed, "we can do that."

"I want to move you on Friday, if that's okay. We are really busy, but if you pack everything up for me, I can get you out of here in four hours or less."

"Friday is the first of April," I replied. "I'll have to clear it with the landlord."

"If not then, we'll have to go into April. Let me know by tomorrow night. Okay?"

"Okay Robert, and thanks," I said weakly, still in a daze over everything that had transpired. "I'm pretty sure it will be okay."

As soon as Robert left, I jumped in the car, took Roy's check to the bank to deposit, and headed over to the Ridge Gardens sales office.

When I walked in the door, the sales girl was arguing with a man. When she saw me she grinned and said, "I'm so glad you were able to make it here early, Elizabeth. This man is the head contractor for Ridge Gardens. He wanted me to null and void your contract because someone came with cash in hand. Did you bring the deposit check?"

"Yes, I have it," I smiled with relief. I sat down, wrote out the check, and felt a wisp of wind go right through my heart. I knew I had just achieved an accomplishment.

Well, that was done, I had made a commitment and now I had to get busy moving. My mind was racing with a list of things that needed to get done. But before I could start the car and drive away, I took a moment. Bowing my head, I gripped the wheel for steadiness, and gave thanks to God, Mary, Mentor, and everyone else who was included in this awesome divine play. "Thank you, Spirit, thank you."

That evening Bill, the realtor, telephoned to see how I was doing with my HUD application. I told him the whole story and he was awestruck.

"How about I call the landlord for you, Elizabeth. I'm sure it will be okay, especially if new people can move in after noontime." Bill suggested.

"That would be great, Bill, thank you."

"You will need to write him a letter tonight to tell him you plan to move out. I'll come over to get it in the morning and bring you some packing boxes. I'm going to have to rent the place as soon as I can. I'll be able to help you pack as well."

Okay, I'll have the coffee on. See you then."

It's lucky that I had nine days to pack because I needed every minute of it.

I got settled in the office in Ridgewood and continued seeing my clients. I was a bit concerned because summer was approaching, and business always slowed down, sometimes coming to a halt. I knew I had to save money for the closing on the new condo and pondered what to do. Then one of those thoughts came to me. I had certainly learned to pay attention by now.

The summer before, through a temp agency, I had worked for a wonderful attorney in Livingston, New Jersey. It was a calm, comfortable legal, accounting, and property management firm. His assistant, Elaine, took the summer off to be with her children. I wondered if I could arrange to work for him again this summer?

Oh what was his name? If only I could remember his name. The temp agency had closed, but I remembered that his first name was Allen. They were both Allen, but the other partner spelled the name differently, Alan. I decided to meditate on it.

In the morning, I awoke with many thoughts racing through my head. All of a sudden I got it. Allen Nimensky, Nimensky and Gallenson, CPA, on South Livingston Ave. I knew the area a bit. Another lawyer friend of mine had his office on South Livingston Ave.

I found the phone number and called the office. Richie, his computer assistant, answered. "Mr. Nimensky isn't here. Who's calling?

Hi Richie, it's Elizabeth Joyce. I worked at your office last summer and wondered if a position was available this year?"

"Can't say, Elizabeth. Why don't you call Allen at his summer home at the shore?"

"Are you sure that's okay? What's the number?"

I gave Allen a call, telling him I had an offer he could not refuse. I explained that I had bought property and needed a summer job. Could I work for him again this summer? I told him I would save him money because the agency had closed, so there would be no fee. I also asked if he would be my lawyer and close the property for me. He agreed to four days a week, to be my real estate lawyer, and I began work the first Tuesday in June.

I'm set, I thought. Got the temporary housing, got the job, and now all I have to do is watch my new building go up. Oh sure!

Right after the Fourth of July holiday, Mr. Nimensky came to me with my real estate file. "Elizabeth, something is wrong here," he said, scratching his head in a funny way. "When are you going to get your mortgage?"

"What mortgage? I'm not getting any mortgage." I said ignorantly.

"You mean you haven't started the mortgage process yet? You only have three more days to get a mortgage, or you lose your deposit and the property goes back up for sale." He said, startled.

Believe it or not, I was flabbergasted. In all of my meditations, moving, finding work, I had not once even thought about a mortgage. Not once. It never entered my consciousness. I knew one thing, I could not get one, and would not need one; Trust, Trust.

I didn't know what to say to Allen. "I'm not getting a mortgage and I know it will all work out."

In silence, Allen stared at me. He stared at me for a while, then he said, "Well if you don't buy this condo, I will. This is way too good a deal to pass on."

The tears came on my drive home that night. When I got back to Ridgewood and the Wilsey Square office parking lot, I was still in shock. I decided to take a walk and try to calm down. I walked up Franklin Ave. and through some side streets. I kept telling myself, "You'll be alright." I talked to God. I began to release the property. "I'll be alright. I don't have to live in Mahwah, I can find a small room or apartment; maybe something in a two family house. It's okay if I'm not supposed to have the property. I know I'll survive and be okay." I had overcome so many disappointments in my life, but it was a bit difficult to work through this one. "Thy will be done," I concluded.

Then I quietly returned to my car and took a drive up to Ridge Gardens Condominiums. I drove down Mark Twain Way to Faulkner Court, turned left and drove to the back of Faulkner Court. I parked in front of Building Fifteen, took a deep breath, closed my eyes, went within and asked for guidance. The two HUD buildings, Fourteen and Fifteen were not built yet. In fact, they had just laid the foundations and the joists were up. I realized the buildings would never be completed by mid-August. I smiled, remembering the packing instructions; hold on to a warm sweater because you will need it. I had a few fall outfits in my small wardrobe at Wilsey Square.

As I came into the back door of the office, the phone was ringing. It was around 8:30 pm. I was emotionally spent, but decided to answer it anyway. "Hi Elizabeth, it's your cousin George down in Virginia. How is everything going with you?"

"Okay, I guess," I said, slightly out of breath.

"Carol and I felt a bit concerned about you tonight, for some reason. How is the HUD property sale coming along?"

Fighting back the tears, I began to explain to George my dilemma. "It seems that I may lose my bid on the property. I need $40,000 and just cannot come up with that amount of cash. I don't believe I could qualify for a mortgage either," I sighed.

"Just a minute dear, hold on." George was whispering to his wife, Carol.

"Elizabeth, we want to send you half the funds, but we just cannot afford to send you out all of it. We can overnight you a $20,000 check tomorrow morning. How's that?"

My head was spinning, I choked as I began to speak. "Oh George, thank you. I just don't know what to say."

"How should I make the check out?"

I paused to think for a moment, then from somewhere deep inside, I said, "Make the check out to my attorney. He'll put the check into his trust account, and if the sale should fall through for any reason, he will return the funds to you." I proceeded to spell out Mr. Nimensky's name and business address.

"That's a great idea, Elizabeth. Just know that you deserve to have a good home that you own, without a mortgage. I'm sure it will all work out for you.

"You have been so good to Uncle Fred and are always there when the family needs you. Carol and I are pleased with all you have done. Just know we love and support you. The check will go out in the morning." George replied.

As I hung up the phone, the floor was back up on the ceiling again. I found it difficult to believe what had just happened. Gratitude and a little bit of fear flowed from my heart. I only wanted a hot cup of tea and then bed.

I was sleeping on a futon on the floor of one of the massage rooms. I had brought my six sided, clear quartz crystals, which were about six inches tall, with me for the summer months. I had about a dozen or so, and placed them around my "bed" every night. I became used to the vibration level this field of crystals created, but to this day, may not realize exactly what they did for me. I was asleep before my head hit the pillow.

The next evening, after work, I decided to go into New York City to Elizabeth Hepburn's meditation group. My friend Donna, who was a nurse, loveed the healing energy she felt there. We caught dinner and drove to the Upper West Side.

About ten people attended the meditation that evening, and afterward Elizabeth offered her "healing stool" to anyone who needed some healing. I often came with one or two of my clients, encouraging them to get a healing treatment and clearing. Tonight was different. We went around the circle and shared. When it was my turn, I could not stop crying. I felt like my teardrops were flooding the room like Niagara Falls.

Elizabeth was surprised and motioned for me to get up on the healing stool. "Close your eyes and relax," she said, softly. Slowly she moved the palms of her hands down my spine, then up the front midline of my body. Suddenly I began to shudder and shiver. Woosh! A strong wind of clear air went directly through my heart center. I "felt" something like a big rock fly out of my body.

"I let it go." I exclaimed.

"What happened?" Elizabeth asked.

"I don't know but something dark and heavy just flew out of my body." Closing my eyes, I smiled and swayed with the energy.

Looking up at Elizabeth with love and gratitude, I said, "The condo is mine. The rest of the money will come tomorrow and I'll be in the clear. I know this for a fact."

"God bless you, Elizabeth. You really deserve it," she replied.

Donna and I drove back to New Jersey almost in silence. As I dropped her off in front of her home, she leaned over and gave me a hug. "I am so happy for you," she said sincerely. "You've helped so many people and really deserve this break. Please let me know what happens."

"I will, I promise," I said, smiling back at her. "Thank you for coming with me tonight. I really needed you."

"Allen's office was very busy the next morning. The phones rang constantly, which was rare for the summertime. Around 11:30 am the phone rang for me. It was an older gentleman that I took care of a few evenings a week, who lived in Livingston. I had met him at the psychic fair at the Scotch Plains Mall, and we struck up a friendship. His living situation with his daughter was not the best, and sometimes she abused him. He loved to call me Betty, the name of his deceased wife, so I allowed it. I became his confidante.

"Betty, what are you doing for lunch?" Steven asked. "I have something important to discuss with you."

"Oh Steven, I have no time. The office is very busy."

"Well you have to eat," he said, laughing gently. "Please ask Mr. Nimensky if you can take a half-hour. By the way, what's happening with your condo purchase?"

"I can tell you at lunch," I said. Allen nodded his okay to me.

"Try not to be long, Elizabeth," Allen asked.

"I won't, Mr. Nimensky. We're only going Chinese across the street." I hastily replied.

Steven seemed upset and began by telling me that he wanted to move out of his daughter's home. He shared how he had taken most of his retirement money and put it into her home, so he and his wife could live there. After his wife passed, his daughter became mean spirited.

"I couldn't do my laundry today because she took the door off of the dryer and hid it somewhere. In the winter she shuts off the heat on my side of the house, and I freeze. I just can't take it anymore," Steven sadly explained. "But tell me about you, Betty. What's going on with the condo?"

I put my head down and told Steven everything, including the call from my cousin last night. "Today is Wednesday, and I have to have that condo money by tomorrow or Friday, at the latest," I muttered.

"We'd better go, Betty, I know you need to get back. However, I really need you to take me by my bank first. There's something I need to do now."

"Okay Steven, but please don't be long.

"Oh I won't," he said with a smile. We stopped at the bank and Steven went inside.

Steven was gone for ten minutes, and I was ready to go in the bank to see what was taking so long. As I reached over to open the door, he came skipping out of the bank, waving a white envelope.

"Here Betty, this is for you." He said almost giggling.

As I began to open the envelope, I realized it was a cashier's check. Turning it over, I saw that it was made out to me in the amount of $25,000. I froze, and then melted like a daughter whose father had just come to the rescue at the eleventh hour.

"How can I ever thank you?" I asked. "Can you really afford to do this?"

"Now never you mind that. We've got to get that condo built, because I may need to stay there if I move out, until I get acclimated. It is a two bedroom? Right?"

Smiling with joy, I replied, "Yes it is, and you are welcome anytime."

I walked back into Nimensky and Gallinson's offices practically dancing on air. Allen was at my desk, waiting anxiously. All the phones were ringing at once.

I handed him the white envelope and began to answer the phones. He walked over to the other desk, opened it up, and saw the cashier's check. "What do I do with this?" He asked, laughing. "Better still, how did you do that? Just tell me, how did you ever do that?"

George and Carol's check had arrived while I was out to lunch. "Well, now you have the funds to buy the condo. Since you are also having me put your paycheck in the trust account, I'm sure you'll have more than enough for the closing costs. Especially with the extra that Steven gave you."

Then he just stared at me for a moment or so. "I will never know how you did all of this, and have never seen anything like it in my life. You are a vey lucky girl, Elizabeth, and many people think a lot of you." He began to shake his head and walked back to his office.

"Elizabeth, come here for a moment," Allen called.

I walked back to Allen's office, and he had pulled out my closing papers file. You're supposed to close on August 19th, and I will be on vacation with my family that week. Do you think you'll close on time? I make it a policy not to do business when I'm at the shore on my week off," Allen said, concerned. "We'll have to go to the government offices of HUD in Hackensack to close. That's more than an hours drive."

"Don't worry Allen, I know we won't close that day." I said with confidence.

"And just how is that? Oh, that's right, you' re psychic," he teased.

Allen, give me your desk calendar," I dared him. "Then I turned the pages until I got to September 22nd and drew a heart around the date. That's our date of closing," I said, giggling.

Could anyone ever know how I was certain? Over the past ten years I learned that astrology never lies. That date was the only logical one, because I had signed the first paperwork on March 21st, the Spring Equinox; was working in Allen's office on June 21st, the Summer Solstice; I knew we would close on September 22nd, the Fall Equinox.

On August 1st, Allen received a letter from HUD Housing explaining there was a delay with construction, and the closing date would be on Thursday, September 22nd at 1:00 pm in their offices.

I spent the rest of the summer working for Allen, seeing my clients in Ridgewood, and doing the weekend Psychic Fairs. On occasion I would take an evening drive up to Ridge Gardens to see how my new home was coming along, taking time for prayers of gratitude.

On an early Saturday morning in late August, I was stretching and reveling in the crystals energy surrounding my futon, when I heard clearly, "You're going to get your furniture today, but you must work with the married couple first." It was my day off; I had no planned appointments and no idea what was going on.

Wanting to get another half-hour of sleep, I turned over to curl up, when the phone rang. Slowly I arose to answer it. "Hi, is this Elizabeth Joyce?"

"Yes. What can I do for you?"

"My name is Mary. My husband and I are at a crossroads, and I saw your ad in the *New Jersey Journal* and wanted to know if we could make an appointment to see you? Are you possibly available today, late morning?"

Remembering my other worldly instructions, I said yes, and scheduled them for 11:30 am. I am not a morning person and rarely take appointments before 1:00 or 2:00 pm. However, I knew Spirit had other plans for me that day as well.

I was in the car, driving south down Route 17 by one o'clock in the afternoon.. I felt a bit confused and did not know which store to begin this furniture search. After feeling no inspiration at Macys and The Cottage Beautiful on Route 4, I decided to try Huffman—Koos. My high school colleague's parents were part owners, and I wondered if Donny would be there on a Saturday. Felling strangely excited, I pulled into their parking lot.

I wasn't sure exactly what to look for, but I definitely needed a dining room table and chairs. My unit wasn't built yet. I did not have measurements, only my Third Eye and inner senses. As I wandered over to the Ethan Allen display, I noticed Thomasville was having an end of summer half-price sale, for the weekend before Labor Day. I decided to browse.

As I entered that area of the store, the Tinker Bell dust came back again. I fell in love with a queen-sized headboard for a bed, a matching hutch and corner hutch for the dining area. Then I found an adjustable kitchen table, with beige padded chairs on wheels. Oh my, how could I ever manage all this?

Hey, twin; are you Beth or Priscilla?"

Smiling, I turned around, and there was Donny, grinning back at me. "Beth," I answered.

"What can I do for you today?"

"I'm not sure. I've just bought a new condo but it won't be ready for another month. Do you know the new condos they are building in Mahwah?" I asked.

"Yes, quite a few of the firemen have bought units, and we're helping with furnishing them."

I showed Donny all of the pieces I had fallen in love with. "You know, Beth, you can have all of these for a song. Thomasville is having a one-weekend sale, which is very rare for them. Let's see if we can arrange for you to get it all." He said. "Come and let's go over to my desk so I can do some figuring."

I followed Donny through the beautiful store to his back office. He asked me to fill out a credit application while I waited for his *figuring*.

It all took two phone calls and about twenty minutes. He came back to me smiling with a twinkle in his eye. "If you can give me ten per cent today. It's all yours over a three-year credit agreement. After the half-price discount, the total amount is about $5,000 not including tax or delivery. I would need a $500 for deposit now. It's lucky you came in today, Beth, because next week I could not have given you this value. What is the property address and what day would you like it delivered?"

I gasped with delight. I simply could not believe it. I went through credit quickly and easily. All four of the Thomasville pieces would be in my new condo.

"I'm in the Ridge Garden Condos off of Ridge Road, The English Tudor style condos, different from the other condos which are plain and boxy. The address is 1502 Faulkner Court, and the Building, number fifteen, in the back, on the right. I'm on the first floor. Please deliver the furniture on Friday, September 23rd, as the closing is that Thursday."

"Oh good, that's plenty of notice for us. Sure am glad it's the first floor. Those stairs are narrow and getting the headboard unit upstairs would have been near impossible. Just sign right here and you're all set. It's good to see you again, Beth."

I didn't even remember the ride back to Ridgewood and Wilsey Square. I was numb with the day's events. "So this is how the Universe supports you when you're in the flow," I thought. A sense of gratitude filled me.

Elaine returned to Allen's office right after Labor Day, and I met him at the HUD offices on the day of closing. "Elizabeth, we need to do this quickly," Allen said. "I know I said we could have a celebration lunch after closing, but I have to be at the shore by 4:00 pm if possible. It's always family first. Sorry to let you down, but duty calls."

Since it was a cash sale, the closing went through easily. I brought a stamped envelope addressed to Roy, hoping there would be enough funds left over to get him paid back for the deposit on the condo.

At the end of the closing, Allen began laughing, as he wrote out a second check. "Well Elizabeth, here's your set of keys to your new home, along with the condo book and some papers for you to keep. We paid Roy, and there was still a little money left over. Here's the extra funds for you; $70.11. You know what? That's craps! You tossed the dice in your world of unlimited probabilities, and you won, Elizabeth. Big time. I will never forget this closing." he called to me as he walked out to his car.

I slowly followed him. Walking over to my car, I was feeling strange, a bit empty, but perhaps it was a void. Jeffrey was in college at the New Jersey College of Medicine, Vance was, heaven knows where. I had so much to do because the furniture was coming tomorrow. Yet, in that moment I felt so alone.

I spent the afternoon packing all of my things at Wilsey Square to take to my new home. It was early evening when I arrived. The building was dark, and I was the first to move into the twenty-four unit building.

I carried in my items and put them away while mentally making a list of what I would need to purchase. The new furniture would be delivered in the morning, and Ridgewood Movers would bring over my storage boxes in the afternoon. I had sold a lot of the storage items over the summer. There really wouldn't be much. Although the condo was small, it met my needs.

Alan Gallinson gave me his son's old boy scouts' sleeping bag; my bed for one night. I laid out my sleeping area in the middle of the living room. I had brought my boom box so I could play some music in my new home. Carefully laying out the dozen Brazilian crystals around the sleeping bag, I prepared for bed.

I sat in quiet for a moment as my mind reviewed all that had transpired over the last six months. I knew I had just walked through a miracle. I remembered Hawaii, traveling through the universe to Mother Mary's loca, the promise on Sunset Court that this new place would be right for me, how the unit and funds arrived, and turning the key in the lock of my condo for the first time on the Fall Equinox. There were no trumpets, no marching band, not a soul around, just the beating of my heart.

As I reflected on the events, my body began to relax and feel peaceful. The landscape outside the large living room window was turning gray at dusk, feeling sweet, loving, welcoming, and comfortable. I could hear the water rippling in the little creek, as the sun faded on the horizon.

Everything seemed luxurious, warm, and supportive. Then I saw it. The trees and shrubs were giving off a bright white light. I could feel Mentor, and the large meeting room somewhere in the universe. I remembered Mother Mary putting the ring of flowers in my hair. I was beginning to see it — I was beginning to see reality consciously as a divine gift, as an emanation of Light. This was my first, true *vision of reality.*

Then my heart began to sing William's latest composition. Smiling with joy, I got up, found the cassette, inserted it into the boom box, and set it on repeat play. With soft tears of gratitude I fell asleep as the vibration of William's voice rippled over my body, piercing deep down into my Soul.

Come to me My Lord,
All in you made new.
Come to me my Lord,
Nothing outside of you.
Oh, Banish every hesitation.
Throw out every last doubt,
Till all that remains is knowing,
Knowing the love you're pouring out.
Come to me my Lord.
Come to me oh my Lord.

Come to me my Lord.
Banish every fear.
Come to me my Lord.
Oh, Let me know you are so near.
Your heart is my home forever.
Your first light's forever everywhere.
All the world by your word comes together.
Every form enfolded in your care.
Come to me my Lord,
Come to me oh my Lord.

Since the condo was a HUD Property, I knew I had to own it for twenty-five years before I could sell it for any kind of profit. I lived in the condo for fifteen years and rented it for ten.

The condo was a magical, mystical place with a very high vibration. I taught classes, held weekly meditations, formed a women's group, and did my healings and readings there.

In the extra bedroom I made an altar to the Divine Mother, and then added all of the Masters. A mirror, candles, and crystals were provided. I would say my morning mantra into the mirror to gain balance and clarity. I worked my chakras and did the "ring of fire" in the shower. While putting on my make-up in the morning, I wrapped myself with white light and asked the Divine to shine its Light through me on a daily basis. I was developing a strong energy field, without consciously realizing the power of doing so.

In that magical condo I helped many others find lost articles, solve marriage problems, make career decisions, uncover deceit, work out emotional crisis with their families, have faith before an operation that all will work out well, solve a mystery or crime, as well as talk telepathically to the departed.

I recall a young woman who came to me in February of 1989. Lisa from Tuxedo Park, New York, came for a reading. She had lost her grandmother's diamond ring. Lisa was at a loss because she had searched everywhere but she did not know where it was. I explained to her that her Grandmother had "borrowed" it for a while and had taken the ring to "the other side." We both said a prayer together and asked "grandma" to return the ring. I told her it would reappear within three days.

When Lisa went home and told her husband about our conversation he was quite angry. He thought I was a quack and asked her not to ever speak with me again. Two nights later her husband was awakened at 2:00 am. He heard a loud CLINK in the bathroom. Startled, he went to the bathroom and turned on the light. In the soap dish, there was the missing diamond ring. Her husband sent me roses after finding the ring. I smiled.

There were many powerful healing incidents that occurred in the condo. In September 1992, Pat and her sister came to my condo in Mahwah, NJ for a reading on a Sunday afternoon, the day after I returned from Cape Cod after my personal healing ordeal. When Pat came in, I noticed she had a physical problem, lockjaw. She had been rear-ended in a car accident six year before. The clavicle bone had moved, locking her jaw tight. Under a doctor's care, she had not enjoyed any solid food since the accident.

As the girls were leaving, I asked Pat if she would allow me to touch her face. I explained to her that sometimes when I touched someone, healing miracles would happen. As I placed my hands over each side of her jaw on her face, a shot of light energy burst through my body. I instantly went into a trance and closing my eyes, began to sway back and forth as my hands held her face. I stood there for about ten minutes.

During the inner visualization I saw three angles on each side of her face. They drilled into her jaw and removed some poison gaseous material. The room began to have an odor, as if one had removed a filling from a tooth. The hallowed out jaw was filled with White Light from the angles. The jaw was plated so the light could be contained within it. Then the healing was complete. Opening my eyes, I dropped my hands from her face, and her jaw fell open.

Pat began to cry. She said, "You are a holy woman." I was a bit uncomfortable and replied, "No, I am not. I am a clear light funnel for the Divine. You were willing to release your pain and gain back the use of your jaw. You did this along with your Blessed Higher Self. I was just a conductor of energy."

Her sister, who was visiting from Florida, stared at Pat in amazement. She could not believe her eyes.

I asked Pat to go into the other room, where I had the alter, and thank God for giving her the courage to heal her body. Pat stayed by the altar for about ten minutes, before leaving. About an hour later Pat called me laughing and crying while she was munching on an apple.

Healing can also happen at a distance. It's not necessary to be in physical proximity to someone. Something people are just beginning to understand- the healing energy transcends time and space. It was in the spring of 1993 when Chris from Mohegan Lake, New York, came to the Women's Group meditation on Friday nights. She had met me in Mt. Kisco at the Sunday Psychic Fair. She became a regular, and later that spring, her son, Scott, was diagnosed with children's diabetes.

One evening at the meditation group, Chris expressed to us that she was upset because Scott was prohibited by his school from participating in sports because of his diagnosis. She came into the healing circle and cried from her heart. I worked on her energy for a bit, then we all went into a deep meditation. Chris was flabbergasted after the meditation. She described seeing a bright violet and sliver flame circling around her. She knew something had changed. I told her that Scott had received a spontaneous healing.

About an hour after the group had left I received a phone call, and it was Chris.

"Elizabeth, I am so excited and thrilled because Scott ran out to the car when I arrived home."

"Who was that lady you were with tonight," he asked.

"Her name is Elizabeth and she is my Spiritual Teacher," Chris replied.

"Well, she came here and healed me," Scott explained, jumping up and down with joy.

I smiled, thanking Spirit as I listened to her. The joy that she shared was profound, and beyond words. At his next doctor's visit, Scott was completely free of children's diabetes.

Random Awareness

One never knows when their psychic powers or intuition may be called upon by the Divine. Just before we entered into the new millennium, people were apprehensive about the ability of computers to turn from 1999 over to 2000. Known as the Y2K Scare, millions of dollars were spent by corporations to make sure their computers would not be shut down as the clock struck midnight on New Year's Eve.

It was mid-morning on a Thursday. I was scheduled to be on a local news show in New York to discuss the Y2K phenomena as a psychic. What did I see happening?

The studio was on the West Side between 10th and 11th Avenues. Despite being close to the West Side Highway, it's a deserted, area and nearly impossible to hail a cab. Luckily I had driven in from New Jersey to do the TV show.

As I was leaving the studio after the taping, I was looking forward to a fast drive home straight through the Lincoln Tunnel. I walked out onto Thirty-Second Street at Tenth Avenue, and noticed a very anxious couple looking for a cab. "It's not so easy to get a cab down here," I said to them, smiling.

"Oh I am in such a hurry," the man responded. "I have several important meetings today and am late already."

"Where is your office?" I asked.

"In the Times Magazine Building on Sixth Avenue," he responded.

"I have my car, can I drive you?"

"Where are you headed?" he asked.

"New Jersey."

"Oh that's in the opposite direction from the Lincoln Tunnel. It may take you forever with this traffic." He said in a disappointing voice.

"No, I insist." I said, really concerned for his nervousness.

Okay then, thank you. This is Karen, my secretary. We were also guests on that TV Show that you were on. I spoke about financials. What was your topic?" he asked curiously, getting into the front passenger side of my Oldsmobile sedan.

"What's the best way to go uptown?" I asked, avoiding his question.

"Tenth Avenue to Fiftieth Street, then turn left onto Sixth up to Fifty-Second."

We arrived pretty quickly for midday in New York City. As I pulled over in front of his building and stopped the car, a burning sensation went down my spine. I had the impulse to touch his arm as he began to get out of the car. Karen had already jumped out of the back door onto the sidewalk.

"Why are you here?" Were the words that jumped out of my throat. "Why are you here?"

He stopped and got back into the car, looking at me in awe.

"You need to go home, and go home now. Your daughter is in the middle of a very serious operation. She and your wife need you. Nothing is more important! How could you put these meetings and stupid TV Show ahead of that?" I said, astounded at my own words.

With tears in his eyes, he stared at me. "How did you know that? Who are you?" he said aghast.

"I am a well known psychic, and I can tell you this. Your daughter will be just fine. She has a lot to give and a lot to do this lifetime. She will be up and about before you know it. Just get home to Long Island. She needs you and will be calling for you when you arrive at the hospital." I responded.

"What's your name? He asked.

"Elizabeth Joyce," I said.

"Elizabeth, I am one of the Vice President's of Time Magazine. I know I may never see you again but I can tell you this, when I hear your name in the future, and I'm sure I will, I will help you from behind the scenes any way I can," he promised.

I just looked back at him and said, "Get home."

He winked at me, mouthed a "Thank you," and ran off.

Working with the FBI

Over the years, I've worked with the FBI on several occasions. One case in particular stands out to this day. On April 29, 1992, at about 3:30 pm, I was working in the living room of my condo, when I had a strong sense to turn on the TV. I turned on CBS. Breaking news flashed on the screen, the President of Exxon, Sidney J. Reso, was missing. "Oh, not another Exxon murder," I thought. Horrified, I remembered another Exxon executive, Don Johnson, being murdered by his wife in Ridgewood, New Jersey, my hometown, a few years ago.

My father worked for Exxon for over forty years. He had helped Don, a good friend of my older sisters, get a job at Exxon. I felt I had a strong psychic connection to the company.

I looked out my large living room window, and a *vista* appeared. A vista is when you see a "movie" in front of your eyes, showing you information. I saw the following movie:

A dark blue Cadillac was backing out of a driveway. The man driving was older, thin, and wearing glasses. He heard a scream, and looked up into his rear view mirror. He saw a blonde woman fall behind his car.

Thinking he'd hit her, he jumped out of the car to help her, leaving the door open and the car engine running. Suddenly another man came out from behind a hedge, stuck a gun in Reso's back, and the couple forced him into a white van. He struggled, and the gun accidently went off, shooting him in his left shoulder. The van sped away, toward Bloomfield, New Jersey.

I was beside myself because it was all so clear to me, and I was certain I was supposed to help the authorities find him. One of my students, Eileen, had three brothers who worked for the FBI. I called her and told her what happened. She told me there was not much she could do, but she would tell her brothers.

Late the next day, an FBI agent, Tom Cattone, called me from Morristown, New Jersey. He told me the FBI had set up a task force, and were widening the search. He gave me a fax number where I could send in information as I received it. When I told him that Mr. Reso's car door was open, and the engine had been running, he knew I was on to something. I also asked about Mr. Reso's heart condition and medication. None of that had been in the news.

I knew Mr. Reso was kept in a small house for awhile, and then I saw him moved to what seemed like a closet. (Actually, it was a storage unit. I could clearly see the number on the unit, which I thought was the house number.) At that time I also knew that he had a heart condition, and was without his medication.

On the morning of May 3rd, 1992, I woke up crying. I knew Sidney Reso had passed away. I faxed Mr. Cattone. He called me on the phone. He asked me when the kidnappers would be found. I told him June 30th.

On May 15th, a frustrated Tom Cattone called me again. They had not been able to get any leads of who kidnapped him. Taking a deep breath, I closed my eyes and said this to him, "The man is a former EXXON employee, who wore a blue uniform. I think the woman is his wife. They buried him in the pines off of a major highway. He's in a shallow grave between two pine trees."

"Well, we're looking around Newark Airport and the New Jersey Turnpike," he responded.

"That's the wrong direction." I responded. "He's in the pines, he's in the pines."

Sidney's Reso's body was found on June 30th, just off the Garden State Parkway, between two pine trees in Pinehurst, New Jersey.

Years later in March of 1999, Richie, Ornstein, who is a retired New York City cop, and I were speaking on the phone when he told me there had been a double homicide in the area. As he was talking, I began to see the details of the crime. I saw a restaurant on the corner, a brick building, an old lady across the street, about three flights up who witnessed the crime while looking out her window, and that there had been an eye witness. I asked Richie if he knew a Charlie, and he was shocked. Charlie was one of the suspects. I gave more details as he asked me questions. This crime was not written up in the newspapers. It had occurred the day before about 150 miles from where I live, and there was no possible way I could have known anything about the crime or the details.

In the late 1990's as e-mail emerged, and before Skype, I was working with a woman in Sydney, Australia via e-mail. It was as instant as you could get back then. Suddenly my hand reached down to pat a dog. Of course, there was no dog there; just the etheric, energetic outline. I wrote to my client in Australia, how do you like your new Golden Retriever? Does she have a bit of an upset stomach today?

The woman was shocked. "How did you know that?" She asked.

"I just petted her." I responded. Then I gave her a natural formula to help her pet get over its upset stomach; ginger water with a bit of cinnamon. It worked.

Texting-Lost Animal

Many years later in 2016, the same dynamic took place via texting on an iPhone. My girlfriend, Joann, could not find her cat. The cat had been missing for two days. She sent me a text asking me, "Where is my cat?" I texted her back, "The cat was tired, laying down under a tree in a wooded, forestry area, and cannot 'get out.' She has given up."

Joann and her daughter went outside to look for the cat. Joann did not have any wooded area on her property. Next door she saw a few trees together in her neighbors' back yard. She walked over to take a look. Calling her cat, she searched in the grove of trees. She found her cat curled up between them. Next she noticed a barbed wire fence around the trees, and realized her cat could not get out without help. Another animal saved!

Our inner technology allows us to connect psychically with people. It doesn't need to be one on one in person. That's the miracle of our connectivity. We can tap into an energy field, get answers as well as receiving healings and communication from others.

Many more powerful miracles happened at the condo over those ten years. As I look back now, I realize that the power that built up between those walls is what everyone is talking about today. It's always with us, but stronger now, in the new millennium, than ever before. There was nothing to do but live in it, flow with it, and accept it. Since this flow has been present with me this entire lifetime, I simply could not imagine life without devotion to the Divine; the flow that washes through me on a daily basis.

CHAPTER 13

The Holy Mother Brought Me Blessings and Grace

Meeting a fully realized Saint—Amritananda Mayi

IT WAS THE SPRING OF 1997 when the phone call came in from Hawaii. Indira was calling to tell me about a Saint she had just spent some time with in Hawaii

"You need to meet her, Elizabeth," Indira said. "Your life has never really known the affection of motherly love. She's a true Saint. Rob and I just returned from the Big Island in Hawaii, where Amma was. This is her first trip to America, but she wants to spread her profound love, kisses, and hugs across the United States. A core group is gathering, and your presence would be an added blessing. You're such a good promoter."

"Sounds good," I responded. "I'm just worried about finding airfare to California."

"Don't worry, you'll be taken care of," Indira responded, trying to reassure me.

I had a working knowledge of the work of the Christ through my healing work and psychic readings. Recently I had been reading and learning the works of Parmahansa Yogananda through Clear Light Therapy and the book, *The Autobiography of a Yogi*. It was only after meeting Amma that I began to understand and accept the wonderful, incomprehensible mysteries of how Her Guru teaching worked.

In sanskrit, gu means darkness, and ru means Light. It took me some time to be able to absorb and work with this energy, but through the years I have been with Her, I began to see that all my spiritual efforts and experiences would be successful. I had been a seeker for higher learning and truth all of my life, and probably for many lifetimes. I was privileged to be able to pass through many challenges, but had yet to learn how all of us can receive and use this fabulous, out-of-this-world energy, as well as experience a deeper love beyond all understanding.

A Guru (spiritual teacher) is implicitly aware of the disciple's faults and weaknesses, as well as their strengths and gifts, and knows unerringly what is best for the disciple at any given moment.

In my lifetime I have had the opportunity to meet and sit with many enlightened beings who have taken on the role as Guru. They are rare, and many cannot live up to the role they claim. However, I found Mother to be something else altogether.

Yogi Bahjan told me that Amma is an Avatar. At the time, that word was new to me. "An Avatar is a world Guru," he explained. "I am a spiritual teacher and have learned to work well with the spiritual energies available to all of us on this planet. Amma is an Avatar, which means "to come down." They are not enlightened beings who have raised themselves up out of the earth and mankind, but rather they are a part of God embodying a human form for the upliftment of humanity. They signify God's descent to humanity. They are reverently and lovingly called *Incarnations of God.*

Ammachi, as she is affectionately known, is a rare mystic soul who makes herself accessible to anyone and everyone. Utterly simple, yet stoically strong, she is humble, unshakable and awesomely self-sacrificing. She's been called a fragrant lotus, born of India's deeply spiritual soil. Through the power of her austerity and spiritual attainment, her fragrance has spread across many countries, where it has attracted and enthralled thousands of spiritually starved seekers.

I have been with Amma's US Tour for thirty years. I was accepted into a core group of sixty people who work hard and long to bring Amma before her children across the United States. I have often said, "My gift back to Mother is to bring Her new people." I have been through many awe inspiring trials and triumphs along this journey.

Amma teaches that the life force is eternal and universal, with a limitless capacity, imbued in all things. It is everywhere! Each person has unlimited power and unlimited potential through this life force when tapped.

It becomes a matter of identifying with that power, understanding its characteristics, and learning how to use it effectively. A Guru becomes the teacher of the Infinite, teaching us how to bring this energy into our lives. This is why we all need a Guru like Amma.

When you utter her name with your voice along with thoughts, you create a constructive energy and send it out into the universe. Amma guides you to actually lock into the power source. Like a plug in a socket, you become poised and ready for the next step. This requires looking at the characteristics of this infinite power within you, and learning how to use your own spiritual energies effectively.

As you walk this pathway, the path of the Initiate, or the devotee to Amma, your perceptions expand gradually to accept the higher vibrations of Self as you begin to understand that we have experienced life through the five senses, the windows to the soul. We are taught at an early age the capacity of each of these five senses, seeing, hearing, touching, feeling, and tasting. Yet, each of these senses has another dimension many times deeper and more sensitive than normally perceived. Each of these dimensions will open up for you as you move toward them. This is called *the Spiritual Evolvement of the Soul.* As you practice your saddanas. (prayers), Amma guides you along the path each day. The reflection of this Shakti energy comes in the form of other people, life events, and challenges that you experience.

Through devotion and inner belief, you process Amma's energies and encourage them to be delivered to you. When meditating, try at all times to remain centered, keeping your thoughts pure, directed, and focused on Amma. If doubts creep in, do not allow them "house room," as my grandmother used to say. Acknowledge the disturbing thoughts, thank them for sharing with you, then dismiss them strongly. Meditate and look at all of your doubts from above yourself. Understand that it is only your mind, creating doubts, worries, objections and roadblocks to your desires through fear and ignorance. Know from the higher plane of communion with Amma, and only through her Grace, will what you set in motion and what you want happen.

As you work with Amma's etheric power, She will show you the next move at every turn. Believe in it! Know that this force within you is so powerful that it will pull you into excitement and adventure beyond your wildest dreams. Keep it pure, remain silent, and always remember to bless the process between yourself and the Divine.

The more you come in touch with and work with the Avatar through prayer, the more you will be in touch with all of life that surrounds you. Everything is one with everything else. This knowledge will become a source of strength for you. The world is here to help and support you. The more you come into the richness of these energies, the more dimensions you will be able to access.

Over the years Amma has instructed me, frustrated me, driven me crazy, while instilling faith in me through countless instances, and I will share some of them now.

I always loved driving up to New Hampshire from New Jersey. The change of air was the first thing I felt, as well as the scenery, and clear lakes and rivers. This trip was a bit different, because I was traveling up to see my "Mother", but a different mother. Amma's summer New England Retreat in 1990 was in New Hampshire, about sixty miles from Grammie's home. My mother was living in Pennsylvania with my older sister, Nancy, and Grammies house was sold and gone. The circumstances made me feel very sad.

Lucille, from Frank Alper's group, and another friend were taking the retreat with me. We arrived in Temple and found we were staying at a farm, with about ten people in a room, sleeping on the floor. These were the early days of being with Amma. Bachti was Her assistant and kept all of us very busy. I ironed Amma's clothes, help bathe Her, swept out Her room, and contributed time in the kitchen to help prepare the daily meals. We had to feed about two-hundred people and thought that was a lot. Amma always served Her children the evening meal, just before meditation and bujhans. (Now we have three to six thousand people to prepare for.)

At this retreat I learned a great lesson. I was in a relationship at the time, and there were no cell phones. The morning of the second day Lucille and I went into town to get some drinks and use the pay phone. When we pulled into the parking lot of the General Store, someone was using the only payphone.

"I'm going to make him get off the phone, I told Lucille, with an angry voice. "I just can't wait to call John."

Lucille grabbed my arm and began her divine lecture. "Now wait just a minute, Elizabeth. You just can't do that. He has a right to have his conversation in comfort. Leave him alone. Go inside and get the drinks we need, relax, take a deep breath. I guarantee you that if you don't, John won't be home, and you'll be even more frustrated."

I was both annoyed and surprised at what she said. Not really believing her, I grumbled and went into the store to shop. As I was coming out of the General Store, the man came out of the phone booth.

"Thank you for your patience, he said. "My mother is very ill and I had to give the doctor some special instructions." Tipping his hat, he smiled and went to his truck and drove away.

I put the groceries in the back seat of the car, and started to walk over to the phone boot when Lucille called to me. "Fill the car with gas first, Elizabeth," she said smiling.

I could not figure out what was going on, but I did as she said. Finally, I got to the phone booth and called John.

"Hello Elizabeth," John said. "You have perfect timing, I just got in the door. I've been out all morning, and was walking into the house while the phone was ringing. How are you doing"

Well, I got it! So much knowledge in a split second. Our impatience is what gets us into trouble, along with "me first" and judgment. When we honor others, and realize that everything happens for a reason, we can grow closer to unconditional respect and kindness. Allow it, allow the delay or change of plans. There is always a reason beyond our reach or knowledge.

Many years ago I promised Amma that whenever she needed me, I would be of service to her without question. One must think very hard before you make a promise like that to an Avatar. You could be called upon to do just that and be tested!

Nakasha, a blind devotee from Philadelphia, Pennsylvania, had been praying hard to the Christ, Mother Mary, and the Nature Spirits for upliftment from her inner prison. Having been born blind, Nakasha struggled to get a basic education. She mastered Braille and graduated from college. An intelligent, avid reader, Nakasha knew there was something more to life. She knew there was something beyond herself, a spiritual power, that she had not yet found, and it had nothing to do with sight. She continuously prayed to be shown the path, the way to her personal enlightenment.

In July of 1991, Nakasha was invited to New York City with some spiritual friends from Philadelphia, who offered to drive her to visit a Guru visiting from India. Her name was Amritianyandamayi, or Ammachi as many called her. Nakasha made the trip and was completely overwhelmed. At her first darshan, she fell completely in love with Amma and the Bliss that Amma brought to her soul within.

Nakasha was so taken with Mother that she returned for something called a Puja and Devi Bhava. She didn't know much about the process, but was told it was a purification ceremony. Curious, and with a strong feeling of the need to be embraced in Amma's arms once more, she took the train, alone, from Philadelphia to New York City.

Nakasha arrived and immediately began to pray. "Please, please Mother, bring me closer to you." Nakasha did not realize this would be an all night affair. She was not prepared, and knew absolutely no one at the Devi Bhava service. Remembering the wonderful feelings of the previous darshan, was all she had to go on.

I had been with Ammachi since She first arrived in the United States in 1987. Over the past several years my prayer had been to experience true enlightenment in this lifetime. Nakasha had the same desire and felt she wanted to wait no longer! One of her friends had advised her that was a dangerous prayer, as all her karma could be brought to her at the same time.

I had already faced a lot of loss and pain in my life, but kept on with my prayers. I was about to be asked to keep the promise I made to Amma four years earlier.

I was the line director at Devi Bhava, with the New York Satsang, as host of this event. There were hundreds of people to manage, and I had grown tired in the wee small hours of the morning. Suddenly Amma sent for me. One of the Bramacheri's came to me and asked me to come up to the place where people sat after receiving Devi Bhava. A blonde woman was wailing with tears of pain. The Bramachieri pointed to this woman and said, "She's blind. Mother wants you to take care of her." Then he was gone.

Stunned, I was hesitant to make a move. She was embraced in the energies of Amma and Devi Bhava. Then Mother turned her head and gazed into my eyes for a brief moment. A warmth enveloped me and the path was made clear. I went over to the woman and asked her, "What is your name and where are you from?"

"My name is Nakasha and I'm from Philadelphia. I am anxious because I have to meet my train at Penn Station to return home at six o'clock in the morning."

"Who brought you here?" I asked.

"No one. I came alone. I had been to a darshan yesterday with some friends, but had to return tonight to be with Amma, I love her so." Nakasha answered.

I slowly got the picture of my beloved Guru's message. This was the beginning of an endearing friendship that is ongoing forever.

"Are you going to the retreat in Rhode Island?" I asked.

"What retreat? You mean I can spend more time with Amma?" Nakasha answered.

"Yes." I responded.

"My parents live in Connecticut, which is on the way. My birthday is July 10th and I usually visit with my parents at that time. When is this retreat?"

"July 12th through the 14th." I answered.

"Oh, I'd love to go. Is there a cost? I have no money." Nakasha responded.

"Yes. It's one hundred fifty dollars," I answered. "Nakasha, I run a Women's Group in New Jersey. Perhaps we could take a collection and sponsor you for this retreat. You will be served all your meals. You need to bring bedding and towels, plus your personal items for a three-day stay. If you are in Connecticut, I could pick you up on the way, and return you to either Connecticut or New York City, where you could take the train home to Philadelphia."

The deed was done. This was only the beginning!

Nakasha has been to every East Coast retreat since and has grown into a much deeper love and devotion with Ammachi. Of course, Nakasha had her own spiritual lessons to learn.

In November of 1997 Nakasha was returning from a Spiritual Seminar in Albany, New York. She carried with her an Amma doll that one of the devotee's bought for her in Rhode Island the summer before. The doll was in her bag, along with money, her credit cards, tape recorder, and other various items. The morning after her return, she searched and searched, but could not find that bag.

Nakasha was distraught and called several friends for help and guidance. Andrea, a neighbor, came over and looked everywhere for the bag. She could not see it and Nakasha thought it was lost forever. She called me.

When I received Nakasha's call, she was sure the bag was not lost. I instructed Nakasha to go within and ask Amma to return the bag safe and sound. I asked Nakasha over and over again to do a visualization

232

and *see* the doll back in her possession. I asked my friend, Iris, also from Philadelphia, to go over to Nekasha's apartment and search for the bag. Iris could not locate it either.

Month's past. Nakasha and I spoke about once a week and each time I reassured her that the bag was not lost. I felt it had been misplaced and would be found soon. I was sure of it. Amma would never let Nakasha down. I asked Nakasha if she was doing the inner prayer and visualization. I reminded Nakasha that was the only way I knew of to have the doll returned.

In May of 1998, Nakasha traveled to Connecticut to visit her ailing mother in the hospital. She spent Mother's Day weekend with her family and was saddened by her mother's poor health. She prayed and called out to Ammachi. "Please, please make my mother well again." Nakasha completely surrendered with her prayers.

When she returned to Philadelphia, a neighbor told her a bag of hers had been found. It was sitting at the door entrance to the home, on the inside, as if it had been placed there by hidden hands. The doll, the money, the credit cards, tape recorder and other various items, were inside, untouched.

Nakasha was amazed, pleased, thrilled and astounded, all at the same time. She ran to the phone and called me. "The doll has returned! The bag has been found."

I laughed with delight and said, "It was never missing, only misplaced until the proper time. How is your mother?"

Nakasha said. "I'm so afraid she may pass away."

I told her, "Call on Amma. She will hear you. She just returned your doll and everything else you lost. Amma will never desert you."

Nakasha knew that was true. Over the next several months, Nakasha's mother has regained her strength slowly improved. Praise be to Amma She managed to remain on the planet for a few more years.

Nakasha learned, when you choose to experience your own spiritual convictions, a new world begins to open up for you. Don't live with a false sense of security, believing that just because you have come to

Amma you will be saved. Reach out to others and live your faith. You yourself must make the effort to know God within yourself.

In June of 1992, Iris and I decided to fly out to Amma's new Ashram in San Ramon, California. We had not seen it as yet, and were excited that Amma had a home in the United States.

Iris Darlington and I travelled together during Amma's US Tour for twenty years. We shared some miraculous experiences and there was always drama around Amma, you could bet on it. Amma's retreats are three days in length, and this was the afternoon of the second day. By that time my body felt lighter, as if I wasn't really walking on the earth at all. We were late for the start of the program. Running to the front door of the hall, we had to quickly remove our shoes. Instead of putting them on the shoe rack along side the door, we just threw them in a corner on the front stoop and ran inside to find a spot to sit.

During the morning meditation I began to feel the fullness of Divine Love welling within me. I realized that Amma's love for us helped us arrive to clear perfection within the mind. I understood the importance of spiritual discipline. What I was feeling with Amma was an infinite expansion of the heart to include all things, all beings in this world and all the other worlds. Although my youth was filled with pain and anguish, I knew that I could transform it, but I could not embrace Divine Love until I had experienced human love.

As the meditation ended, I began to laugh from deep within my belly. I laughed so hard that tears were running down my cheeks.

Iris became concerned. "What's going on Elizabeth? What's happening to you?"

I tried to speak through my hiccups. "They are moving our shoes because we left them in the wrong place," I said, still laughing.

With that, Iris began to laugh too. Then she suddenly got serious. "Goodness Elizabeth, there are over a thousand people here. How will we ever find our shoes? How can we know where to begin to look?"

"Don't worry Iris," I responded, still smiling. "They are showing me exactly where the shoes are on the shoe racks."

We had arrived at the morning program at ten o'clock in the morning, and left to go back to our room at the Marriott around nine that evening, after dinner and seva. Even though we had been in the hall for almost twelve hours, when we walked outside, I went directly to our shoes. Iris was flabbergasted!

As I prepared for bed that night, I marveled at how my third eye had opened up for me to "see" others in a different area, moving our shoes. I felt that Amma was asking me to accept this simple act so that I could expand into a deeper knowledge. I was on a new road, a new dimension of direct contact with the Divine. "What was She opening up for me?" I wondered.

"I love seeing you act out your awareness," Iris said in a teasing voice, "The drama is like watching a thriller feature film."

We both giggled.

Mother came to the Columbia University campus in New York City the summer of 2004. Iris and I got to stay in a women's dorm with two other girls, Sudha and Prana. By this time Amma's programs were packed, and it was difficult to plan on the supplies needed. Amma gives rose petals and a chocolate kiss to everyone She hugs. Most people don't realize that She fills the chocolate with Her powerful energy, so when it is eaten and savored, the energy goes all through your body.

The rose petals are just as powerful and many people transfer them to their gardens after the program.

As part of our seva (volunteer work) Iris and I were asked to run out and get some bags of chocolate kisses. We were so far uptown in the City that we didn't know how we could do that, but I remembered a Duane Reed drugstore on Broadway, about a block away, so we decided to try there. Luckily there were about six large bags, so we bought them all.

The sun was setting on our way back to the hall, and we were in a hurry to get to the evening program. As we walked up Broadway, I noticed a young man sitting on the corner, with a cup in his hand, begging for quarters.

"Mike," I said. "What are you doing?"

Startled, he answered, "I'm trying to get enough money for dinner. I had to drop out of college because my family ran out of funds," he stammered on.

With brown, sad eyes, he looked up at me. His hair was brown, curly, he was rather thin, and stood about six feet tall. I bent over to help him up. "You don't belong here," I said sternly.

"I know, but I just don't know what else to do. I am lost and confused," he admitted.

"Come with me," I insisted.

"Elizabeth, what are you going to do?" Iris asked.

"Iris, we have to get him over to the men's dorm and in the shower," I said in an excited voice. "Please help me."

Between the two of us, we managed to get him over to the men's dorm about a block and a half away. Mike offered no resistance. It was as if he were in another world.

I found Bob Weiner, one of the New York Satsang leaders, and told him Mike's story. "He needs to get to Amma's feet somehow. He needs to be at the program tonight."

I left Mike there and Iris and I hurried back to the hall to deliver our goodies for the evening program.

Later that night I was doing another seva called *prasad*, when you put a rose petal and chocolate into Amma's hand for Her to give to the devotee she is hugging. As I glanced at Amma, while handing Her the prasad, I saw Mike sitting at Her right side, right next to Her. He was cleaned up, dressed in white, and his curly hair has been combed back so you could see his eyes and full face. He looked like he was in total bliss. My heart jumped for joy.

In 2008, Iris and I attended the Albuquerque, New Mexico Retreat. We had just arrived to the hall to help with the set up, when all of a sudden I heard my name called.

"Elizabeth! Are you Elizabeth from New York?" A very handsome young man was walking toward me, with a grin on his face.

"Yes," I replied, but I did not recognize him.

All of a sudden he quickened his step, ran up to me, and with a big hug, picked me up off the floor, and twirled me around. "Hi, I'm Mike."

"Mike?" I asked.

"Yes, don't you remember? You saved my life in New York City a few years ago. You got me to Amma's feet," he explained.

"She's always doing something like that," Iris chimed in. "I was with her that day and you seemed to be in bad shape."

Smiling, Mike explained the aftermath from that random act of kindness. "Since I couldn't return to school, I left New York and came here to Santa Fe for a quieter life. The people at Amma's ashram here were very helpful. I have a small job, but I am healing. Perhaps I'll be able to finish my education in a year or so. Elizabeth, what made you stop and pick me up? How did you know my name?"

"I smiled and said, "Sometimes Amma makes magic happen when a soul needs to get to Her feet. This is such good news, Mike. I am honored to be a part of your rescue." We hugged and that was that.

Later I said to Iris, "Isn't it great when an Earth Angel comes along? I'll bet most everyone has that experience once or twice in their life. I know that William Vitalis saved my life years ago. Why, if it wasn't for him and the Clear Light Group, I wouldn't even be here in Albuquerque today."

In 2010 my life focus expanded and grew one more time. A couple from Japan, Devananda and Pujitha, who ran a sacred temple and were priests and spiritual practitioners, joined Amma's ashram in India. From 1992 to 2007, Devananda and Pujitha worked with this energy together to benefit thousands of people with every kind of health problem, including many "incurable" conditions. One year after Devananda's passing in 2007, Pujitha received Amma's blessing to carry on this healing tradition.

Radiance Healing is not part of any previously existing healing system or discipline. It does not conflict with any other healing systems including western medicine, ayurveda, acupuncture, etc.

Pujitha has said, *"The Universe is permeated with a radiant white light that is the highest vibration of energy in existence.* This healing energy is all around us, but most of us have forgotten how to "tune into this powerful source" on our own."

The minute I learned about Radiance Healing, I recognized it as a part of Mentor's message to me. I quickly joined thee Radiance healing table to help in any way I could. I consider Pujitha the highest healer in the world, because she brings in the Double Helix, which was our gift that came from the Universe on December 21, 2012.

I resigned from the New York Welcome Table that I had managed for twenty-five years, and began to work with Radiance Healing. Although I recognized that I could never reach Pujitha's status, I want to move along toward that goal.

Radiance Healing is very unique because it flows into the mind, body and soul on a fundamental level, providing positive effects in all these areas. This energy pours divine light to your soul and gradually dissolves accumulated negative qualities in you. It can also help to arouse peace and love shining through within. Radiance Healing is the divine loving energy healing that has been brought back to the earth plane by Amma's blessing.

Pujitha's gift is her ability to re-connect us to this universal healing energy, profoundly healing and uplifting our body, mind and spirit. The longer we receive this energy, the healthier and more radiant we become; the softer you feel inside reflects out to the world around you. Relationships improve, as well as your self-esteem and inner talk. Then grace and peace can become a part of your life on a daily basis.

The new level to our aura, the fourth level that is amber gold, has strengthened our bodies with this energy in a natural way. The function of the fourth level of the aura is to hold this energy so we can draw on it as needed. This information is explained in my last book, *The New Spiritual Chakras and How to Work With Them.*

CHAPTER 14

Jacques the False Teacher

A BUTTERFLY MOVING FROM ROSE to rose in your garden can inspire more profound thoughts than many books of wisdom. Animals can provide spectacular examples of unconditional love and great courage. Everyone we meet has the potential to teach us. Every single human experience is an opportunity to learn and can be a source of inspiration when we practice withholding judgment of ourselves, and others. For the most part we need good human role models and teachers who can help us develop a loving spirit and a clear, well functioning spiritual system.

Seek out people who live up to the high ideals and standards, people who move your heart and mind profoundly. They don't have to be perfect. In fact, anyone who looks perfect is usually hiding something. But they must be people who, you feel, genuinely care for others, and are seeking truth. They don't even need to be physically alive, such as Mahavatar Babaci, Yogananda, Mentor, or your invisible guides. My three favorite teachers were Meg Stettner, Marc Tremblay, and Louise Hay. I gained great insight from Dr. Frank Alper of the Arizona Metaphysical Society, Indira Ivie and the Clear Light Group, and Dr. Deepak Chopra, too.

Even if some teachers turn out to be flawed, they can help you along your path. The message they bring can deeply move your soul, becoming a real spiritual treasure that helps you grow. Perhaps you already know how to tell a good teacher from a bad teacher, and the same criteria applies to both incarnate or disincarnate teachers. Evaluate the message of any teacher objectively, as though you heard it on the radio, saw it on television, or read it in the newspaper. Trust your instincts. Look for the implied purpose. Ask yourself, "Where is this teacher coming from? What does he want? What does he want me to do — or be?" It really isn't difficult.

Many of us give our power away in the beginning, because we idolize them, especially in the United States. Our ego says, "If I know them, then I am better, I am somebody, I am important." How foolish! However, teachers can have the habit of teaching but not practicing what they preach. You can listen to lectures about nirvana, leaving the body at will, or floating out there, but you will never know the feelings and sensations until you have had that experience for yourself. Neither can the truth of any teaching be known except through direct experience. You have to begin to live the teachings of the masters, gurus, and the great ones. Once their truth has become your own, you can realize that truth is demonstrable and Universal. Direct experience is the best guide.

It was 1989 in Sedona, Arizona that I knew I was complete with Indira and the Clear Light Group. My oldest son Vance and I flew out for a Spiritual Retreat. I thought the experience would strengthen Vance, the way it had for me. Vance did a sweat lodge for the first time, and even climbed up to the top of Bell Rock, while we all watched from below. He turned around in a circle three times shouting, "I'm Free! I'm Free!" It marked a significant turning point in his life, and I took a breath of relief.

However, I did not feel the same inside as I had at other retreats. Something was wrong. Indira had changed. She became almost tyrannical. The forgiving grace was William and his ever-blissful music. It got me through the week.

On the last day of the retreat I was walking along a trail with Lucille, who had joined us for the retreat. Suddenly my crystal necklace broke, and crystals went flying into the sun, creating shimmering rainbows as they fell to the ground. As disappointed as I was with the necklace falling apart, it was a beautiful sight to see.

"Do you know what that means, Elizabeth?" Lucille asked.

"I haven't a clue," I responded as I knelt down to try to retrieve the tiny clear quartz crystals. "Boy, these things are small and almost impossible to see. I don't think I can get them all."

"Let them go," Lucille said firmly. They are carrying a message. You have outgrown the Clear Light Group. It's time for you to move on."

I knew she was right. I meditated on that day for many months afterward.

In the early 1990's I began working psychic fairs in other cities. Donald Nesbaum called me and became one of my strongest contacts. He produced fairs in the upper Midwest and Canada. My first fair with the International Psychic and Holistic Festival was in Toronto, Canada. Eventually, I did three fairs in Ottawa, Canada, and a few in Vancouver. It was wonderful meeting new people from different cultures, until I came under *Psychic Attack*.

A Psychic Attack is a malady that can be overcome by specific metaphysical and/or spiritual treatment. The mental equilibrium is disturbed, resulting in nervous disorders and agony of mind caused by continuous states of excitement (for good or for ill) along with excessive stimulation of the senses. This is experienced as continuous fear, anger, melancholy, remorse, envy, sorrow, hatred, discontent and worry; sometimes there is body pain as well. A person could suffer from lack of the necessities of life or a purpose in life. He could be coping with a disagreeable work situation, the loss of a close family member or friend, or an inharmonious living situation. By not eating the right foods, not exercising regularly and not getting enough sleep, he could weaken his physical condition. All or some of these maladies are caused when someone is under psychic attack.

Part of one's job as they follow their Spiritual practice is to learn to recognize attacks. Some attacks masquerade as confusion, disorientation, illness, and others as mental illness. You should always discuss any severe symptoms with a physician.

These symptoms seem to have a life of their own. For example, a sensation of paralysis may rise like a wave or a fluid through your body which does not make physiological sense, but which makes psychic sense. Or, pain may shift around in ways that don't make physiological sense. Or, it feels like you're fighting for your mind against an invisible force field, a pressure on your *mind* to let go and let something else take over. Some attacks like these are strong enough to knock someone out — they can be truly dangerous.

Beware; a preponderance of symptoms will be stronger at night. They worsen when you are half-asleep, a few hours after sunset, and finally relent near dawn. I don't know *why* there is a diurnal relationship, but there is one.

Psychic attack is no simple problem. The power to send out negative energies to others is not recognized by mainstream society. But unfortunately, some people who have built up their inner power, have done so to "take over" other Souls and have them do their bidding, on many levels.

Psychic attack is in reality our deadly enemy with far-reaching effects. Physically, it is difficult to heal any disease so long as it is aggravated by the powerful energies of a psychic attacker. Spiritually, an imbalance of the life force that is created in the body makes it extremely hard for the victim to concentrate mentally, or to meditate deeply enough to acquire any freedom, peace, or wisdom. However, psychic attacks can be cured or handled. The victim must be willing to analyze his condition and remove the disintegrating emotions and energies along with negative thoughts that are, little by little, destroying him. This is how the evil forces take Souls and render one helpless or perhaps even dead. I call this SBD (silent but deadly).

Because of my life karma, this was an important lesson that I needed to learn. I had not had the experience of being taken over, although I had seen the effect of it on others. All these points are extremely subtle deceptions, but the danger is real. The road begins quite plain and straight and wonderful, but slowly, slowly, it curves away. Be alert of your thoughts, and the energies you receive. Always ask your invisible guides or teacher if they are "of the Light." If so, they will stay with you and grow brighter; if not, they will instantly disappear. Know your invisible teachers and from what astral plane they come from! These people who practice psychic attacks can cause psychic damage, interfere with you, influence your thoughts, and even astral project and harass you physically (especially if they dabble in the occult-the dark side of these energies. There is an apparent epidemic coming as we enter 2020. Be careful and be alert.)

Exercising our spirituality is one of the best ways to spiritually grow. The experiences we have while interacting with other people, the mistakes we make, the responsibilities we accept, the trials of our faith we endure — these things give us tremendous insights and opportunities for soul growth.

One of the people I admire most, Marc Tremblay, is a wonderful man, and powerful healer, who helped me escape from a horrible, two-year long, psychic attack. I met Jacques Marin, the false teacher, and Gaeton Tremblay, Marc's brother, at the Psychic Fair. Had I not gone to Ottawa, Canada at that time, I would never have met him.

Jacques was a small man, very dark and very French. He did not speak English. His wife, Yolane, was an educated brown haired beauty. She translated for him so that we could have a conversation. They lived in Hull, Quebec Province, just outside of Ottawa. Jacques, who was psychically gifted, became my teacher for about eighteen months. He claimed he was from another planet and was sent down to earth to teach. I should have known better. The relationship ended badly and I was under his psychic attack for three months. I felt as though I had been spit out of the sky, completely unworthy of God's love. Jacques put a devastating spell on me. I could not work; I could not function at all.

During this time my close friends in New York, Elizabeth Hepburn and Gordon Clark, were working with me to help me free myself from this influence. They called me everyday. I had also confided in my minister, Rev. David Bach of the Wyckoff Reform Church in New Jersey. It was not a good time, as I felt as though I had been overtaken and possessed by the devil. All I could do is play blessed mantras on my tape deck and pray. I had no energy for anything except for very basic day-to-day living.

Surprisingly, a few weeks after returning from Ottawa, a phone call came from a kind, loving, gentle man who asked me if I could send him a photo of Mahavitar Babaci. His brother had met me in Ottawa and had seen the photograph on my table at the Psychic Fair. What a miracle, or was he truly God sent?

This is how I met Marc Tremblay from Quebec, Canada, a truly gifted, great healer. He knew of this false teacher, Jacques Marin, and he sensed right away exactly what was going on, and began to work with my energy field.

I am going to tell you a part of this story to help you understand what it took to escape this force field that had been placed around me by several people.

It was mid-week and I was deep in slumber, having a nightmare that a group of people, some who I recognized, were throwing me into a snake pit. The snakes were black cottonmouth cobras. I fell into the pit and began a pleading mantra to the Lord. "Lord Jesus Christ, have mercy on me. Lord Jesus Christ, have mercy on me." I repeated over and over. After what seemed like forever, I saw three Angels come down into the pit and pull me out. The snakes jumped and snapped at me, and I was covered with white venom. As I lay sobbing on the ground, halfway delirious, the Angels worked on my energy field.

In the morning when I awoke, I ran for the shower. As I bathed, I discovered red marks, like bite marks, all over my body. They were everywhere. I was frightened and very sore, but the mantra never stopped running through my head. "Lord Jesus Christ, have mercy on me."

Fixing myself some coffee, I put *"Ardas"* on the tape recorder, and played it continually day and night. I meditated all day, and slept deeply at night. My support system, Elizabeth, Gordon, and Marc, knew what had happened.

Of course, I never went outside, except to buy food and gas. I wasn't working, either. But every time I went to my purse to find money for milk, coffee, food, or gas, there were always three brand new hundred-dollar bills. They appeared magically through the ethers. This happened about six times.

Finally, at summer's end, Rev. Bach came over for a visit.

"I'm worried about you, Elizabeth. You have to snap out of this. What can I do to be of help?" he looked at me with sadness. "Do you need to go up to the Cape for a rest and to be by the ocean?"

"Oh that would be wonderful," I responded.

"Well, I brought you the key. All the renters are out, it's just after Labor Day, but there are some lovely September days ahead." David replied, smiling with relief. "All I ask is that you stop at the rental management office when you arrive, and let them know you are there. Then stay as long as you need to. When you leave, please close up the house, like you have done in the past, and drop off the key with the rental office. I will give you a call from time to time, to make sure you're doing okay."

With a tear in my eye, I thanked Rev. Bach, and somehow I knew the worst was over.

I left for the Cape the next morning with a few clothes, an umbrella for the beach, a boom box, my crystals, some of William's music, and *Ardas*.

Cape Cod is another magical place, and I had spent sixteen years there with my children at David's house in North Eastham, at the mouth of the northern protected seashore. I knew some of the "townies" there and enjoyed a meditation circle, while visiting several new age bookshops in Chatham and Provincetown. The Willfleet drive-in movie theater was still open to enjoy as well.

I slept in my field of crystals, meditated almost continually every morning, drove around and visited with the townies in the afternoons, and went down to the beach at night to "talk to the moon." With *Ardas* playing continually, my body and mind slowly began to come back together again.

The tenth day was a Saturday, and I'll never forget it. I awoke as the sun was rising, stretching my body and reveling in the peace that was present. I did not want to get out of bed because I had not felt this good in months. I looked at the beautiful, tall and green, bamboo plant I had just purchased in Provincetown the day before, and almost felt that it bowed and gave me a smile.

Suddenly my body went zip, zip, zip, and I felt a soft, light, comfortable energy curse down my spine. I began to giggle. I was "cooked." I was "done." Marc had told me the Cape would complete my healing. With great joy, I began to clean up and pack for my ride home.

Marc taught me a great deal by his words and explanation of events that happened during that time, and helped me learn how to recognize true light in a person, as well as in myself. He also helped teach me that God's presence, as Spirit, is where people work willingly and honestly for others, out of compassion and caring. He took me under his wing. Giving me his time and encouragement, as I began to lean on him for strength, helped me to trust again. These lessons are now such an ingrained part of me that I can scarcely imagine what I would have been like if I hadn't met this person. Marc Tremblay saved my life in many ways.

I realized, as Marc said, "This is what is meant by trusting the energy flow, and above all trusting the Universe. Who else could do it but you Elizabeth? Bravo!"

As for Jacques, I knew he was not an honest man, and later found out that his wife's best friend bore his illegitimate child. That I had suspected all along. His wife, Yolane, left him, taking her son with her. He eventually died of lung cancer.

Back in Mahwah, I began a new prayer to the Divine. "What do you want me to do?" I cried. "I will go wherever you guide me. I will stop all my spiritual work if that is your wish. I will go back and work in a lawyer's office or in aviation. I surrender. Please direct me."

It was the next morning that I received a call from Pat and her sister. (See pg. 217)

CHAPTER 15

My New Teachers

Working with Dr. Deepak Chopra

I MET DR. CHOPRA AT a Louis Hay seminar in New York City in the early 1990's. He had just arrived with his family from Massachusetts. I liked him immediately, and we chatted about the differences between Eastern and Western medicine and healing. I believe that Dr. Chopra has fused the wisdom of Eastern healing practices with practical Western healing techniques. Through ancient knowledge and modern cutting-edge research, his work has become internationally known and respected. His workshops and books inspire, and bring practical, new strategies for clearing away obstacles to create health, love, and peace in your life. His workshops can restore boundless Soul love, and perhaps open the door for you to find romance that will last a lifetime. This purpose is the main reason he came to America. He has fulfilled his Soul's assignment.

I knew I wanted to attend Dr. Deepak Chopra's seminar on the chakras. Curious as I am, I wanted the experience to enliven my chakras, feel them spin, and work within me. I sensed this workshop would bring that to me.

In 1993, musician Richard Shulman and I put together a guided meditation called, *The Chakras and Your Body.* I feel it's the best work I've ever done. It was a big accomplishment. Richard, with his divine Ascension music, and I began giving Spiritual Intensive Workshops in, the New York City and New Jersey areas.

It was late winter, 1995. I heard of Dr. Chopra's latest workshop, *Seduction of Spirit.* He had relocated to the San Diego area of California and opened the Chopra Center. I began to visualize attending that workshop, scheduled in late April, 1995. I told my meditation group about it and we began to visualize my attending the workshop as a group. The workshop was cost prohibitive for me, and I knew I could not go without some kind of help or Divine Intervention.

In March, the group gave me the workshop, paid in full, as a birthday present. I was shocked! The next hurdle to conquer was the flight out to San Diego and back. I called United Airlines, and found that I had enough miles to cover the ticket. Wow! Next was room and lodging.

Richard and I had signed up for a table at Whole Life Expo in New York City the second weekend in April. I was still struggling with the room and lodging issue for the workshop. Although I had my airline ticket, and the workshop was paid for, I had no lodging and the rooms at Coronado Bay were $400 plus a night.

"Why don't you just surrender it, Elizabeth," Richard asked. "After all, if you have the ticket and workshop taken care of, the rest must be too. Trust in the Universe."

"I know, Richard, but I can get worked up and full of worries." I admitted.

Richard just smiled and said, "It's all good. I sense you have a few nice surprises ahead, Elizabeth."

It was the second day of the Expo, and Richard was away from the booth, playing for someone's workshop. A man came up to the table and said, "Hi, I'm Brian, Brian Anderson, are you busy? I would like a reading. I've walked around this expo for hours, been on all three floors, and you are the one I need to have a reading from. I'm a bit fussy about whoever reads my energy."

Flattered, I smiled and asked Brian to sit down. I asked for his birth information, and where he was from. "I'm from San Diego, but I'm looking to move soon," he responded.

"San Diego, California?"

"Yes, that's right."

"What are you doing here in New York?" I asked, shyly.

"I really have no clue," He laughed. I had a dream I was supposed to come here for the Expo, but I still don't know why. I always listen to Spirit," Brian confided.

We got down to business and I gave Brian a lengthy and informative reading. He was very pleased.

"I'm supposed to go out to San Diego on the 25th for a workshop with Dr. Deepak Chopra," I shared. "Do you know of any place I can stay near Coronado Bay that is affordable?"

Brian began to laugh. "Are you kidding?" Coronado Bay is on a peninsula off of the Bay area in the most expensive part of town. That's like looking for a bargain in the middle of New York City." Still smiling, he suddenly reached into the back pocket of his jeans.

Brian laid a key on the table. "Elizabeth, now I know why I was sent here and to you. For some reason you are supposed to go to this workshop without worry. This is my house key. My girlfriend and I need to drive over to Dallas, Texas, to pick up a car. It will take about a week to get everything done. However, I have two dogs, and did not want to take them, board them, or leave them alone. I'm about twenty minutes from your workshop. How about you stay at the house and take care of the animals for me?"

I stared at him for a minute or so, and then the tears of gratitude began to fall. I remember Richard's words as we set up for the Expo. "Just trust."

Dr. Deepak Chopra's workshop was perfect in more ways than one. As I was packing for the trip, an inner voice said, *"Take as many crystals and oils as you can fit into the suitcase. You will sell them all."*

Delighted, I did just that. Brian met me at the airport and took me to his home. Later that day he showed me the drive to the hotel where the workshop would be held. "I have an extra car for you to use while you're here, so you don't need a rental," Brian said. He and his girlfriend were off to Texas bright and early the next morning.

The workshop was amazing. I met some wonderful people, and was truly in a magical, mystical space. Deepak was very gracious, and remembered me from when Louise Hay had introduced us years before. I sold every crystal and my oils at the workshop, which paid for my food and gas, plus a souvenir or two. The tools I learned I use in my teachings today, as they are timeless.

1995 was a number seven year for me, and certainly proved to be educational, spiritual, and quite different from my other years.

On another note, the energy I gained at the workshop opened the door for my next experience, the fated trip to Egypt with the Schor Foundation.

Dr Joseph Schor — Egypt

Later that year I met another gentleman who proved to be a teacher to me as well, Dr. Joseph M. Schor. Dr. Han Holzer, considered one of the world's leading experts in the paranormal, had been tracking my psychic work for many years. We met at the New Jersey Metaphysical Society in the early 1980's, and became good friends. He had included me in his book, *The Directory of Psychics,* which was published in 1995.

I was living on the Upper West Side of New York by the end of 1995. Hans was at Riverside Drive at the mid-80o's. We became neighbors, and lunched together often.

Filmmaker Boris Said also knew and respected Dr. Holzer. The 1994 NBC TV feature documentary that he produced with John Anthony West, "*The Mysteries of the Sphinx*" hosted by Charlton Heston, won an Emmy.

Boris first learned about the mysteries surrounding the monuments in Egypt and the questions about their origins from John Anthony West, while helping make the documentary. West was working with Boston

University Geologist Dr. Robert Schoch whose groundbreaking work indicates that the age of *the Sphinx* is thousands of years older than the Egyptian civilization itself.

Boris had been invited to document and film a new, private research expedition to Egypt, which was to be headed by Dr. Joseph Schor who was conducting a series of scientific investigations of the Giza Plateau. Technically, the Egyptian license for this activity only allowed for "exploration of underground geological faults and cavities ... possibly injurious to tourists and the ancient monuments," many have inferred that the scope of the "Schor Expédition" extended far beyond this public disclaimer. Some (because of his extensive connection with "ARE" -- the "Cayce Foundation") have implied that Dr. Schor had been interested in nothing less than confirming Edgar Cayce's fabled "readings of Atlantis" and actually discovering the legendary "Hall of Records."

Both Boris and Joe Schor felt that if they brought a good and clear psychic along, perhaps they could be directed to some new findings and answers. To that end, Boris approached Dr. Holzer to help with this mission.

Hans set up a meeting between the three of us, Hans, Boris, and myself. In the meeting Boris asked me many questions, read through some of Han's accounts of my work, and asked me if I would be willing to go to Egypt and support this expedition.

I had read all of Edgar Cayce's books, and had healed several people using the Cayce formulas. I was a member of the ARE for more than ten years, and was thrilled by this opportunity. Grammie Hemphill told me many years ago that I would go to Egypt.

I told Boris I would love to go and bring along Marc Tremblay. I felt that together, we could be more than powerful. Boris was pleased. The next step would be for me to interview with Dr. Schor.

Boris and I met with Dr. Schor the following week. Dr. Schor explained to me the secrecy of this journey, and that I could not tell anyone I was a psychic. I signed a contract to that effect. He would bring me over as his secretary, and Marc as his advisor. He was impressed with my aviation background, and that I had once had top security clearance, as well as Dr. Holzer's recommendation. It assured him that I could keep secrets very well. He phoned Marc in Quebec, Canada, who agreed to go on the trip too. Arrangements were made to depart from New York's Kennedy Airport in mid-April, 1996.

We flew together on British Airways, and Boris Said's good friend met us at the Cairo Airport. He would also be Boris' assistant on this excursion. "Giza is about ten miles away, " the driver said, grinning through his broken teeth. The Mena House is right across the street from the entrance onto the Giza Plateau. You are lucky to be staying at this beautiful Swiss hotel." He added.

"Yes," Dr. Schor chimed in, "The hotel is beautiful, well run, has about six or seven restaurants, and you can trust the water and the fruit, as well. I stay here every time I come to Giza."

"Marc and Elizabeth," Dr. Schor continued. "You cannot trust any raw food or water here. Please have bottled water with you everywhere you go. You will need it. Also do not eat any fruit that is not from the Mena House. We don't want you getting sick here," he added, smiling.

"The Great Pyramid of Giza is an Ancient Egyptian landmark. Known as Khufu's Pyramid, it is the greatest pyramid of the nine-pyramid complex: a truly overwhelming sight. The pyramid is placed right in the center of the earth, and as one of the seven wonders of the ancient world, it is the only one still standing to this day! When gazing at this colossal structure, there's no way to escape the feeling of being dwarfed. The two smaller – but still huge – pyramids in Giza are those of Khafre and Menkaure. A few steps to the east you will notice three small piles of rubble: the Queens' pyramids, tombs of Khufu's wives and sisters. Nearby, on the Giza Plateau, you'll also find the Great Sphinx and the Solar Boat Museum. The site is also where the Sound Light Show at Giza takes place once a week, and where every newcomer to Egypt experiences Giza camel rides for the first time," the driver explained.

With its rich, colorful history, I had read that The Mena House is one of the most unique hotels in Cairo. Surrounded by verdant green gardens, this palatial hotel is located in the shadows of the Great Pyramids of Giza. I was so excited, and pleased to be so very well taken care of by the Schor Foundation.

The royal history of the hotel is reflected in luxurious interiors that are embellished with exquisite antiques, handcrafted furniture, original work of arts and magnificent antiques that are rarely found in luxury hotels. Mena House has hosted kings, emperors, Heads of State, and celebrities.

The Mena House offers unmatched views of the pyramids. You can gaze upon the magnificence of the pyramids from your rooms at sunrise and sunset. Marc and I would enjoy breakfast, and then meditate for at least one hour, facing the Great Pyramid, on the grounds of the Mena House, in complete safety and comfort. We began our walk up the road to the Great Pyramid, and then once behind it, we went down the road leading to the Sphinx.

After dinner at one of the many restaurants, we would see the Pyramids lit up for our private viewing. We would meditate from our balconies at night. It was a journey of discovery. We explored Cairo's ancient treasures and unraveled the many mysteries of Egypt's past.

Marc and I were on the plateau everyday with Dr. Schor. We worked in and around the Sphinx. Together we drew diagrams of what we sensed there. There was a large group of people, about thirty, and we all had our jobs to do. Since Dr. Schor (we called him Joe) did not want us identified, we also ran errands and such. However, Dr. Schor made sure that Tom Dobecki tested the ground with his radar after we showed him where to look. Of course, they looked in other areas as well.

Dr. Schor, along with the University of Florida, Tom Dobecki, and the ARE were conducting extensive new scientific surveys of the Giza Plateau. These included several in the immediate vicinity of the highly controversial Sphinx. They involved seismological investigations, ground-penetrating radar of the subsurface Plateau geology, and sound experiments conducted inside the Great Pyramid itself.

Marc and I helped draw sketches mapping the interior of the pyramids using our psychic abilities. We both inwardly knew there were underground tunnels between the Sphinx and the other pyramids. (There are nine in all.) I also "saw" steps going down into the tunnels at about fifty feet in front of the Sphinx claws.

Below are some of the sketches:

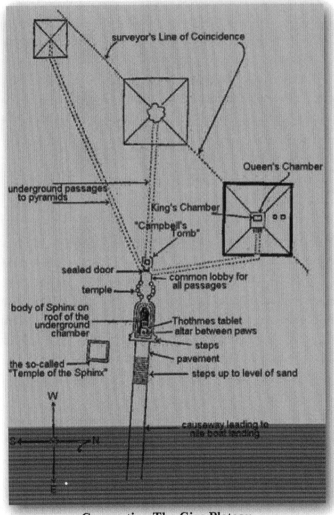

Connecting The Giza Plateau

The Sphinx – Giza, Egypt

Dr. Robert Schoch, in the first trip to Giza, explained why *the Sphinx* was older than 4000-5000 years, and it just made perfect sense to Marc and I. Nothing was more obvious. The marks were there,, it was in the stone, and, right from the start. an alternative viewpoint to the age, and perhaps the meaning, of these monuments began to resonate within me. We were especially awestruck from the Rosetta Stone in front of the Sphinx, and decided to meditate in front of the stone every day as soon as we arrived.

The film crew was there, and I wanted to be filmed walking the paw of the Sphinx. I walked the left paw, because that's the receiving side. What a thrill that was, however, although we were promised copies of all the pictures, we never received any because of the unfortunate events that followed.

Marc and I waited four days before entering the Great Pyramid. We were deeply involved with the energy at the Sphinx and waited to be invited by Spirit.

On the fourth day, with permission from Joe, we headed up to the Great Pyramid. Joe gave us the pass required to enter. As we approached the entrance, after climbing up a precarious staircase along the side of the pyramid, the gatekeepers saw us, and began to bow down to us. "You are Holy People," one of them uttered.

Then the two gatekeepers ran inside the pyramid and ordered all tourists out! I could not believe this was happening, and just observed in wonderment.

"We are at your service," the Gatekeepers told us. What is your pleasure? Both Marc and I had read the New York Times bestseller, *Initiation* by Elisabeth Haich, a fabulous novel by a respected German teacher of metaphysics. We wanted to walk through the *Initiation* conducted in ancient Egypt for the Initiates to become the Hierophant, the great teachers of wisdom described in the book. In order to do that, we had to crawl down into the "pit" under the pyramid. It was 280 feet below the main floor.

I almost didn't make it because half way down I wanted to turn around. However, Marc, who was leading the way, would not allow me to quit. "Elizabeth, you must do this. It's a once in a lifetime experience. Keep going." Finding strength in his voice, I kept going.

We were actually crawling on sand and stone through a very narrow, natural tunnel, with sand seeping down along the way. Part of me thought the sky could fall in, but we made it. Behind us, one of the Gatekeepers crawled along as well.

Once inside, we could see how the Initiation worked. There was an area that once held a lake of water. On the other side of the room, along a narrow, rocky and sandy ledge was a small door. That door opened up to another tunnel, leading up to the Queen's Chamber, in the middle of this Great Pyramid. Supposedly, alligators were put in the lake. The Initiate had to crawl through the tunnel, work his way around the narrow ledge to the door on the other side, in the dark, and make his way up to the Queen's Chamber.

If it were not for the alligators, swimming across the lake would have been easy. If they made it to the Queen's Chamber, they were considered worthy enough to teach. They would then ascend up to the King's Chamber to be honored and complete the initiation.

Marc and I found a ledge to sit on and meditated for at least an hour. The Gatekeeper joined us. A very intense power filled us, and we knew we were blessed. As we rose to leave Marc gave the Gatekeeper a mini-reading.

"You are worried about your mother, who is ill, and your living situation. Don't worry, your mother will be well soon, and you are safe. You will not lose your animals and home, because you are protected by Spirit. Don't allow yourself to become discouraged," Marc told him.

This young, handsome Egyptian thanked Marc and with a tear in his eye, led us back to the tunnel opening so we could crawl up to the main floor and continue our quest.

When we arrived at the Queen's Chamber, we realized that the tourists were not allowed to enter or disturb us. The Gatekeeper stood at the door, instructing the tourists to go up to the King's Chamber first and check the Queen's Chamber for availability on their way down.

Marc and I knew we had something to do for Spirit, but were not sure just what. "Let's just sit and meditate awhile," Marc suggested.

"Marc, did you know that it is believed that whatever is requested in the Queen's Chamber in meditation is supposed to be granted? What can we ask, for the world?" I asked.

As we meditated, our energies were brought together, and we viewed the same image and received the identical message from within. Place the gems of the chakras above you, and ask for the total healing of AIDS.

"Oh my," Marc exclaimed. "Okay, let's begin. We'll use the number eight for extra power. Visualize the fin to a ceiling fan, in pure gold, with an emerald filling and place it in the center, at the top of the room. Then follow with a sapphire, ruby, and diamond filling. You will see that it becomes a ceiling fan," Marc explained.

In unison, both of us began the visualization. We both completed it at the same time. Suddenly we were hit with a powerful Light, which lit up the entire chamber. We knew the "fan of jewels and gold" was placed perfectly at the center of the ceiling. We were finished, and Spirit would take it from here. We both got up and quietly left the Queen's Chamber.

Now it was time to ascend up the rickety stairs to the King's Chamber. Again, we were asked to wait until those inside could come down, because the chamber was being emptied for us. It was very exciting.

As we entered the King's Chamber, a blanket of "knowing" energy enveloped us. We instantly knew that the Great Pyramid was a treasury of Divine wisdom embodying chronological, meteorological, astronomical, mathematical, historical and Biblical truths. This storehouse of wisdom remains sealed by Divine appointment. These truths would only be revealed to individuals when the knowledge was most needed. Although Marc and I had many things revealed to us, we knew there was centuries more knowledge still to come.

We sensed there was the King's Chamber, as well as an Ante-Chamber, and other parts holding the secrets of the Universe. The Great Pyramid enshrines knowledge and was built with guidance, help, and support of the Divine. The pyramid and sphinx sit directly in the center of the earth, from where all math can be deciphered, and all longitudes and latitudes can be measured.

We completed our meditation, and began our descent back to the pyramid entrance, and then back to the hotel.

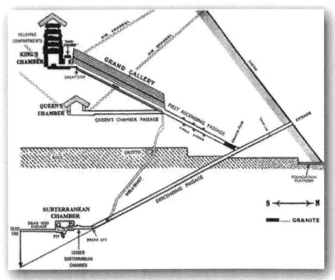

An Inner Map of the Great Pyramid

As we returned to the Mena Hotel, directly across from the entrance to the Great Pyramid and Sphinx, Marc and I realized that the giant echo chamber enhanced the vibrations of both sound and the body. It was a place of higher consciousness and perhaps held the clues to other life in other worlds.

Later that evening I typed up the spiritual notes Marc and I wrote on a daily basis while meditating at the Rosetta Stone in front of the Sphinx. They are included at the back of this book, *"Within The Heart of the Sphinx." (See pg. 309)*

Besides my daily experiences on the Giza strip, I found a new teacher within in the form of Isis. This was the goddess Howard had mentioned years ago. I didn't know much about her at the time, but on the plane ride back to New York, she joined Marc and I in our seats. Telepathically she assured us that we both had strong past lives in Egypt and were great teachers. She also advised us that her energy could be called upon anytime we wished.

NOTE: Scientist Richard Hoagland says, he envisions the builders of the Pyramid designing it to amplify tones that would literally twist the calcium carbonate crystal back and forth in a rhythmic pattern in such a way that you could also *twist space and time itself* and potentially create extraordinary changes of consciousness." He goes on to say that, "Because the pyramid, through the plateau, is anchored to trillions and trillions of tons of this limestone stretching a quarter of a way around the planet to Indonesia, you literally could change the resonant characteristics of *Planet Earth* itself if you pumped enough energy into the pyramids. This effect is an example of *hyperdimensional physics and could be done, in theory, because all things are vibration.* (I met Richard Hoagland when we were both teaching on Dannion Brinkley's Intuition Cruise in 2011.)

We were in Cairo for three weeks, and then were forced to return to New York. We had wanted to continue on, past Mt. Sinai and into Jerusalem, but some terrorists' activities in Cairo made us forgo that option.

I met to Dr. Schor in 1996 and he agreed to fund an expedition to try and record the opening of that tunnel. Dr. Schor had a permit to explore the *Giza Plateau,* as well as a permit to film. Dr. Schor took over all the science and the government negotiations, including paying hundreds of thousands of dollars to the Antiquity Commission.

The result of The Schor Foundation's excursions came to naught. As it turned out, Schor's "situation," after making its sensational discoveries, was unable to get permission to *follow through* with the next logical step because of politics. He was blocked from filming or from seeing *behind* the door discovered along the side of the King's Chamber.

Schor was forced to indefinitely sit on these exciting new archaeological discoveries, brought to light by his initial investigation. Schor hoped to inform *other* members of the government of Egypt of the apparent "agendas" of Zawas and others and to create sufficient *public political pressure* to bring this intolerable situation "to a head." It was never done.

With Dr. Joseph Schor's *Sphinx Expedition,* the publicized goal seemed to be locating unknown cavities and geological faults beneath the *Sphinx, and they were there!* Those pursuits have long since reached an impasse, and hopes they could ever be resolve, faded.

The repercussion of the inexplicable and dramatic discovery in the Great Pyramid, by *Schor* consultant Thomas Danley, as well as achieving the *Schor Foundation* goals, or those of any other unorthodox expedition were permanently preempted, and Dr. Schor knew it.

The Egyptians were very resistant to suggestions that Schor (1) drill a hole down into the room; and (2) excavate a tunnel at the back of the Sphinx, thought to lead to that room. For whatever reasons, they denied us permission to do the excavations. They kept Dr. Schor waiting, with promises of completion, for years. Eventually, Dr. Joseph Schor became ill with Alzheimer, and passed away without ever completing his desired project.

I met with him at his office month after month after month, ready to go back to Egypt with him and provide more guidance. Because of jealousy, greed, lies, deceits, around this project, it was simply abandoned. Of course there are many others who have picked up the reins, but to me, what was done was tragic.

The bottom line is that it is Egypt's country and the pyramids - their monument. It is hard to be miffed. The Schor Foundation also discovered a tunnel at the bottom of a well, about 120 feet down, and it is about halfway from the back of the Sphinx up to the Great Pyramid. They were trying to find a way to get permission to open that tunnel, because they thought it might lead to the Sphinx as well. It would support *the Rosicrucian* theory that the three pyramids are connected to a temple-like structure, which is then connected to the Sphinx.

I took several trips to England, and met with Dr. Schor, his wife Laura, and author Adrian Gilbert, co-author of the *Orion Mysteries*. Adrian has a deep interest in the the mysteries of Egypt, the Sphinx, and the Hall of Records. Adrian is a frequent guest on *Coast to Coast AM* and speaks at the ARE (Edgar Cayce) Center at Virginia Beach, Virginia.

On one of the trips, Adrian Gilbert took us to South Wales to tour the area where King Arthur dwelled. Supposedly there were two King Arthurs, as explained in Adrian's book, *The Holy Kingdom*.

Although Dr. Schor and his ensemble did not feel the trip to Egypt had been successful, Marc and I shared a different point of view. We pulled our notes together and found a synchronicity of the journey, and what it may have brought to mankind. We wrote our impression of what the Sphinx communicated to us about the state of this planet and where it might be headed, if we all could just get it together.

I remained friends with Dr. Schor until his death, two days before my twin sister died, in July 2013.

JOSEPH M. SCHOR Obituary

SCHOR--Joseph M., Ph.D., 84, died at home peacefully after a long illness on July 14. Beloved father, brother, husband of Laura S. Schor and the late Sandra M. Schor, grandfather and friend. A brilliant man who lived many lives: biochemist, executive, astrologer, farmer, Col. NY Guard, saxophonist, archaeologist, Zionist. Retired VP of Forest Laboratories.

Published in *The New York Times* on July 16, 2013

CHAPTER 16

What in the World is Happening?
Finishing Up The Twentieth Century

THE WORLD BEGAN TO CHANGE as new technologies had their first beginnings at the end of the twentieth century. Global expansion and instant communication with anyone, anywhere, took its first baby steps in the last years of the 1990's.

My life changed during this last decade as well. My mother passed in 1991. Jeffrey married his first wife, and moved to Nashville, Tennessee to begin his residency. My worldwide consciousness grew as I attended an International Holistic Health Conference in Geneve, Switzerland. Vance moved out of my condo and for the first time, I rented it. I met Don Swaim and fell in love.

It was in November of 1993 when I began to "feel it." I had just returned from Switzerland and found myself dancing around the living room in my condo. I dug out every love song I could find and began waltzing with the "handsome Stranger." This ritual went on for days.

One afternoon the phone rang. "You've really been on my mind a lot lately," Brenda said as she greeted me, "What's going on?"

"I have no idea," I laughingly responded. "I just know that I'm falling in love, and I'm doing it before I even meet the guy."

"That's interesting," she responded, as she usually does when I tell her something 'off the wall.' "Tell me about it."

Excitedly I responded, "Do you remember when Meg told us to visualize? She told us to make a vision board on the New Moon. Well, we're going into the Holiday Season, and I decided I need a new love. It's been more than fifteen years since Joe passed, and I'm ready for a new beginning. I found a magazine, cut out a picture of the handsome stranger, and hung it on the wall near my bedroom window. I gaze at it every morning as soon as I wake up, just before I go into my morning meditation. Then I thank Spirit for my new love and partner."

"And," Brenda asked.

"It's working. I can feel "him." I said slowly. "His energy came into my field about three days ago. This reminds me of the words of Rumi, the great poet from thousands of years ago. *True lovers don't meet somewhere. They're in each other all along.*

"What are you feeling," Brenda asked.

"Well I can't get his name but he's about five eleven, has blue eyes, and the only thing I know about him is that he was born in Wichita Kansas. However, I can feel his form as I dance with him around the condo."

"Amazing," she responded. "Well, keep me posted."

Don Swaim was a friend of my twin sister. She had suggested I give him a call, because I had begun writing this book, *Unlimited Realities*. Knowing he was well known for his show, *Book Beat* on CBS News Radio88, I was shy and not comfortable calling him. Don was an author, interviewed famous authors all around the world on his radio show, and was well respected.

It was December 5th when I had the second dream. "Call him, call him," my guides were instructing me. At the urging of my twin, I had called Don in September, 1993. We had talked for a while, and that was it. How could I call him again?

I always try to follow what Spirit asks of me. Reluctantly, I called Don again. We visited for a few moments, then I suggested that I come into New York so he could read some of what I had written. "How about dinner," he suggested? "When can you drive in?"

Looking at my calendar, I responded, "Not until the seventeenth."

"Fine, what's your address? I'll send you directions."

The date went well, and we talk until four in the morning. I got up to leave and Don insisted that I not drive back to New Jersey at four in the morning. He just wouldn't allow it. Pulling out the sofa bed, he said, "Don't worry, you're safe with me. Tomorrow we can do Christmas." Too tired to question or argue, I feel asleep as soon as my head hit the pillow.

The next morning, and it was almost lunchtime, Don had fixed breakfast and was talking excitedly about the day's plans. "Let's do New York," he said.

"What do you mean, Don," I asked. I had no clue as to what he meant.

"Elizabeth, you're in New York the week before Christmas. This is the time of year when New York is bursting at the seams. It's filled to the brim with people from all over the world, seeing the sights with their families. So many people would give their eyeteeth to be here now. We'll start in Battery Park and work our way up. I want to show you everything beautiful about this city. I'll even teach you how to ride the subways."

What a fabulous day we had. We did Chinatown, Barnes and Noble at 14th Street, Union Square, then up 5th Avenue to St. Patrick's Cathedral and Rockefeller Center. We walked and walked, stopping into any shop I desired; Godiva Chocolates, The Museum, Gift Shop, and many specialty shops. It was overwhelming and especially beautiful. As we got to 59th St and The Plaza Hotel, across from FAO Schwartz, Don suggested we go in for a drink at the famous Oak Bar.

It was dark when we headed back to Don's apartment. On the walk back we went through Central Park, which was beautifully lit up with all of the holiday lights. "You must be hungry," Don said. "It's way past dinnertime unless you're a New Yorker."

Smiling, I shook my head yes. "I'm going to take you to a nice restaurant on Broadway near my apartment. It's called Dock's. Do you like seafood?"

"It's about my favorite," I responded.

After we sat down at Dock's, Don turned my face to his and said, "Elizabeth, you surprised me today. We've been out for more than eight hours, walking and enjoying ourselves. You never complained once. You are so different from your twin. You two are not at all alike. I like you and have truly enjoyed today. I hope you will give me the chance to get to know you."

Wow! Little did he know that was the best thing he could have said to me. My heart was filled with new feelings I had not enjoyed for years, I was smitten.

Upon arriving back at the apartment, we talked until the wee small hours. Don pulled out the sleeper couch again, and said, "See you in the morning."

It was almost noon when we sat down to breakfast. I was a bit jittery and nervous. "I must get back to the condo immediately, Don. I have people coming at three o'clock this afternoon. Also, I have to leave for Tennessee tomorrow morning."

"I understand," he responded, "Thank you for giving me Christmas, because I will be alone on that day. When will you be back? Can I see you for New Year's Eve?"

"You told me you had a party to go to on New Year's."

"Well, that's not as important as you. What would you like to do for New Year's Eve? Have you ever spent New Year's Eve in New York City?" he asked, smiling.

"No I haven't," I replied. "Yes, there is one thing I have always wanted to do for New Year's Eve. I'd like to attend the candlelight service at St. John The Divine."

"Done. By the way why are you going out to Tennessee?" Don asked.

"My son, Jeffrey, is doing his residency at Vanderbilt University in Nashville. He's becoming an ophthalmologist. I am going with his wife's parents and my ex-husband, Dick to celebrate Christmas. We are driving out and we'll be back on the twenty-eighth."

"Yes, I can come into New York for New Year's weekend. My foster daughter, Caroline is coming to visit on New Year's Day. Since she will be staying in New York, can I invite her here? She just got engaged to Chuck, her high school sweetheart, and I am sure her fiancée will be with her."

"Absolutely, " Don said. "We can all plan on having lunch together."

As I walked to the door to leave, Don stopped me. He lifted my chin and looked into my eyes. "I just want you to know that I feel you won't be driving out to Tennessee with your ex again anytime soon. Merry Christmas and see you next week."

My heart was flying over the car as I drove across the George Washington Bridge and back to the condo.

Don and I spent New Year's weekend 1993/94 together and have never been apart since.

On New Year's Eve we went to the candlelight service at St. John the Divine on the Upper West Side. Don was able to get CBS press box seats, and we were up front, sitting next to the new Mayor, Rudy Giuliani and his wife. She lit my candle to pass on the Light, and Rudy lit Don's. Then we went out for Indian food.

Caroline came by the next day and introduced us to her fiancée, Chuck DiVone. We went to the American Museum of Art to see a Christmas tree decorated with four hundred year old ornaments, carved out of wood. The angels were spectacular.

Later we had dinner at the Tavern on the Green in Central Park. It was fairytale perfect.

After about a year of dating, I moved into Don's apartment on New York's Upper West Side. Although I still gave personal readings, these years were dedicated to building my relationship with him. I worked as a temp in lawyer's offices, and went back to doing extra work for commercials and films. All this work kept me very busy.

Computers were Don's expertise. He fell in love with Apple when they first arrived on the market. With the help and guidance of Don, I sent my first email and created my personal website in the spring months of 1996. I learned html and the concept of webhosting. I also created my Paypal bank account for my internet business, never imagining what the concept would fully become. My webhost Amy told me I was creating virtual money. I felt her insight was way ahead of mine. These Apple computers were really something and way ahead of any PC. I loved the learning curve and creativity of my new found hobby.

I would write articles and people would actually read them. Several of my astrology articles were published nationally. I created a webpage and began a monthly astrology newsletter. This was great!

I purchased the domain name for my new website was www.new-visions.com. At the time, people asked me why I would ever want a website? I smiled enjoying the concept of these new web hosting companies who were about to make a fortune. My first email was Tibet@aol.com, and I gave readings through email.

I was fascinated by the worldwide access, and the fact that people could read my articles from anywhere in the world. Yes, they would have to have a computer, but soon I was listed in "Ask Jeeves." In the message from Joe years ago, I knew that I had a book to write.

1996 was an active year. Prince Charles and Diana got divorced. Ask Jeeves became popular on the computer, the first digital encyclopedia. Bill Clinton was re-elected and I took my fateful trip to Egypt.

1997 ushered in female power. Madeleine Albright was appointed as the first female Secretary of State in the United States. Scotland, trying to break away from the United Kingdom, created its own Parliament. The first Harry Potter book was published by author J.K. Rowling. Scientists at the Roslin Institute unveiled "Dolly" the first successfully cloned sheep. The Hale-Bopp comet made its closest approach to Earth.

Many people on the young Internet predicted a comet would hit the earth and cause destruction. I knew that would not happen, but this began a new trend in society.

In September, 1997, I made a prediction about the Monika Lewinsky and Bill Clinton affair, published in several publications as well as posted on my website.

A dark haired girl named Veronica will upset the White House in January, 1998, and President Clinton may not give his "State of the Union" address. An angry blonde will bring forth the truth, and Clinton will be impeached in the fall months of 1998. Welcome President Gore.

Oh yes, and Don proposed.

1998 opened with the news of the Bill Clinton, Monika Lewinsky affair. Google was founded.. The United States had a budget surplus for the first time in thirty years.

To Don's delight, Apple Computers revealed the iMac computer. I took a trip to Florida. While visiting friends in Boca Raton, I was able to purchase my first Apple IMac Computer for a nice discount, and managed to fly it home to surprise Don. At that point, I settled in to the computer world, learned word processing, Quicken Books, and how to post articles on my website.

In the summer of 1998, Don Swaim and I bought a house in Bucks County, Pennsylvania. After thirty years, Don retired from CBS New Radio88, and we moved out of New York City.

That year, at Amma's annual summer retreat in Albuquerque, at darshan, Anna lifted my left hand. She circled her fingers and ran them down my ring finger, smiling and laughing with pleasure. Although Don had complications with his ex and family, I knew at that moment Don and I would marry in 1999.

As 1999 came to a close, I reflected over the happenings of the last year of the 1900's. President Bill Clinton faced impeachment proceedings. (As predicted by me in 1997) The computer file-sharing service Napster is created. The Dow Jones closed above 11,000 for the first time. Eleven countries begin to use the Euro as their currency. After a number of years fighting between Iran and Iraq, Saddam Hussein needed additional funds and invaded neighboring oil rich Kuwait. The UN showed it's strength and a coalition force fully backed by the United Nations first bombed and then a month later mounted a ground attack to send the Iraq army back to Iraq and retook possession of Kuwait. (This was known as *The Gulf War*)

The 90's saw a world wide increase of the use, production, and smuggling of the drug trade, with the drugs becoming more addictive and destructive. Many initiatives were tried to stop the growth and production, including education, but even today it continues to be a growing. problem in our society

Also, in 1999, Cosgrove Muir Production Company called and asked me to film a show for *Unsolved Mysteries*. As I accepted, my question to them was, "What took you so long?" I was in the show, *Suddenly Psychic*, along with Richard Harlan, a wonderful and gifted psychic from Massachusetts. These shows still air on the Lifetime Channel.

Don and I were married on June 12th, 1999, outside, at the historic Barley Sheaf Farm in Holicong, Pennsylvania.

CHAPTER 17

Entering the New Mellinnium
and a New Worldwide Lifestyle

EXCITEMENT WAS BUILDING AS WE entered the year 2000. New Year's Eve was eagerly awaited by millions around the world. Several people feared the stories of thee Y2K and that the computers, the stock market, and the banks would shut down, creating widespread chaos. The concern was that the computers would revert back to 1900 instead of moving ahead to 2000.

Think about it. There were no iPhones, no smartphones, no Facebook or Twitter, and no going through the airport security, like we have to now. Our Internet was shiny and new, forging a new frontier. We believed that its function was to deliver food, packs of gum and cigarettes to our front door, and we still used cassette recorders and large car phones. Google was in its infancy and no one had ever heard of YouTube.

In 1999, *Friends* was the country's favorite comedy, a weekly peek inside a whitewashed Manhattan apartment, and how the "singles" lived. On HBO, *Sex and the City* celebrated their successful first season. The most popular TV show, was *Who Wants to Be a Millionaire.*

On New Year's Eve 1999, a record number of revelers gathered in Times Square to wear funny glasses, peering through the zeros in 2000. They joined Dick Clark, anxiously waiting for the apple to drop, to see if the Y2K would really happen. Would the world's computers fail, and jets start falling from the sky?

To my joy, the Clinton's hosted a TV Special showing New Year's Eve around the world, beginning with Australia. Many nations were shown throughout the world, celebrating New Year's Eve, as the clocks flawlessly struck midnight in each country.

Yes, the New Year and the future arrived time zone by time zone, encircling the globe, without incident or apocalypse. Dick Clark counted down the seconds for us as the *Apple* dropped in Times Square. With this beautiful celebration, the new millennium began. We'd all asked anxiously, "What's going to happen next?" The answer was no Y2K, no drama; we are safe! However, all would unfold in due time.

We needed to move into the actual millennium, 2001, for the Twin Towers to fall. The decades overlapped as they usually do, and the nineties didn't truly end until September 11, 2001.

We'd been wondering what was coming, and then we found out. We saw clearly what it was, the end of a world as we knew it, but we didn't yet know and couldn't possibly anticipate or comprehend what laid ahead for America and the world.

On New Year's Day, 2001, Kathy Sasso, one of my students, had a New Year's luncheon at her house for our Women's Group. After lunch, the girls sat me down, and gathered around me, "What's coming for us this year?" They asked, wide-eyed. Taking a deep breath, I closed my eyes, and began searching the energies to see if there was anything significant I could find.

"Washington will beat Purdue at today's Rose Bowl," I began. "Apple will bring us a new way to listen to and purchase music. The Ravens will beat the New York Giants at the Super Bowl. There is a nasty crash at the Daytona 500, possibly killing a famous driver. Russell Crow and Julia Roberts win the Academy Awards for best actors. Crow for "The Gladiator" and Roberts for "Erin Brockovich," and the Twin Towers will fall like pancakes. It will be an act of terrorism, taking place in September, right after school starts.

Then the girls stopped me. "We only want to hear good predictions, Elizabeth. What can you tell us individually?"

"But this event will change to world, and we will all lose some of our freedoms." I replied.

"Oh we don't care about that now. What can you tell US?"

Smiling, and loving them in their ignorance, I began telling each on of them a tidbit of what 2001 would bring to them personally. They could never understand what energy had just moved through my body.

It was August when I received the invitation to Gina's, my favorite cousin's wedding in New Hampshire. I was excited to be "going back home" to Grammie's, and thrilled for my cousin Kathy's happiness about her daughter's wedding. It was on September 9th, and I wanted to take a break and spend several days there. In mid-August, before purchasing my airline ticket, I began to meditate on what day I should return. Should I come back on Monday the tenth, or Tuesday, the eleventh? The answer that came was:

You must return on Monday, September tenth, because there will be no planes flying on Tuesday

"Oh my, why couldn't Spirit be more specific?" I wondered. Of course, I wanted all of the details. I booked a ticket to Manchester, New Hampshire for Sept. 6th, returning on Sept. 10th.

A few days later, Iris, called to ask me about her flight back to India. "I'm returning in September, Elizabeth. I have picked two dates, September 11th or September 18th. Which one should I take? I want to be back in time for Amma's birthday celebration."

"Well Iris, I know you can't go on the eleventh because no planes will be flying. It's best to go with the eighteenth."

"How do you know that?"

"Because I will be in New Hampshire at my cousin's wedding, and was told I had to fly back on September 10th as there will be no planes flying on the eleventh."

"Why, do you suppose?"

"I don't know. Maybe there'll be a pilot's strike or something." I answered, a bit frustrated.

"Oh well, that would just cover the USA Airlines, not Kuwait. I think I'll go on the eleventh," she said.

"I still advise against it, Iris. You will have to change your flight, I'm sure." I replied.

These were the warnings I received well before that fateful day.

On Monday, September 10th, I boarded the USAir flight for my return to Philadelphia National Airport at 12:30 pm. About midway through the trip, an announcement came over the intercom from the pilot. "We are going to have to land in Bader Field, in Connecticut with a forced delay. There has been a fire at Newark Airport and all flights have to be diverted," he informed us.

I had a cell phone, so I called my husband to ask him what was going on. Don is a computer wiz, and would know how to find the information online quickly. He told me that somewhere near Terminal C there was a small fire.

"This fire doesn't seem very threatening, Elizabeth. I don't know why you would have to land at another field and have such a delay."

We were at Bader field for three hours. When we asked the stewardess if we could change to a different flight, we were told that no planes were landing at Newark, so we may as well stay safe and wait it out.

We landed at Newark around 5:30 pm and were told that there would be no more flights out of that airport. The airport was closing down and booking rooms for all stranded travelers. Stunned, and having worked in aviation, I recognized all of the secret service personnel running around the airport.

I went to the private office at the back of USAir's baggage claims to find out about my luggage. I was assured it would arrive at my home the next day.

"What in the world is going on?" I asked the agent.

"I don't know, but it must be big. We began to close the airport at noontime. By the way, the last bus to Doylestown leaves in twenty minutes. You'd better hurry along," she informed me.

I rushed over to the bus stop, boarded, and tried to relax a bit on the two-hour bus ride back home. Don met me at the Doylestown bus stop, and as I stepped down onto the sidewalk, I told him something bad was happening.

"Nonsense," he responded. "Why do you always think the worst?"

Nonetheless, my body was shaking with fear and dread. I had the inner warnings and *knew* things were about to change for everyone.

That night I had one of my penetrating dreams. I was in a subway station, at Franklin Street on the west side of New York City. There were two trains coming at me with piercing bright lights. Suddenly, they both disappeared in a ball of fire in front of me. Needless to say, I had a very restless night's sleep.

In the morning, from somewhere far away, I heard the phone ringing. As I awoke, I realized the phone *was* ringing. It was my cousin, Kathy.

"Beth, do you have the TV on?"

"No," I responded, still in a daze.

"Put it on right now," she replied.

"What channel?" I asked.

"It doesn't matter, it's on all the channels."

Turning on CBS, I saw that one of the Twin Towers in New York City was burning. "Oh my God," I said to Kathy. "It's actually happening."

"Yep, you were right," she said. "Keep listening, I think there's more planes elsewhere. We're under attack."

For the rest of the day, I watched the events as they unfolded. The second tower was hit as well as the Pentagon in Arlington, Virginia, and the fourth plane was stopped in air over a field in Stony Creek Township near Shanksville, Pennsylvania. There were 343 and 72 people killed respectively. Within 45 minutes both 110 story towers in New York City "fell like a stack of pancakes" with debris falling everywhere. The resulting fires caused a partial or complete collapse of all other buildings in the Twin Tower complex, as well as significant damage to ten other large surrounding structures.

In those 45 minutes, the United States and the world was *changed forever.* Suspicion for the attack quickly fell on Al-Qaeda. The United

States responded to the attacks by launching the War on Terror and invading Afghanistan to depose the Taliban. Afghanistan had harbored Al-Qaeda. Many countries strengthened their anti-terrorism legislation and expanded the powers of law enforcement and intelligence agencies to prevent further terrorist attacks.

The impact of the 9/11 attacks, which killed nearly 3,000 people, is still being felt in 2017, as I complete this book. Industries have upgraded and strengthened security policies. The government formed new agencies and the hearts and minds of Americans have been changed forever.

Psychologically speaking, Americans have changed since 9/11 as well. In some ways—whether it's further awareness of foreign threats or the idea that the U.S. is not completely safe—Americans underwent an existential crisis. "Despite the technological advantages, relative safety and general happiness, there's also an underlying fear. Beneath the surface, there's a profound malaise about life and uncertainty about the future. *We've opened up a new dimension that reverses the natural sequence of how things have always been,"* Charles B. Strozier, a psychoanalyst from John Jay College of Criminal Justice in New York City told *Psychology Today.*

Just remember, as Sonny and Cher always told us, *The Beat Goes On, The Beat Goes On.*

It took Don and I some time to adjust to our drastic move from New York City to Bucks County, Pennsylvania. The first year, I worked in Blue Bell, while Don tried to adjust. He finally found a writers group, joined it, and now is the leader of the *Bucks County Writers Group,* helping many authors learn how to write better, and get their books published. Between that group, handling the website for CBS News Radio88, and several others, he keeps very busy.

In November of 2001, a little more than two months after the 911 attacks, Amma came to Michigan for a retreat, and more than sixty people from the New York Satsang were there to gain comfort and understanding. Being near Amma gave us an inner peace, as so many wondered why this event had happened? Would there be any further attacks in New York City? What could we do to help others cope with this disaster?

Throughout her life, Mata Amritanandamayi has embraced and comforted more than 34 million people. Amma inspires, uplifts, and transforms through her embrace, her spiritual wisdom, and through her global charities. Exactly what was Her explanation and thoughts about this experience in our country? Many of us were very troubled.

The first night of the retreat I sat next to Amma during meditation. As I sat there going into the meditation, all of a sudden my third eye opened and it seemed like I was watching a movie. As we were all singing the Bahjans, the energy in the room was building and gaining more power. As the room moved into a higher vibration, I saw an orange, red, and gold ball of light. It was expanding, similar to blowing up a balloon. Suddenly I felt as if I were flying, holding the balloon of Light, and heading somewhere. Where I did not know.

I opened my eyes for a moment to look at Amma. She was looking back at me with a somber smile. It seemed She knew my question, "Where am I going with this?" She nodded her head, and I closed my eyes again.

In my vision I saw Amma and I flying over New York City until we were directly over Ground Zero. The ugly, thick grey and white smoke was rising up from the bowels of the World Trade Center. We took the shimmering ball of Light and dropped in right in the center of the gaping hole in the ground. The ball exploded and Light went everywhere. It was a powerful event. Slivers of *the Ball of Light* began moving down the streets of New York, and across the Brooklyn and Manhattan Bridges. The shimmering Light rays were everywhere. I knew Amma was sending a strong healing energy through the wounded areas. I had great difficulty holding back my tears.

I looked up at Her again, and She nodded her head once more, and I quickly closed my eyes again. Soaring up once more, we flew over the Pentagon and dropped another ball, then headed over the fields of Pennsylvania to where another plane had crashed, for the third drop.

There was truly such an enormous fountain of energy, love and compassion within the Balls of Light. I think if all of the people and earth who received this energy were to absorb even a fraction of it within their own beings, it would bring the living as well as the departed, relief from pain and fear, by uplifting their souls. Whatever little I had to do with Her inspiration, I strived my best to accomplish it. Suddenly I was enveloped in a scent of roses. It was a powerful experience and a powerful moment of realization for me. Overcome with a profound sense of comfort, clarity, and calm, I staggered off stage and over to a chair to complete the Bahjans and meditation.

This is the century that I came into my own. After being the student for more than twenty years, it was time to become the teacher. I formed a new Women's Group, and with the help of Pam from the local New Age shop, *Spirit Song*, I began my readings and healing work.

An Alternative Medicine organization, attached to Doylestown Hospital, opened up and I applied for office space there. I opened that office in 2002, and began seeing clients with mental/emotional concerns and worries. I also began teaching my *Opening Up Your Intuitive Awareness* classes at Pam's apartment on South Main Street in Doylestown, above the Doylestown Book Shop. I was very busy, and loving it.

It was at the Alternative Medicine Clinic that I met Kathy Sasso and Jackie Lutz. Kathy was going through a divorce and Jackie had marriage problems as well. I had known Jackie a few months when she decided to gift her mother, Kay, a reading.

At midday on a Friday, Kay called me from Ohio. She was having a half-hour reading on her lunch break. As I looked at her astrological chart and "tuned in," I gasped at the message.

"Kay, do you have a daughter on the West Coast?" I began.

"Yes, her name is Joan, she lives near Seattle, is married and has four children." She answered.

"How friendly are you with your boss? Will he allow you to have some time off, beginning now?"

This was one of the few emergency readings I have ever given. My body was shaking and *I knew, without a doubt,* that her daughter's life was in danger.

"You need to get on a plane and get to your daughter's home tonight, or she could come to serious physical harm," I told her.

Kay began to cry. Sharply I asked her to remain calm and focus on getting to her daughter's side. The energy pouring through me was full of fear and dread. My body was shaking beyond belief.

"I will go now," she said.

"Please keep me posted, and you can call me, day or night." I responded, in a calmer voice. "I am here for you."

Kay went out to Seattle to find that her daughter was bleeding internally, and her husband would not allow her to go to the hospital to check it out. Kay told him to stay with the children and she would drive her daughter.

The doctor found that Joan was being drugged and sexually abused by her husband while she was sleeping. If she had not gone to the hospital, she could have bled to death.

The important thing here is that the truth came out. It was a rough road, but Joan recovered, divorced, and is fine today.

In the meantime, *Unsolved Mysteries* filmed my segment in 2004, in New York City. Shortly after that another production company called and asked me to film for the show *Beyond Chance*, with Melissa Ethredge, on the Lifetime Channel. I loved her insight and music, and was thrilled to be a part of that production.

In 2006, *The Psychic Detectives* called. The production company actually came to Doylestown to film, and many of my Women's Group members were extras in the film. My concern was they always told the same story, the Texas oil explosion and body I had located from New Jersey. There had been so many others that I would like to film, but these stories had not made the newspapers. At least *Unsolved Mysteries* added the Exxon case I had worked on.

Here are some high profile cases I worked on via telephone, email, and posted on my website:

Jon Benet Ramsey   December 25 - 26, 1996
Was murdered by a man known to Pat Ramsey. He was in the house when she arrived home with the children from the Christmas party.

Elizabeth Smart   June 5, 2002.
She was rescued by police officers nine months later on March 12, 2003 – a workman with a long beard took her. He had been doing roofing at the house. She was kept in a commune and would be found alive and well, as stated on my website all along.

Chandra Levy   Disappeared May 1, 2001
Her body was found on May 22, 2002
I said she was randomly murdered and her body would be found in Rock Creek Park. I also was certain Congressman Gary Condit had nothing whatsoever to do with this crime. I told this to Bob Woodward of the Washington Post, at the recommendation of Dr. Hans Holzer. I even drew a picture of the crime scene – and was right on the money.

The DC Sniper attacks—a serial killing spree in October 2002.
I drew their sinister plan, where they would hit next and why – with the final target being the White House. I knew they were in Frederick, Maryland the day they were caught.

Natalie Halloway vanished on May 30, 2005, while on a high school graduation trip to Aruba, a Dutch island in the Caribbean. I literally "saw" the murder in my third eye, and saw her body thrown overboard from a ship in the middle of the ocean.

After visiting Amma's tour in July of 2007, I received a call from a woman who lived in Philadelphia. She wanted to come to my semi-annual Intensive Workshop in September. She also wanted a reading. She had been a victim of psychic fraud for several years and was trying to recoup some of the money that she had been scammed out of. I helped her by advising her to go to the police and report the crime. She was frightened, but listened to the advice given. A court case ensued and I testified on her behalf. She won, and about a third of her funds were returned to her.

This was the fourth legal case I had been active in. It got me to thinking, perhaps I should write a book about this matter. I knew the drill very well, and how these scams were set up. From that case my first book, *Psychic Attack—Are You a Victim,* was born.

In September 2007, I had another one of those penetrating dreams. I had left the Alternative Medicine organization, Pam had moved, and I was at a loss, going through transition.

I dreamt of a logo. It was powerful. The logo, consisted of two triangles, one straight up, and one inverted, and were in a circle. The words outside of the logo were oneness, universal, power. The words inside were creation, spirit, universal law, as well as thinking, talking, action, the three steps to manifestation.

For years I had been a member of the New Jersey Metaphysical Organization, and felt as if I needed to create one in Bucks County. That was the birth of *The Bucks County Metaphysical Association,* or the BCMA.

I called my women's group together, and told them about my dream. I had even been able to draw the logo given to me in my dream. With some difficulty, we began the organization. I went through legal channels and set up a non-profit organization, set up the by-laws, and chose the Board of Trustees. We decided to hold holistic events and donate the funds to local Bucks County charities. The BCMA opened up in October, 2007 and lasted through 2013.

In the fall of 2010, I had a reading with Richard Schoeller, a true medium. I had met him at a TV studio in New York City, while we filmed a pilot for a new psychic series planned. In that reading, he told me that extra angels were around me because my sister was going to pass. He was certain it wasn't my twin, but one of my older sisters. He expected it to happen within three months. (To me, Richard Schoeller is the best medium one can find, at least in this country.)

I went to visit my older sister, Nancy, in Wilkes-Barre, Pennsylvania over the 2010 Thanksgiving weekend. We enjoyed a long talk about our lives as sisters. She apologized for not being a good sister to me. She was aware of the many times that she had let me down. I reminded her of some good times we had also shared.

We did the Louise Hay forgiveness prayer together.

Nancy, I forgive you
For everything you've done
And everything you haven't done,
Past, present, and future.
And I ask that you forgive me
For everything I've done
And everything I haven't done,
Past, present, and future.

Then she said it back to me. I told her of Richard Scholler's prediction, and she said, "It's me. I know it's me."

"No Nancy, it can't be. I will miss you too much," I wept.

She explained how much she missed her husband, Wesley Kemp, who was a Methodist Minister, and had passed in 2005. Nancy had read my book, *Psychic Attack—Are You a Victim,* and knew that my second book, *Ascension—Accessing The Fifth Dimension,* would be coming out soon. She knew that she did not want to linger and wait for death to arrive, like many of our ancestors had. She had been unable to drive or leave her home without help for several years.

Nancy was visibly depressed, as she had some recent disappointments regarding her children, and found it difficult to accept. She had a recent upset with her second daughter, Patricia, and was deeply sorry for her part in it. She asked me if I knew how she could leave the body and join her husband. She said she was truly suffering, was on way too much medication, and needed the release from this earth plane.

Believing in after-life, Soulmates, and the continuity of life, I gave her these instructions:

As you lay here on the couch, close your eyes. Visualize Wes standing in front of you, holding his arms out. Feel your "essence," your *Universal Body*, get up and walk into his arms. Do this everyday and ask the Lord to grant you the wish. Then, feel Wes take you in his arms, and bring you back to your original home.

My older sister, Nancy Ruth Reich Kemp, passed away on December 19th, 2010, the day before I was to drive out to see her and share Christmas. She suffered a sudden stroke and was gone within ten minutes.

In the summer of 2010, I was at the Manhattan Center for Amma's yearly visit. I had worked very hard at the New York City Information Table, a position Amma assigned to me at the very first New York City event. For my "reward" and for the first time ever for me, I was given the opportunity to sit close to, and in front of Amma for twenty minutes, while she gave darshan. There was no way I was going to miss this one!

I decided in my mind what I wanted to do the day before this special moment. For twenty minutes, I held in my mind a request for world peace, and for me, I asked for Her support and blessings in writing a book with the golden pen of angels; a book to touch the hearts of people all over the world. Something She would want written, and would empower me to write. That is the time that *Ascension—Accessing The Fifth Dimension*, the Ascension Workbook, the Divine Seals, and *the NEW Spiritual Chakras* were born, although not yet conceived. This would be a three-year effort with many steps and processes in between.

This was also the first year that my identical twin sister, Chris, would choose to visit Amma. At the time, I did not know that I was also being asked to do something else. Amma wanted me to take on the responsibility of helping my twin through her ascension experience.

Because the New York City event is so crowded, and I had been on tour with Amma from Albuquerque, New Mexico, with several chances for darshan, I could not have darshan in New York until Devi Bhava. Mid-afternoon, my twin came in the hall and sat with me and the group at the Information Table. She was all dressed up wearing a dress and heels. I smiled because she did look very pretty, but it was hardly the attire for sitting on the floor, climbing over crowds, or for being comfortable.

After a few minutes, my favorite Swami, Ramakrishnananda Puri walked over to us, smiling a beautiful, gentle smile. "Is this your sister?" he asked.

"Yes Swami. She's my identical twin."

"You both must have darshan together." He replied.

"But Swami, how can I? I am supposed to wait for Devi Bhava." I stated, feeling myself resisting the thought.

"I will bring you the tokens." He said, and promptly walked off to the backstage.

I knew this was a command from the higher forces, and wondered why this was being arranged. My twin and I had been estranged since 1991, after she stole the family home in New Hampshire, hit my mother around, and sold everything in the house that belonged to many family members. Mother had disowned her, and my older sisters and I had taken her to court to have mother's funds returned. Of course I wasn't thinking of how we began life, or of how neither of us had received much motherly support. Not at that moment. Most importantly, I was blind at the unconditional love I desired so much, and that Amma continually gave.

Two hours later, Swami returned with the tokens for afternoon darshan with Amma. Much to my surprise, he took us by the hand and walked down to where Amma was sitting, giving darshan. In front of the lines and crowd, he nodded to Her, and a path was made for my twin and I to have darshan. She grabbed my sister to Her breast, and held her for a few moments. Then with a deep, piercing look, She had me kneel and pulled my body over my twin's, holding us both for what seemed like forever. It would be three years later that I recognized the significance.

I began the first of four books, *Ascension—Accessing the Fifth Dimension* in August of 2010. I needed good editing for the book as I moved along, both content and grammatical editing. My twin was a retired English teacher in the New York City school system, so I decided to ask her to do some line editing. The content was edited by Barbara Cronie, also from New York City.

My sister relished this editing. She loved it, read about many spiritual truths she'd had no idea of, and began to open her mind and grow. She kept telling me it would be a best seller. I found that amusing. I explained to her that I just wanted to bring forth the information for others to know, about what was happening on our planet Earth, as well as in the solar system.

The following summer, when I was at a summer retreat with Amma, I took her the Ascension book and Workbook and gave them back to Her. "They're yours," I explained. "I want to teach this work around the world, but it's not happening. Why Amma?"

Smiling, Amma looked down at me and said, "You're too weak."

At the time, I did not understand it. Then She said, "How did you get all of this information into one place?"

"You gave it to me, Amma." I replied. "And now I give it back to you. Thank you for allowing me to write this material. I am truly honored."

Still smiling, Amma looked at the drawing of the new spiritual chakras, and took Her right index finger and traced it around the sign of infinity at the twelfth chakra. She lingered awhile.

Full of joy, I watched Her. "That's where you're from, Amma, the Twelfth Dimension. I know you miss it. Thank you for choosing to be here with us." I whispered.

Seeing my tears, She leaned over and patted my cheek. A shot of energy began to flow through me, and breathing a sigh of relief, I was at peace. Then Amma blessed the books and returned them to me. I knew they would get out to the world at the right time.

William Vitalis from the Clear Light Group was at the Amma event, and I shared with him what had happened. He suggested that I find a good energy healer and work with them for a while, at least through the end of 2012. He knew a lot was ahead for all of us.

I did not care for most of the energy people around New Hope. They were not on the same spiritual path, but there was one located nearby.

Luisa Rasiej and her husband John, had taken my classes when I first moved to Doylestown. At times Luisa would attend the group dinner parties. As soon as I return from the Amma tour, I called and asked her to work with me on a weekly basis. She is a top of the notch energy healer. She agreed, and my four years of weekly sessions began.

Moment by moment, layer by layer, the shackles and hooks were removed and lifted off my soul. Luisa proved to be a gifted and compassionate healer. From the insights gained, and the expanding conscious, I felt my anger and confusion leaving me. Luisa works in a silent, kind, and loving manner and is totally supportive. My friends were able to notice the change, and as time went on, I was more at peace.

Then, along came 2012. I had been going through so much emotional turmoil for the past year or so, and felt completely out of alignment with my body and spirit. I knew I needed some deep healing work. After eighteen months, I had finally finished the *Ascension Workbook*. What a test that had been. During that time I had a horrible falling out with my assistant, Bonnie, lost the women's group and BCMA. What a nightmare it had been. I felt hated and rejected by everyone. All I could depend on were my meditations and my devotion to Amma.

It was Thanksgiving of 2012. Don and I decided to ask my twin, Chris, and her husband David, to our home for the Thanksgiving weekend. Chris and I had been in touch since her visit to Amma in 2010. She and David attended the Amma Program in Washington, D.C. in the summer of 2011. Both Don and I worried a bit, because David had begun dementia, and Chris could have some strange behavior patterns, but we decided to brave the storm. We planned to eat out Thanksgiving Day and catch the movie *Lincoln* over the weekend.

The morning of their arrival, I was walking downstairs for my daily cup of coffee. The sun was shining brightly through the window in my entryway with a cathedral ceiling. I stopped midway down the stairs to give thanks for this glorious morning, when I noticed a wave of blue light with a golden hue. Stunned, I stopped and watched. The Light came in stronger and stronger. It was shaping into the form of the Holy Mother, Mary. Silently, She reached out to me. There was a moment of merging, and I knew She was consoling me for my loss. She was giving me compassion and strength, but for what I did not know.

The feeling stayed with me for an hour or so, and then I went on with my day. Chris and David arrived for the weekend Wednesday, in the late afternoon.

On Friday morning, after Thanksgiving Day, Chris woke up with horrible stomach pains.

"I don't know what wrong with me, Beth. I just can't go out to a movie. Take David and go. I just want to stay here and sleep."

"Okay," I said. By the way, do you take Tylenol?"

"Yes, why?"

"On the news last night they announced a recall for Tylenol, saying that some broken glass had been found in the pills. I hope you didn't get any, Chris. Get to a doctor as soon as you get home."

"I will," she said, trying to smile.

Because of her pain, Chris and David drove back to their home in Delaware a day early. She called me the following Tuesday, telling me that the doctor had possibly found the result of her pain, but some tests had to be made.

"Do they know what it is?" I asked.

"Not for sure, but they think it could be pancreatic cancer," she quietly responded. "I won't know for sure until next week."

"Oh my gosh, Chris. May I ask you a question?" I responded. After all that had happened, I was not surprised.

"Yes, of course. What?" she said.

"How long have you been praying to die?"

"How in the world did you know that, Beth? She answered. "For at least two years. With David and his Aspersers Syndrome and dementia, I have not been happy. I sleep all the time. I know I have things to do, but I can't make myself get up to do them. I have even neglected my rose garden. It's like I've given up on myself.

"Well, it looks like you're about to get your wish," I said. "Are you willing to explore the healing modalities available for you? Do you want to heal?"

"No, I don't think so," she said. "Thank goodness we had the Wesley College 40th year reunion. I did the yearbook, and all the girls were reunited. Those years at Wesley College were the best, most loving years of my life," she explained. "I think that brought me another year of life."

I knew there was nothing much I could do but support her. Her decisions were her decisions, and not to be interfered with.

"Would you and David like to come back for Christmas?" I asked.

"Oh no, we can't," Chris said. "We always go to June Smith's in Wilmington. We missed last year. I know June finds me a trial, but she does like David, and I feel I cannot miss this year."

"Okay, then how about New Year's?"

"Oh, I'd love that, Beth. Will Don be okay with it?" She asked excited.

Hearing the thrill in her voice, I said, "Of course. You can come directly from June's, or the day of New Year's Eve, whichever you'd prefer," I said.

"We'll come back home, feed the cats, and arrive New Year's Eve, mid afternoon."

"Good, see you then."

New Year's Eve morning, I was walking down the stairs again on a sunny day, and the blue, gold cloud appeared again. Mother Mary had returned, bearing such a beautiful, compassionate smile. "Twice within a month? What's going on?" I thought to myself. Then quickly I sent out the thought, "Oh Mother, thank you so much for supporting me. I am honored by your presence. Thank you for bringing me the strength to get through this experience."

Before Chris arrived I called Luisa to ask if she could give my twin a healing while she was visiting. She agreed and we set the date for New Year's Day, in the afternoon.

Just after Chris had her healing session, I began mine for accepting our de-twinning and eventual separation and detachment. It was quite a tough few months.

On June 19th, 2013, my identical twin sister, Priscilla Evelyn Reich, checked into Johns Hopkins Hospital for cancer surgery; the Whipple method for pancreatic cancer. After weeks of great pain and suffering, she passed on July 18th. Her husband, David, was at her side every day. They had a very strong love that began when we were just seventeen, when they met at Palisades Amusement Park in New Jersey. Although they did not marry until both of them were in their fifties, the love connection between the two of them was always strong. Five days after Chris, David passed as well, from natural causes. Although it was very shocking, this was a blessing, as David had dementia and would be absolutely lost without his wife, my twin.

During this time, I had two special spiritual experiences. My twin and I were trying to re-establish a relationship that had been estranged twenty years before. I had an inner knowing that I needed to be at the hospital before June 26th, for whatever reason. I drove to Baltimore on June 25th, to spend the week taking care of David, and share time with my sister.

When I arrived at her bedside that afternoon, finding that she was in intensive care, something happened inside of me. I simply knew that I could not leave her. I arranged to spend the night at my sister's side, not knowing what lay ahead of me, but completely trusting my "gut instinct messages" and the comfort of Spirit.

Just after midnight my sister went into a bit of distress. I'll admit that I did fear her demise, way before she chose to undergo this surgery. (In her age bracket, there is only a 20 percent survival rate.) I reached for her hand, forgetting that her wrists were tied to the bed for protection. I wanted to hold her hand, and in order to compensate, entwined our pinkies, as we had done in our infancy.

Suddenly Chris spoke to me telepathically, clear and distinct. "Oh Beth, we used to do this as kids." She was smiling and her etheric essence was full of Light. All concerns, worries, and judgment were swept away. There was nothing present except our "Twin Souls," floating around the intensive care room at Johns Hopkins. The personalities were gone and we were together in the Oneness of unconditional Love.

I sensed a deep opening in my Solar Plexus and I knew a spiritual healing was taking place. I was blanketed with a sense of gratitude and Divine bliss. It was then that I thanked her for coming in and choosing to be my twin in this lifetime. I honored her pain, confusion, and turmoil, and realized that had been a part of my younger years as well. We had just both processed our experiences differently. I realized that I was the person I am today because she had chosen to be my twin sister. The joy, freedom, laughter, and bliss was incredible. I never wanted it to end!

I snuggled closer to her and then a complete Peace came. The message received was, "It is done." All necessary forgiveness had been completed and I knew then that she would soon pass.

In the morning I went back to the condo Johns Hopkins provided the families, to freshen up, check on David, and bring him over to her bedside, where he spent the day. Finding again that I could not leave her side, I spent another night with Chris at Johns Hopkins, in the feeling of Oneness.

It was suddenly Friday, and I had been in the intensive care unit since Tuesday. I called the shuttle to go back to the condo, and during the ride "felt" the personalities return, and began to cry. The "floating" feeling disappeared and I was back in the present moment. I would miss it. How could I ever know what was next?

On Sunday, driving back to my home in Chalfont, Pennsylvania, I reflected on my time with Chris that morning. She told me that she wanted to die and asked me to untie her hands so she could pull the plugs and tubes out of her body. Distressed, I quickly called the nurse, and we decided to have the Chaplin come to visit. By this time, David had returned to the room, and he and the Chaplin chose the 100th

Psalm to be read out loud. David and I both held her pinky, one on each side of the bed, as the Psalm was recited by the Chaplin.

Psalm 100
King James Version (KJV)

Make a joyful noise unto the LORD, all ye lands.
Serve the LORD with gladness: come before his presence with singing.
Know ye that the LORD he is God: it is he that
hath made us, and not we ourselves;
we are his people, and the sheep of his pasture.
Enter into his gates with thanksgiving, and into his courts
with praise: be thankful unto him, and bless his name.
For the LORD is good; his mercy is everlasting;
and his truth endureth to all generations.

After about a half-hour she seemed to calm down. It was time to drive back to Pennsylvania, and as I hugged David good-bye he sobbed a bit and said he wished I didn't have to leave.

Then I turned back to Chris for a minute. I pulled out a photo of Amma, the hugging Saint, and told my twin to "go inside" and work the problem out with Amma. This had to be Chris' decision and no one could help her with it.

Amma was coming to Alexandria, Virginia the next weekend, and I was looking forward to spending some time with her. I knew that I would also stop back at Johns Hopkins to see Chris again.

While with Amma, I had more that an hour of private instruction with Pujtha, from the Radiance Healing sessions, who is deeply respected. She told me my sister was in the process of passing and that I needed to pray for her Soul. It was midnight, we had both been working since morning, yet she and her assistant, Sahasra, gave me another hour of their precious time to help me disconnect and unhook from my twin's energy field. This was one of the most sacred and blessed times I have experienced.

291

Although I had stopped at Johns Hopkins on my way to Virginia for a few minutes, I was compelled to stop by for another visit. This was the last day I saw my sister. I stopped by the condo to see if David could go with me, but there was no answer at the door or by phone. Now I realize that this visit had to be personal and private. It was definitely a Divine set-up.

They had removed the breathing tube from my sister and she could talk a bit, although sometimes it was in a whisper. She was anxious to call Susan, the daughter of her close friend, Jo, who had recently passed. I took out my IPhone and we dialed the number. She spoke with Susan for almost ten minutes. She seemed clear-headed, although a bit unstable, and had a beautiful conversation with someone whom she respected and cared about. She was so very happy at the end of that call.

I brought my sister a small photo of Amma in a plastic stand, so she could have it in the room with her. I showed her how to "talk a prayer" to the photo, and she practiced a bit. I explained that she could also "think" any message or prayer, and know that Amma would hear it.

Suddenly Chris told me she felt very tired and needed to sleep. I prepared to leave. Although I was pleased with her progress, my gut didn't trust the rally. As I was walking out of the room, I heard her say, "I love you, Beth." In tears, I turned around, went over to her side, looked straight into her eyes, and said, "I love you, too." That statement came up out of me somewhere from my toes. It was sincere, and very different from other times. Leaning over, I kissed her on the forehead, and left. That was on July 9th, and although she didn't pass until the 18th, it was the last time I saw my sister alive.

As I was leaving the Intensive Care Unit at John Hopkins Cancer Care Center, I heard a nurse say, "Do you have the bed ready for Mrs. DiVone?" I stopped short in my tracks. "Mrs. DiVone? That's a rare name," I thought. "That couldn't be my Caroline. No! I just spoke with her last month and would surly know if she had cancer." I dismissed it and kept walking. I think my body and soul just couldn't take any more sadness.

Amma moved on to New York City on July 11th. I went to the program and intended to work with Pujitha at the Radiance Healing table. This year, New York had other plans for me.

While working at the Radiance Healing table, my favorite swami, Ramakrishnananda, came to me again. He asked me if my twin sister was dying? I nodded yes, and he advised me to go sit on the stage with Mother. He said I needed to pray for her Soul, because she was in Darkness, and needed help to go to Amma.

I immediately went up to the stage and remained there the entire day! This is unheard of around Amma, but by Her grace, it was permitted during this watchful time. I sat there for more that six hours, watching as Amma hugged hundreds of people, one at a time. I saw the faces of pain turn into tears of relief and peace. Many of my friends joined me from time to time, and we visualized my sister reaching for Amma's arms, as her Soul prepared to Ascend into the Light.

It is said that Mother's hugs lift karma and helps life situations that are askew and messed up, turn around and right themselves again. Another belief is that one hug from Amma lifts you from darkness into the Light.

Mata Amritanandamayi is known throughout the world as Amma, or Mother, for her selfless love and compassion toward all beings. Her entire life has been dedicated to alleviating the pain of the poor, and those suffering physically and emotionally. She is truly a fully realized Saint. The Mata Atman.

I was staying in my condo in Mahwah, New Jersey, which is just outside of New York City. This was convenient for the New York City part of Her tour. My close friend, Danuta, drove me into the city that day, and we left the hall at the Javits Center just before midnight, to pick up our car and return to the condo.

On Friday morning, I found that I was too exhausted to return to the city. I spent the day in quiet prayer, resting and meditating. Saturday, July 13th, was Divi Bhava, the time when Mother goes into full power for Her "children." Danuta offered to drive me into New York City again because she was concerned about my physical ability to do so. Two of my close friends from Bucks County, where I now live, came up on the train as well. Again I was asked to sit on the stage with Amma during the afternoon program. I spent another six hours there, visualizing my sister's Ascension.

That evening, after the Puja, I prepared to get on the darshan line for my hug. First, I went in for a Radiance Healing with Pujjtha, to free up any and all past negative energies that I may be subconsciously holding on to.

When I reached Mother's feet, I had but one desire. I asked Mother to please take my sister into the Light if it was her time. Amma's face became filled with fear and pain - for a moment. Suddenly She shrugged Her shoulders, and then, miraculously, broke into the most beautiful smile, filled with Light. I closed my eyes as She hugged me, and "saw" my sister being lifted up into the brightest, most blinding triangle of Light; Mother Mary was on her left side and our Lord, the Christ was on her right side. Then Mother smiled, held me back, looked into my eyes, and tapped my Third Eye, twice!

Then she handed me an apple to thank me for bringing Her Chris' soul. This was on July 13th, 2013, and was my father's birthday. Chris adored him. *I knew her soul had left the body* and the rest was only a matter of time. Astonished, I did not know what to say. At that moment I thought the double tap on my forehead had been for me and my twin. Little did I know that it was for her husband David, who died quietly in his home in Delaware, four days after my sister had passed. It was the night before her funeral at Wesley College in Dover, Delaware.

The next morning I received a phone call from June, my sister's friend, caretaker, and Power of Attorney. She told me that I had to get down to Baltimore immediately because some decisions had to be made. My sister was passing and I had to "get there @#$%^&* it!"

I tried to explain to June that I knew that, and to just let her go. She needed to be allowed to go without any machinery to hold her back, as stated in her legal declaration. I suggested they remove the breathing device and let her pass. Well, I was called every name in the book, including a "piece of s--t sister," followed by very cruel statements and threats. This woman had no clue about what had just happened, and would not allow me to tell her.

Feeling guilty, I went within and asked Spirit to advise me as to what I should do. After a bit, I went out to my car, and found that the battery was dead. I was going nowhere, and spent the day getting it repaired. Somehow, I felt I could not go to a place where I was being sworn at, screamed at, and abused. Besides, I had witnessed my sister's beautiful and glorious Ascension the night before.

I had intended to drive back to Pennsylvania on Tuesday, but could not do so. I was so disoriented, dizzy, and spinning that I did not dare drive. I called my husband ant told him I would come back in the morning and go to Baltimore on Thursday, if need be. Then again, I meditated and slept. The energy with Amma had been very powerful.

I drove back home on Wednesday, July 17th, arriving late in the day. I told Don I would get up early and drive to Baltimore in the morning. At four am the phone rang. It was Chris' doctor, telling me that she had just passed away. Breathing a sigh of relief, I reached for the phone to call Elizabeth, David's daughter, who lived in Connecticut. Four days later, in the late afternoon, the day before my sister's funeral, Elizabeth called me back to tell me they found her Dad's body at the house, and he had passed away from an aneurism of the heart. David died of a broken heart, joining his wife and soul mate on the other side.

Yes, I was shocked! More about the feeling of a Lotus flower opening at my heart center, than the news about David's departure. Because of my training, I knew David's passing had been a matter of choice. I was feeling grace, happiness, and a jumping for joy sensation, once it all sunk in. A song my sister loved to sing ran through my body for several hours afterward, *"Ho-Ho-Ho, who's got the last laugh now?"*

That night, as I slept, I "saw" Chris and David in the heavenly Ethers. His head was on her shoulder, and they both were in a revere of Bliss and Oneness.

Beloved's, Soul mates, many say, "That's hogwash." Well -- I ask you -- Is it?"

FOR CHRIS AND DAVID
FOREVER TOGETHER ALWAYS
When I needed a shoulder to lean on
When I needed an ear to listen
It was you I could turn to.
It was you who would help me
Hold me and
I could find myself again.
After all the years we shared
I find a deep peacefulness
Knowing, believing it's still love,
You're still the one,
You'll always be the one
Now we're together
On the other side
Put your head on my shoulder
As we eternally abide.

—ELIZABETH JOYCE
7/22/2013

Two month's after Chris passed away, I received a call from my younger son, Jeffrey. He told me that Caroline Henning DiVone has just passed away from a rare cancer. He decided he would not let me know until after she had died and the funeral services were over. Can you imagine? Luckily, Meg had taught me years ago that you don't have to "be there," to mourn. That night Caroline came to me in my sleep. She lay down next to me and I held her essence and wept.

On December 1, 2013, my close friend and travel companion, Iris Darlington, passed away from a brain aneurysm. 2013, the year after the entrance of the new planetary energies, had been the year of letting go and transition for many people.

As 2014 opened I knew it was time for me to sell the condo. The tenants weren't working out, and I had not been able to work, because of so many losses right in a row. Since I was living in Pennsylvania I had lost many contacts in Northern New Jersey. However, after our fiftieth Ridgewood High School reunion, I was able to reconnect with several classmates, and they were there to lend help and support me in this process. With kindness, loyalty, love, and support I accomplished the complicated task.

The night before the closing was my last night in the condo. Everything had been emptied out and I was sleeping in a sleeping bag. Around 4:00 AM I felt as if someone was working on my body energetically. I opened my eyes into a squint, and saw a pair of black shoes in the corner by my closet. The left foot was tapping slightly. I realized it was Stephen Gould, the older gentleman who had helped me purchase the condo twenty-five years ago. As my eyes moved back to me, I broke into a soft smile. I saw Amma sitting over me, working on my body. She was giving me Darshan and in the middle of the hug, I whispered, "Amma, I've never been hugged by a ghost before." With a gentle and loving stroke across my right cheek, She was gone. I realized I had returned the condo back to Her, while feeling a deep gratitude for the gift.

In September of 2014, almost to the day of his sister's passing the year before, my foster son Nilas joined her on the other side. Again, I was not told until after it was over. My heart ached for months.

During this time, I could not write another book. To fill the void, I took all of the classes I had taught over the last thirty plus years and put them into book form. The *Opening to Your Intuition and Psychic Sensitivity Trilogy* was born. These books have many exercises and information to help you develop cosmic awareness, as well as your sixth sense. They are great for beginners as well as ones who are on their way toward inner development and cosmic connection.

While at the Amma Programs in 2014, I again sat in front of Her and asked to write another book. I felt so blocked and void of life and desire.

Two weeks later, as I was walking around my home, this mantra came; *Seeding and Nurturing the Garden of Your Soul. Seeding and Nurturing the Garden of Your Soul, Seeding and Nurturing the Garden of Your Soul.*

"What is that?" I asked Spirit.

The answer came back immediately; *The title of your new book.*

It was time to write an inspirational book about the underlying, natural Universe. *Seeding and Nurturing the Garden of Your Soul*, became a practical guide, with many exercises to teach you how to "hold down" invisible essences that are difficult to understand. I loved writing this book, and asked Luisa Rasiej to add a chapter as well. This book was completed in six weeks. I feel it should be in every church and on every bedside table for reference and guidance. It transcends man-made religion and, in fact, embraces them all, while adding more. It came inside of me, as if stuffed into my mind by the wise, caring hands of Amma.

Just after attending Amma's 2015 summer programs, I kept hearing *"Why have you hidden them? Why have you hidden them? It's time to bring out this information."*

Frustrated, I asked for clarity. A new book title came; *The NEW Spiritual Chakras and How to Work With Them* was born. I had put together the Ascension Workbook in 2011, during a very painful time for me. Within that book I had written about the Spiritual Chakras, and composed an Invocation to help activate them.

In the summer of 2015, I pulled out from the Workbook the new chakra information, added additional insights, and published *The NEW Spiritual Chakras and How to Work with Them*. The exciting part about this book is that the information has never been available before on this planet. It was an instant hit and became my best seller. With the help of Sara Sgarlat Publicity and George Noorey of *Coast to Coast AM* the word got out and I have sold 8,000 copies of this era changing book.

I began writing *Unlimited Realities* in 1986, let it go for awhile, picking it back up again after Dr. Chopra's Intensive, *Seduction of Spirit*. At that time, I worked with two editors, Barbara Cronie of New York City, and Linda Banks, a member of my husband's writers group. We joined forces and worked on this book for about four years. Then Linda passed away from lymphoma, and I put down the book once again until now.

I have noticed since the energy shift in 2012 that my classes have dropped off. So many things have changed with my work. The weekly Divine Healing Sessions have turned into quarterly Spiritual Intensives. My readings continue, but at a lighter pace. I have my weekly YouTube *Stargazing* report and radio show, *Let's Find Out*, on BBSRadio.com. So much has changed as I walk into a new era of my life.

2017 is giving me an invigorating burst of energy and initiative. I am sure this is an excellent time for making a fresh start, turning over a new leaf while starting new projects. All possibilities are on the table and I have put myself at the center of plans for my future. Old habits, behaviors, and beliefs can be questioned and put aside as I search for new and inventive ways to make progress.

I have written my first *Treatment* of a movie, and am in the process of writing my first screenplay for *Unlimited Realities*. Since I completely believe in magic, let's see where this new road will lead.

CHAPTER 18

Ascension
Gratitude Brings It All

ON DECEMBER 21, 2012, A rare celestial alignment occurred, moving Earth into the galactic center of the Milky Way Galaxy. This marked the end of the Mayan Calendar and the beginning of the Great Shift into the Fifth Dimension This movement is called by some the Ninth Wave, involving Quantum Physics, Holographic Evolution, and the destiny of humanity. Now is a time for the planet's enlightenment called *Ascension*. This dimensional shift is a cosmology cycle known and described by the ancients and brings forth the double helix energy for our destiny as Souls to evolve.

Embassies of beings keep heading our way from superpowers at the outermost and innermost locations and areas of the cosmos. They come both for our wellbeing and/or our demise. How few are the unique, glowing teachers and avatars that are truly shining with the mystery of truth. Such a journey, such a visitation can only happen in layers, as the planetary vibration opens and accepts the new, higher energy. Yes, there are now thousands of "walk-ins" in the First Universe, with many walking the planet Earth. In the First Universe there are billions of Earths with as many forms of life as the Earth has heritages.

These teachers are two separate vibration forces, sent from two different locations within the Universe. One comes from the border of the

Fourth and misinformation. These teachers are of a darker variety and belong to a lower form of duality and teach great knowledge for *their* benefit, while not for the growth of the Universe as a whole. These are shattered Souls who have not completely been able to heal and purify enough to come into the pure Light Beings needed to help all of us ascend into the Second Universe. This is why the Law of Karma, Akashic Records, and Reincarnation have been set up in the First Universe. However, out of ignorance, people bow down and worship or exalt these dark beings. They are not recognized as who they really are. Soul stealers.

It is difficult to explain to such beings and earthlings how to discern the difference, yet it can be done. Every Soul has free choice, as well as the ability to rise up to a new level of Light during a lifetime. This is true of all locations of life in the First Universe. These Souls know that something is missing. They know they have not attained the Light of perfection in this lifetime, and this continues through the Soul's essence throughout all lifetimes, until merging, release, and the true purity of Love is achieved. (The human mean is 400 to 600 lifetimes)

One cannot achieve self-realization without working through the imprints left on the Soul after each lifetime experience. This process is known as *working through your karma.*

Finally, after hundreds of thousands of life lessons, a Soul is purified enough to ascend into the Second Universe, where more purification occurs. However, the Second Universe does not contain duality, separateness, or choice. The character has been firmed up and "set" and ascends in its own time and its own way. The Second Universe brings more love and balance to the Soul while eliminating illusion and duality.

I have been asked to explain this to you – and I never have taken the time to do so since this knowledge was impaired to me in this present lifetime in Hawaii, at the base of Haleakala.

Some true avatars have been sent to the planet Earth but they are few and far between, and lifetimes apart. Many "high" teachers have been sent carrying the *Truth*, and, since you are in a duality Universe, some have been pulled down into darkness and defiled through their personal choices. But, more importantly, is the need to recognize that the dark forces have their angels as well, with as many powers, but they are ALWAYS used to pull down and destroy, not ascend.

One problem has been worshiping a human form. When these teachers are "recognized" they are put on a pedestal and bowed down to. Socially you are "in" if you go and learn from them. Most don't realize that they are "THAT" as well, or how, in this worshiping, they give their little power away.

In this lifetime, I have had two Soul changes, or "walk-in's" as you refer to them. Once when I was 36 and one when I was 42. At age 36, it was a head on car crash – where I had the *"Out of Body"* experience and learned about the continuation of life. At that time I was given the Divine power to teach, write, and heal energetically. I had the Akashic lineage to do so, and the portal was opened for my by invisible forces.

I learned about the continuity of life and that there is no fear with death. The Soul continues on, and if they choose, can enjoy another lifetime on the planet Earth.

During that time, in the late 20th Century, there were many closed minds. Most people were indifferent to spiritual concepts or so attached to various religions (which are man made). Then they received opinions or beliefs that they no longer felt they needed to consider a perspective other than their current view. The one who has no doubts that his convictions are about the Truth will indeed, have a closed mind. This leads to prejudice and judgment.

This was just before AIDS broke out, and the entrance of Louise Hay and Dr. Deepak Chopra, while Dr. Bernie Siegel and Dr. Raymond Moody were in the process of their personal awakenings and before Amma came to the US as well as thousand of others.

As you may know, when a walk-in arrives, there is an agreement between the two Souls, the one who departed and the one who enters. The departed Soul was praying to be delivered, and to leave the current life because the Soul could no longer bear the pain. The higher vibration Soul enters, and agrees to complete the karma of the lifetime for the departed Soul. (This is usually a seven-year process, but could prove to be longer.) The "walk-in" has a higher vibration, is usually from another area in the Universe, and cannot, ever, be too high as to destroy the body it enters. During a Soul exchange there is a lot of chemistry and high math going on.

The second Soul change was in Hawaii, when I met Mentor. Mentor is like St. Michael, but he is head of the Souls who are in the true process of Ascension, as well as all of the soul pods in all three universes. Somehow, in my meditation in Hawaii, I was "taken up" and was able to pierce the veil of all three Universes, I was taken through the Seven Rings of Light, right to the feel of the Divine Mother. This loca is beyond-beyond.

After a high class with Mentor, I was sent back to "teach." It has taken me so long to get there. I had to complete karma of three people. It has JUST been accomplished at the end of 2016.

I am not only here to teach, but to prepare the human body to open up to the higher energies, and guide them on the True path. Mentor and Amma actually put the book *Ascension* inside of me --- as well as *The NEW Spiritual Chakras*.

A question you may ask is, "Why is a healer able to heal? Why can he create changes by laying on his hands with intention or send healing impulses through energy work or thought? Why can't everyone do this if it's an ability that exists in each of us?"

The answer? Everyone can send healing energies. Expanded consciousness allows one to do it!

"So what exactly is expanded consciousness?"

Simply put, it's nothing but experience! The understanding and experience that you are able to heal enables you to heal! Experience creates the expansion of consciousness. To know something that you did not know before is to experience expanded consciousness.

At Amma's programs Swamij teaches, "Think of a penniless person living a life of poverty in a run-down shack. If he knew there was a treasure buried right in front of his house, he would dig it up. He would not be poor anymore and he would stop feeling poor too. If he doesn't know he can change his circumstances with meditation and thought, and nobody tells him, then his wealth stays hidden from him despite being so close."

As we practice consciousness-expanding exercises that make our brains activate cells to produce new neural pathways, our consciousness expands and cosmic love flows into our body system. This gradually awakens and nurtures our previously inactive healing abilities. A worldwide awakening is happening on this planet now. We are entering a new era of tapping into our Spiritual Consciousness, or Universal Body, to bring forth a higher form of life—one of love without fear.

Through many spiritual exercises found in the many religions around the world, we can open our minds. This will unlock the keys to other plains of experience. We create connection with our intuition that enables us to develop new thoughts that are both genuine and brilliant as well as the ability to recognize synchronicities that go far beyond the limited mindset of our current society. In other words, we expand our horizons and they become unlimited.

Thus we realize that energy is everywhere. Here, there, sitting on a park bench, a subway, a bus, driving a car, a quiet building, walking alone, a busy thoroughfare, or a lonely street. A smile, a nod, a kind word passed, a look of appreciation can be communicated without a word spoken. Invisible rays of living energy, sent out with a kindly thought of infinite love, can fortify another with renewed courage and a greater power.

The art of listening is strengthened as you gain the discipline of daily meditation. *The Gift of Listening* is very sacred and sometimes more useful than the gift of speech. It is how you see "character." This gift of attentive listening develops one's "ears to hear." These ears of the Universal Body are the ones contained deep within the soul. To sharpen this power you must begin to feel, sense, and develop a deep understanding of what's going on around you. This power of listening holds the key to Divine Service, and this service is given out according to the needs of those around you as well as to mankind. Here is when you know how and what to do with any situation.

This listening is not of the ears but of the heart. This greater listening eliminates all surface chatter. When one listens only to his own words, this energy becomes wasted on bankrupt minds. With a deeper ability to listen, you develop the ability to discern not only the worth of other's conversations, but your own words as well.

When this art is cultivated, then it is that words become sacred, and one's spoken word begins to go forth endowed with divine meaning. These words need not be shouted to have power and force. A yes means yes and a no means no. There is no need to be profane to substantiate the remarks. No one will doubt his words. The world itself will feel the impact of his speech and give ear to his message.

It is this listening heart that is so much needed among men at this time on our planet. It is the listening heart that is prepared for the full outpouring of knowledge from the Gift of Light.

"It is the listening heart alone that can hear the word of God."

—GRAMMIE HEMPHILL

To sum it up – I bring to the planet preparation for the continuation of life, release from the cycle of karma, the art of dying, the darkness of the astral world of spirits and trapped souls. This new energy, the double helix, brings union with the Golden Triad, in preparation for entering the *Temple of Eternity*.

Since December 21st, 2012, the new Double Helix energy had been able to be sent to this solar system. It has taken over 300 billion years to do so. This is a simple, powerful energy system streaming in from the *Second Universe*. The existence of the Second Universe is in the process of being discovered at NASA and many scientific laboratories around the world.

Everything that man can comprehend of the profoundest mystery of his existence, both here and beyond this planet, have been made available now. All things you may have heard about the *after-life* up to 2012 is pure fiction. They are products of mere speculation, and nothing more than baseless theories.

One should not believe in baseless theories just because it is popular to do so. For never shall your Soul experience lasting love and peace until you have found and merged with your Self again — as the eternal Soul expression of what is absolute Reality.

One more thing, then I am complete.

What is required for true Ascension is, first and foremost, the attainment of a constant orientation of one's thinking process, one's emotions, and one's temporal desires, all of which must be directed towards their desire and focus. The human being must first gradually transform its *Self* - build up its proper energies, before the *higher beings of intelligence* can reach the Soul with true Spiritual help. It's of little use to realize this orientation from time to time, as many people are accustomed to do. Daily meditation and Soul connection to the Divine energies is essential for self-realization.

The awakened or ascended Soul has now the potential to become, for the sake of illustration, a receiver for a special kind of spiritual – as well as otherworldly—transmissions, through the *NEW Spiritual Chakras*. However, no physical experiment can even prove they exist.

Events, abundance, relationships, healing, achieving desires, creativity, knowledge, etc. are only known, accepted, and absorbed, through each individual's experience; by man's becoming one with the desire. This is not easy peasy, and cannot be done overnight. To be accepted by the invisible forces as an apprentice, a Soul must be prepared to surround its *self* with the Light energy of patience.

It's all happening and it's all good. Mankind is evolving. It is said that Ammachi is the last Avatar to be on this planet. Once Amma passes and leaves the Earth plane, it will be the *Light Workers* who will guide the planet into Ascension. Along with that process, as promised, we will enter into 1,000 years of Peace.

As I enter my Golden Years on March 16th, 2017, my prayer is this:

May I always experience the joy of helping and uplifting those who come to me for help and guidance. It is truly by the will of the Divine that man can touch, access, and attain his eternal will. It's and eye-opener to realize that we all live in a world of Unlimited Realities.

307

Marc and I wrote our spiritual insights at the Stella Stone during our three weeks in Egypt. Following is the worldwide message for everyone.

WITHIN THE HEART OF THE SPHINX
BY: ELIZABETH JOYCE AND
MARC TREMBLAY
GIZA, EGYPT—APRIL, 1996

MARC TREMBLAY (QUEBEC, CANADA) AND I, having long devoted ourselves to the training of our consciousness and the conditioning of our nervous system. We traveled to Egypt with the Schor Foundation with the intention and expectation of having some deep perceptions. Our devotion has paid off. Especially notable is when at one point during our journey to the Pyramid Plateau at Giza, Marc and I focused our awareness and began to merge with, and "go within", the Sphinx. We became aware that Holy Mother Ammachi, a fully realized Saint from India, who visits the US every summer, and whose audiences we attended, joined and prepared our energies for just this mission when she came to New York in July, 1995. What follows is a description of our experience.

Going deep into meditative telepathy, we connect with the Sphinx. At the start we see a hidden underground chamber carved in bedrock. It has a fitted pyramidal stone lid or capstone, which is 30 to 40 feet below the surface of the sand. It measures 4 cubits on each side and is 2 cubits tall. The volume of this cover stone is 161.4 cubic feet. We are uncertain if it was made of limestone or granite, but sense the weight is 12 to 15 tons.

The chamber it covers is 20 meters deep with a square base of 32 meters per side. Around the perimeter of the chamber are 28 clay tablets. There is a small, man-made lake, although the water drained away over the centuries, and a green boat with a head painted in gold on the front. It is 7 cubits in length and made of papyrus. We see a pyramid 20 cubits tall in the center of a platform of solid crystal encrusted with gold ornamentation.

We sense there are many of these rooms underground and that they may stretch as much as 400 feet behind the Sphinx. We get a strong intuitive hit that these constitute the legendary Hall of Records, containing teachings of Sacred Geometry and records of Earth's history extending back to the 4th Dynasty of Egypt and including the history of Atlantis and Lemuria. It is part of the "House of Wisdom," an underground complex of chambers and corridors connecting the nine Pyramids and other parts of the area, which has been hidden for ages.

Next, at about fifty feet in front of the Sphinx's paws, we become inwardly aware of an undiscovered stairway of thirteen steps leading from the surface down to the capstone of this first chamber. Each step has engravings that will provide very useful and important information to mankind. At the bottom of these steps is a large Stele, or proclamation stone, which has many encrypted equations of physics, including "integral and differential maximum equations," and something called the "Epsilon Equation" along with the method of computing the number of atomic elements. These equations prove we are connected to every particle in the Universe. It's like a *Unified Field* that Rumi wrote about thousands of years ago.

My sense is that they relate to the Albert Einstein's work, and address levitation or the manipulation of the forces of gravity. Part of the meaning of this will be found in the inscriptions on the thirteenth step.

On the west side of the capstone we sensed a door leading into another inner chamber, housing the rarest of objects: works of great artistry, gems, crystals and precious tablets. Along the back of the Sphinx is an indentation. We perceive there is a room here, and within it there are two ciphers, or burial chambers: one 18 feet long and the other 12 feet. We sense that bodies of the 1st Dynasty were laid to rest there.

Our vision deepens and the purpose of the experience becomes clearer as an *Illuminated One* appeared to me wearing gold and blue vestments. In his hand he held the Sevenfold Key to Eternity.

He speaks telepathically: "The Mind is the capstone of man. The Spirit is the capstone of the mind. God is the completion, the capstone of Spirit. As the mind and spirit of man meld into the field of consciousness, the mind expands and becomes aware of the new knowledge to uplift mankind into ascension and cosmic awareness."

We are informed that the Temple, this Hall of Records, will be uncovered only when Man The Initiate becomes the living apex, or capstone, through which the Divine Power is focused into a structure, one's body and life in this world. (Hence, the importance of strengthening the nervous system and learning about and working with the New Spiritual Chakras.).

It is confirmed that the "Lion Faced Hierophant" contains the entrance to the *House of Wisdom* and in here there are also chambers hidden externally. (The Sphinx is being referred to here, although it has the face of a human. This is not explained.)

Rediscovery is close at hand. These structures in Egypt have existed for the purpose of inspiring mankind to search for the higher truths and to yearn to rise above materialistic ideals. In the new millennium, Man will become more spiritual and grow to understand the workings of life and God on the metaphysical levels. Once the above-mentioned capstone is unearthed and discovered, man will once again meet the Masters who are silently waiting. Their teaching will remove all clouds of dogma and re-clothe him in the vestments of Truth and Life. Glorious chants of the Illuminated will again resound throughout the ancient passageways and chambers. Man will discover many secrets of the ancients, techniques and technologies that will advance our civilization beyond our wildest dreams. Only the "Final Secret" cannot be handed to us - Ascension must come from within our hearts. The way is shown, but we must travel it ourselves.

The secret of life, and all her manifestation will be revealed to those who have prepared themselves for higher awareness. The Eternal Wisdom also relates to "travel" between worlds, of "being" someplace or some way else—teleportation and transformation. This Knowledge I will call *The Gateway*. A hint of this was seeded into the minds of the writers of the movie *Stargate*, yet it is not a device. It is a "talent" of higher consciousness. By attuning to a time or space through the will, raising your vibration and concept, by "setting a condition" through the alignment of thought, in a process related to the telepathic connection described above, one "moves," one becomes "there."

We are standing by the Stele Stone in front of the Sphinx. Marc is greeted by the Egyptian goddess Hathor and a being identified as Harrem Baaub. They welcome us—the first to be greeted here in over 4,000 years.

"There will be many in this Sacred Society who will meet with others in the planet at a later date. We are an invisible civilization." Ptah says, "I am your Teacher. You have been here before. Be patient with your bodies as you absorb these new energies. Go slowly".

Marc responds: "I surrender. I want nothing. I am a man of Love. I am here to serve my mission and to help Humanity. I am here to declare the Truth to all lands and nations."

We become aware the Stele Stone is not a mere stone. It possesses a consciousness and can reason. A chant comes to us spontaneously:

"Whe He Chak E AdTe." We are to learn and for five days the Stele will "speak" to us. Through it, the Masters will give to us much information. In the meantime, we are instructed to wander and follow where our inner knowing leads us. There will be another special message for us within the King's Chamber. We will be directed and we will be illuminated. Again, the message, "Go slowly."

There before us is Isis facing the Sphinx, throwing water and chanting incantations. We kneel and place our foreheads onto the ground, then chant: "Amen, Christ, Hil Ha Ha, Alla, Islam, Shalom, Shalom! We salute every religion on earth with one heart!"

This intense initiation was one of many awesome experiences we participated in. We had to assimilate powerful energies from that experience for five days and the Master Guides gave us further instructions during our visit. We slept for about twelve hours after this initiation. We were informed that the energies would be very powerful by the end of the week and that there would be automatic energy infusions available to us when we encountered such great inner Teachers. We accepted this, however it came.

Our Vision returns to the great monument. The scent of the White Lotus Blossom emanated from within the Sphinx. We walked around the Sphinx three times in silence in a clockwise spiral. We sensed that there are four rooms within the Sphinx itself. At different levels there are stairs, on the left paw and behind it, there is a stairway that goes down into the center of the Sphinx. It was also revealed there is a passageway within the right neck of the Sphinx. The room accessed from the shoulder of the Sphinx, is very important.

Ptah speaks: "In the back of the Sphinx is a powerful energy that is focused in the neck and shoulder area. The Sphinx shakes and rotates in a clockwise spiral. Its rotating vibration seeps into the center of the Earth, and they are spinning faster and faster."

The Egypt God Occodon, operating on the inner planes, will supervise the great discoveries to come regarding these chambers in the

Sphinx and the Pyramids. He will function as a telepathic "transceiver" in this third dimension and will lead those who will eventually open the monument. The opening of the right paw is anticipated for this fall-if there is no interference. There will be chanting and trumpet fanfares from three angels of Gabriel.

The conservators of the Sphinx will not succeed with their repairs because when the Hall of Records, which is the famous, mysterious "Secret of the Sphinx" is revealed the Sphinx will not be needed as a reminder on the planet anymore. It was the Guardian of the Old World's wisdom, a reminder that there is something more to know. Now, with the revelations, there will be a New World. Some Intuitive Light Workers have foreseen the Pyramids and Sphinx actually disappearing, perhaps during a sandstorm, but they will actually be "lifted off the planet with lasers through the various air shafts." This may be quite a stretch for some, and perhaps there is another explanation.

In the future people will be able to levitate, bi-locate, and travel at will. This will be a giant step for mankind.

Elizabeth Joyce

BORN AS ONE OF TWO sets of identical twins, Elizabeth Joyce has been psychic since birth. Named one of the *World's Greatest Psychics* (Citadel Press, 2004), she is profiled in twelve books. She is a teacher, spiritual healer and gives personal psychic readings worldwide. Ms. Joyce is a professional Astrologer, Spiritual Counselor, Energy Healer, Medium, and Clairvoyant who interprets dreams and teaches the new energies of the Fifth Dimension

Elizabeth has been a writer and columnist for thirty years and is currently writing Astrology columns for *Wisdom Magazine* and *Natural Awakenings.* Her articles have appeared in the *New York Daily News* and the *New York Times.* She has been published in many publications worldwide

Elizabeth has been teaching metaphysical classes for the past thirty years. In 1986, just before the Harmonic Convergence, she was blessed to be initiated into the Hopi Tribe by Grandfather. She was included in the revised book, *America's Top 100 Psychics. (2014)*

Elizabeth has studied with Margaret Stettner, Indira Ivey, Louise Hay, Dr. Deepak Chopra, Yogi Bhajan, Marc Tremblay, and Ammachi. She has trained with Dr. Eric Pearl and is a Reconnective Healer. She is a licensed minister in Worldwide Religions

Elizabeth is one of the very few psychics worldwide that picked up on the Indonesia Tsunami, Haitian Earthquake, the Philippines and Japan earthquakes, tornados, and the Twin Towers tragedy in New York City. Thousands of people have witnessed Elizabeth Joyce's incredible psychic powers on TV shows such as *Unsolved Mysteries, Beyond Chance* and *The Psychic Detectives,* as well as *CNN News*; She is a frequent guest on radio shows across the country, including *Coast 2 Coast AM*, with George Noory,

Her website is one of the top-rated in her field. Elizabeth facilitates her own healing classes, using the Divine Seals and Spiritual Chakras from her books—*Ascension—Accessing The Fifth Dimension WORKBOOK and The NEW Spiritual Chakras and How to Work With Them.*

Located in Doylestown, Pennsylvania, (Bucks County) Elizabeth works on behalf of more than thirty charities, including the Red Cross and Veteran's Administration local offices to benefit the Philadelphia area, and the homeless. She is an accessibility advocate for people with disabilities. Her charities have reached out to Operation Homefront, supporting the families of our deployed troops, and brushes aside the question of time when pushed for an answer, saying she still has to support non-profit organizations that donate to local charities, such as families of children with cancer and extra activities for private schools for children with autism and special needs.

Elizabeth's books are available at Amazon.com and her website as well.

Website: *www.new-visions.com*
E-Mail: Elizabeth_joyce@verizon.net
201-934-8986 — 24 hour answering service

66505516R00188

Made in the USA
Lexington, KY
16 August 2017